# The Watchful Clothier

THE LEWIS WALPOLE SERIES IN EIGHTEENTH-CENTURY
CULTURE AND HISTORY

The Lewis Walpole Series, published by Yale University Press
with the aid of the Annie Burr Lewis Fund, is dedicated to the culture and history of the long eighteenth century (from the Glorious
Revolution to the accession of Queen Victoria). It welcomes work
in a variety of fields, including literature and history, the visual
arts, political philosophy, music, legal history, and the history of
science. In addition to original scholarly work, the series publishes
new editions and translations of writing from the period, as well
as reprints of major books that are currently unavailable. Though
the majority of books in the series will probably concentrate on
Great Britain and the Continent, the range of our geographical
interests is as wide as Horace Walpole's.

# The Watchful Clothier

## The Life of an Eighteenth-Century Protestant Capitalist

*Matthew Kadane*

Yale
UNIVERSITY PRESS
NEW HAVEN AND LONDON

Published with assistance from the Annie Burr Lewis Fund and the Louis Stern Memorial Fund.

Yale University Press books may be purchased in quantity for educational, business, or promotional use. For information, please e-mail sales.press@yale.edu (U.S. office) or sales@yaleup.co.uk (U.K. office).

Set in Fournier type by IDS Infotech Ltd., Chandigarh, India.

Printed in the United States of America.

Library of Congress Cataloging-in-Publication Data

Kadane, Matthew.
The watchful clothier : the life of an eighteenth-century Protestant capitalist / Matthew Kadane.
        p.      cm. — (The Lewis Walpole series in eighteenth-century culture and history)
Includes bibliographical references and index.
ISBN 978–0–300–16961–4 (hbk. : alk. paper)
1. Ryder, John, 1695-1768.   2. Merchants—England—Leeds—Diaries.   3. Clothing trade—England—Leeds—History—18th century.   4. Leeds (England)—Commerce—History—18th century.   5. Leeds (England)—Economic conditions—18th century.   6. Leeds (England)—Social conditions—18th century.
7. Leeds (England)—Social life and customs—18th century.   I. Title.
HF3504.6.R93K33 2013
381.092—dc23
[B]
2012022790

A catalogue record for this book is available from the British Library.

This paper meets the requirements of ANSI/NISO Z39.48–1992 (Permanence of Paper).

10  9  8  7  6  5  4  3  2  1

# Contents

## Note on Style

For the most part I have kept Joseph Ryder's prose intact. Mainly this means that I have not corrected his spelling or standardized his capitalization. For readability, I have, however, replaced the thorn with "th" and extended otherwise confusing contractions (so "ye" becomes "the," "yt" becomes "that," etc.). I have also occasionally inserted punctuation in brackets where its absence would make the syntax unreadable. Words he underlined for emphasis have been italicized, and all italicized words in quotations from him are his, unless I indicate otherwise. Although he seamlessly wove scripture and the works of other authors into his prose, he virtually never explicitly referenced texts other than the Bible, and even here only occasionally. Where his references and allusions did not seem obvious to me, I cite the relevant passage in the endnotes. Note too that Ryder's diary spans the periods when Britain used the Old Style and New Style calendars. I have kept the dates consistent with the former for all entries written before and including September 2, 1752, and with the latter for those written from September 14 on. I always take the new year to begin on January 1 rather than March 25 but preserve the slashed dates that Ryder himself used when I quote him or reference an entry in the notes (February 1, 1742/43, for example). Ryder advanced overnight from his entry on September 2 of the year Britain switched to the Gregorian calendar to his next entry, labeled without comment, "September the 14 New Stile." In his diurnal account, as on the British calendar, September 3 through 13, 1752, never existed.

# The Watchful Clothier

# 1. Double-Minded Men

A soul hung up, as 'twere, in chains
Of nerves, and arteries, and veins;
Tortur'd, besides each other part,
In a vain head, and double heart.
—Andrew Marvell, *A Dialogue Between the Soul and the Body*

A double minded man is unstable in all his ways.
—James 1:8, King James Bible

Thanks to an ongoing debate Max Weber started a century ago, we know more than we once did about the relationship between capitalism and Christianity. Most historians could now agree that spiritual and material interests can be complementary, that devout Protestants have been gifted (though not uniquely) in their commercial pursuits, and that the seventeenth and eighteenth centuries in Britain together represent a major episode in the long process by which amassing wealth beyond need ceased being a Christian sin. We still know less than we should, however, about the birth pangs of modern capitalism felt by the pious people whose commerce and labor brought it about. In a history rich with images of titans and victims of the market, and celebrants and skeptics of consumerism, the obscure figure is the godly entrepreneur on the cusp of industrialization, wrestling with the moral meaning of unknown economic opportunity.[1]

This book brings that figure into clearer light by telling the story of Joseph Ryder, a clothier who spent his entire life, from 1695 to 1768, in Leeds, and who for his last thirty-five years kept a spiritual diary that death finally ended after two and a half million words and forty-one bound volumes. Ever since it left private hands in 1925, Ryder's massive handwritten journal has been sitting in the archives in Manchester, almost untouched. As a Leeds source in a different city's library, it generally escaped the notice of local historians. Its unquantified prose (and poetry) made it an ill fit for economic historians. A few nineteenth- and early-twentieth-century religious scholars were more interested, but these were doctrinal Unitarians who mined the diary for what it could tell them about their faith. A short article from the 1920s, the only other published study of the diary, saw value in its lay perspective of theological change. But "much that [Ryder] chronicled is 'small beer,'" concluded the eminent Unitarian historian and minister Herbert McLachlan: "no reader of the Diary would willingly return to it or be tempted to esteem its author a man of any mark."[2]

It is true enough that Ryder left a faint trace, a point driven home by the paltry and at times indistinct signs of his life in the archives. In the local parish records his full name also describes a Joseph Ryder born in Leeds just over a year after our protagonist's birth date, one whose funeral at age four our Ryder witnessed in 1751, another whose burial at age five he saw thirteen years later. There were "Joseph Ryders" everywhere. Assume a wider angle and the man at the center of this book fades even farther into the crowd: a loyal Anglo-Saxon subject of the crown; a compulsive churchgoer, living in the geographical middle of the nation, in the very middle of the middle class; a worker—a dyer of wool, the basis of manufacturing for most of the eighteenth century—in Britain's and Europe's vast cloth industry.[3] But to admit that Ryder was no one of any mark is to begin to make a case for studying his life. If there was nothing unique about being a clothier and worshipping God while giving allegiance to the reigning monarch, then from a distance Ryder was a kind of eighteenth-century everyman, the sort of person whose very ordinariness historians since McLachlan's generation have seen as key to understanding social and cultural change and continuity. By virtue of his diary Ryder also has a discernible voice, which points to what others who were like him (if less audible) may also have noticed and felt. Having that voice in the form of such an immense diary makes him more unusual, but spiritual diary keeping was not so rare that it restricts a diarist's outlook to his or her specific interests. Reformers in England encouraged laypeople to write diaries to maintain a pious course and find evidence of God's providential hand. By the mid-seventeenth century, expressing this watchfulness in writing had become a cultural preoccupation, at least for pious types with literacy and some leisure; and throughout the eighteenth century, even amid the rise of more secular forms of writing, the production of spiritual diaries continued to increase.[4]

And yet what makes a single artifact like this widely reflective and its maker worth studying goes beyond mere statistical normalcy or the constituent role Ryder can play in the inductive construction of social history. The outside world is always present in the pages of the most confessional diary, where, as E. P. Thompson once wrote, "we have evidence not of a spontaneous unmediated attitude but of this transcribed into an approved self-image (perhaps with approved doctrinal after-thoughts), like someone arranging his face in a looking-glass." In the ostensibly private pages of Ryder's self-account, his encounters with people, places, and events put him through spiritual trials that he often deciphered by reference to the encounters themselves. Even where he does not so explicitly turn his watchful eyes outward, he made his decisions in life by talking to his pastors, reading a Bible whose meaning was shaped by various externalities, and considering the consequences not only for his salvation, but for his family and godly community. The pages of the diary regularly evidence the culture, language, people, and material forces that gave his self-image approval or sent him looking for ways to improve.[5]

Like the diary that reflects it, Ryder's world was especially thick with commercial and religious meaning. This was true, in part, at the national level. The year of his birth, 1695, was bracketed by the founding of the Bank of England, which subsidized Britain's economic ascent, and the lapsing of the Licensing Act, which created print possibilities for decades of religious controversy. By the time of his death nearly seventy-three years later, parts of Britain were noticeably beginning their industrial take-off, while heterodox Dissenters, along with some like-minded Anglicans, were inventing a new mode of religion in the form of doctrinal Unitarianism, in the process radicalizing Christianity in exactly the direction that the limits of religious toleration legally set in 1689 were designed to avoid.[6] Yet Ryder did not need a broad perspective to notice how much his life was dominated by religion and the economy. Many of the more secular cultural possibilities of the Enlightenment were rarely available in the Leeds he knew. The town's first lending library, built at Joseph Priestley's urging, would come only after Ryder's death, even if by mere months. Its first permanent theater didn't appear for another three years. Operas and plays could still be performed without permanent settings, but they were far less common as local options in Ryder's lifetime than horse races, cockfights, and football. What defined cultural life in the town for the pious middling sort were its various Protestant chapels: Call Lane, home to the Congregationalist Independents, the more consistent heirs of Puritanism and Ryder's nearest coreligionists; Mill Hill, where the Presbyterians met, where Ryder regularly sat between his more frequent visits to Call Lane, and where Calvinism eventually gave way to heterodoxy, with Ryder wincing in its pews; Leeds's three Anglican churches–St. Peter's, St. Mary's, and Holy Trinity–a trinity themselves of the town's political power; the Quaker meetinghouse on Water Lane, on the more forlorn south side of the river; or by the early 1750s the Methodist chapel on St. Peter's Street.[7]

Just as defining of Ryder's life as Christianity was the "story of textiles" that one historian of Britain's eighteenth-century economy has called "the epitome of the whole story from protoindustry to Industrial Revolution."[8] The smokestacks we typically associate with full-fledged industrialization would wait to overtake the skyline commanded by the churches until after Ryder was dead and buried. Were we somehow able to look out the windows of Ryder's home on the northeast edge of town, where a beck running into the River Aire gave dyers the ready water they needed to finish their cloth, we would almost certainly be struck by how much closer we were to pastoral England than to William Blake's "dark satanic mills." But it is misleading to think that the material transformation of the English landscape waited for steam power or mechanized industry. Obscuring Ryder's bucolic view would have been a yard filled with tenters used for drying the cloth that he and his workers saturated with dye. Taking a walk only a few blocks southwest and farther into the town, we would have stumbled upon cloth warehouses springing up along the River Aire, the lifeline of a booming export trade, after passing by dozens of houses of other clothiers, busy, like Ryder, making wool cloth with a sense of calculation and ambition that was itself helping to make the structure and ethos of modern capitalism.

In fact, in few places in England–and in all of Europe–was the cluster of prefiguratively industrial characteristics that historians mean by that word "protoindustry"–entrepreneurship, proletarianization, and production for extraregional markets–so profitable and transformative. The Dissenter and commercially savvy traveler Celia Fiennes could write as early as the decade of Ryder's birth that Leeds was "esteemed the wealthiest town of its bigness in the Country." Around the time Ryder was establishing himself as a clothier

Leeds in 1715. "1" identifies the Anglican church, St. Peter's, and "6" Ryder's Dissenter chapel, Call Lane. Reproduced by courtesy of the Carl A. Kroch Library, Cornell University.

in the 1720s, Daniel Defoe began publishing his massive survey of Britain's economy, in which he called Leeds's local industry "a Prodigy of its kind . . . perhaps not to be equalled in the World." During the next several decades, still before cotton eclipsed wool as the primary stuff of textiles, the West Riding would come to dominate cloth production, and Leeds was its entrepôt, with its busy roads likes spokes on a wheel, running to the pious, industrious towns—York, Hull, Wakefield, Halifax, Bradford, Ripon—that encircled it and sent their clothiers and merchants to trade at its cloth markets twice a week.[9]

Because of this dominance of economic and religious life, Ryder's Leeds can be seen in hindsight as a sort of laboratory for testing the interaction of two major motive forces. The quick pace at which his life was coming to be capitalized meant confrontation with rising and more unrestrained consumption, intensified production, aggressive trading, and the emerging ethos of profit maximization. Both the rationalization and persistent traditionalism of Dissent meant, at once, confrontation with theological change, the broadening of religious diversity, and plenty of advice to stay true to the ways of previous generations. The spiritual meaning of the economic shift threw Ryder most off balance, but he held to his religious traditions with a watchfulness that had the effect of exposing additional layers of moral ambiguity in his commercial life.

This is not to say that Ryder is interesting simply because his religion made him ambivalent about commerce. The bulk of this book comes from what the diary can tell us not only about how he and other eighteenth-century Britons worked and worshipped, but how they wrote about themselves, raised their families, measured the worth of their lives, and confronted their own inevitable demise. To borrow Linda Colley's phrase, this is a book about "a world in a life and a life in the world," and it therefore attempts to follow the affinities and tensions arising from varied interactions and experiences.[10] But more than a decade spent with Ryder has led me to conclude that informing almost everything he did and thought was the relationship between the watchfulness his religion encouraged and the countless hours a day he spent as a clothier. His life in the world turned on his methodically vigilant engagement with *the world*, a potent coupling of words that in his diary, as in the godly culture that shaped his outlook, was the quickest way to signify material temptations designed to test spiritual resolve.

To briefly offer a definition considered later at greater length, "watching," as Ryder and others used the word, meant a relentless, self-perpetuating, and salvational examination of the self, the external world, the divine, and the very process of examination. It was in many ways the doctrine of providence put into daily, diligent, and often written practice; and much as could be said of providentialism, it was linked to a general trait of English Protestantism, even if it was more visible in the lives of strenuous believers. It was this watchfulness (more than predestination) that encouraged Ryder to write his spiritual diary, while it was his entrepreneurial life in Leeds's booming textiles industries that generated the endless spiritual anxieties that led him, in particular, to write so much. What distinguishes him as a "Protestant capitalist" was thus his experience of this spiritual vigilance and industriousness with equal degrees of intensity. And that experience meant living in a state in which disciplined and consistent examination both sent him looking for business success as an indication of salvation and regularly offered troubling evidence of the spiritual dangers latent in those very successes.[11]

To put it another way, the relationship between Ryder's religion and his material life had both positive and negative meaning. In one sense, it was sustained by an "elective affinity," as Weber enduringly named the process by which some religious ideals survive over time, or define a group, or resemble in some way a vocational ethic by lining up with nonreligious interests.

British capitalists could thus become more single-minded in their pursuit of gain not only by discarding their religion; they could reshape their religion amid material needs and ambitions. It is precisely this sort of dynamic relationship between the cultural and material that Weber found in Puritanism that helps explain, for example, the spiritual meaning Ryder found in the tempered material successes that augured his salvation. A different sort of elective affinity that we will consider at length also drew together Dissenter heterodoxy and a mode of material acquisitiveness that intensified as the century advanced, easily surpassing what Ryder would have regarded as suitably moderate.

As striking as any affinity between the spiritual and material, however, was the stress. The line between poverty and abundance was easier to imagine than locate, and if diary writing could in theory help to hold a watchful clothier like Ryder between the extremes, in practice it could throw him off balance. As long as his business prospered, he needed his diary; as long as he wrote in his diary, he was acutely aware of the dangers of his prosperity. Ryder's case therefore brings explicit economic meaning to a tension at the root of the model of selfhood implied by godly diary keeping and at the root of one of the seismic cultural shifts of early modern Britain and the modern West more broadly. The general tension implied by the spiritual diary arose from the relationship between self-writing and one of the central premises of the religion that recommended it. "Without self Denial we can't be Christians," the Plymouth purser Pentecost Barker put it as bluntly as anyone in his journal in 1730, quoting a friend who "always drops some good expressions." True to this religious mandate, the diaries of the sort Barker, Ryder, and countless others wrote were designed to be self-abnegating. But by virtue of their authorship, and by a degree that rose as the genre developed, these diaries were also, in varying ways, self-focused. In the messy, marginalia-ridden entries on the physical pages of the earliest spiritual diaries from the late 1500s there may have been relatively little authorial concern about an audience beyond God or the diarist. But by the mid-seventeenth century, the Essex cleric Ralph Josselin could revealingly tell his diary "I desire to loathe myself" (shouldn't pure self-loathing preclude any desire at all?); Katherine Gell, a pious correspondent of Richard Baxter, worried that diary keeping could itself be overdone; while the lay diarist Nehemiah Wallington handmade a table of contents and frontispiece for his massive journal, which, when all was said and done (what surely would have been to Gell's dismay), amounted to some twenty thousand pages. As writing spiritual diaries spread, the "I" that writing was supposed to mute ran the risk of stealing the show. Certainly in more ways than not, Ryder's neatly bound, carefully and cleanly written octavo volumes–manuscripts really only in the more literal sense of being handwritten–are the products of a self-aware author.[12]

This general paradox could be troubling enough: how can one in good faith make the self the protagonist of a narrative of self-denial? The Devil might inspire the spiritual diarist, as one essay on the genre aptly puts it, just as easily as God. But to a traditionally pious soul living through a cultural overhaul of self-interest itself, this paradox could feed a more serious crisis. More secular-minded Enlightenment luminaries repeated to Ryder's generation, with a frequency suggesting the message was difficult to digest, that the very thing against which godly behavior was prescribed to help one cautiously watch was now the basis of commercial success–and happiness more generally. This was why Bernard Mandeville, David Hume, Adam Smith, and many other economic theorists of the era spent so much time trying to demoralize and redefine the emerging keywords of the psychology of capitalism–approbation, vanity, acquisitiveness, self-love, and so on: not everyone in the eighteenth century had abandoned their traditional meanings. It may be easy enough to locate commercial types who blithely accumulated. But not if, like Ryder, they were as pious as entrepreneurial–the very sorts of ordinary industrious people whose full economic potential Smith and others theorized the validation of self-interest would release. This was the more acute tension in Ryder's life: more than his diary alone, his commercial life actively promoted the self-interest that his spiritual life told him to subdue.[13]

We might now begin to find additional layers of significance in entries that otherwise read as typical Puritan hand-wringing. Sunday, April 26, 1741, for example–a day of no particular significance: Ryder sat in Call Lane chapel, in the shadow of the towering Anglican St. Peter's but within view of the Aire and its ships freighting manufactured goods to Hull and a vast European trade. The intermittent spring rain had enlivened the meadows, so he told his diary the day before. Four days later, in a more sullen mood, he would call the same rain an "undeserved bounty" and remark on God's kindness "to the Unthankfull, & to Evill." But in church on this particular Sunday the weather was too uneventful to merit an elaborate providentialist reading. He had returned two days earlier from one of his regular regional trips to pick up or deliver pieces of wool, and he was grateful for divine preservation from natural dangers, highwaymen, and the treacherously underfunded roads that ran through the West Riding.[14]

Likely seated beside Ryder was his wife of six years, Elisabeth, born Wheelhouse, a woman whose husband leaves her nameless throughout his tireless but detail-deprived writings. Around them in the chapel pews would have sat a large, socially varied group of friends, family, and acquaintances: textile employees, clothiers, some of the town's more prominent merchants. And at the pulpit stood the even-handed Thomas Whitaker, Call Lane's minister of fourteen years, and for what beyond 1741 would turn out to be thirty-seven more. Whitaker was adept at consoling the suffering and counseling the doubtful. When he began preaching on this late April Sunday he was speaking to no one if not to Ryder, who later that evening recalled and recorded in his diary the resonant points of the sermon and the products of his self-reflection:

> This day Mr Whitaker preacht from Psalms 119:113, I hate vain thoughts. Vain Thoughts are & Ought to be the Object of a Good mans hatred as they show Great Irreverence of God in the time of his worship. Its what would be offensive to an Earthly prince to see such as were petitioning of him, or pretending to serve him to trifle in his presence. It shows also great hypocrisy for what will it avail us to Draw nigh to God with our Lips and with our Lips to show much Love if our hearts be going after our covetousness. This may lead us to Examine How we stand affected to Vain Thoughts. For hereby we may judge of our Spirituall state if we Indulge pride, vanity, malice, or revenge we hereby declare us to be full of hypocrisy, the Outside seemingly Clean, but the Inside as it were full of dead bones and all uncleanness. . . . Again let us consider Whether or no we have occasioned these thoughts our selves by crowding our selves with Worldly things and filling our hands too full of the World. Again persons of a melancholy frame are much to be pitied who are harassed with blasphemous thoughts in Duty, but this is often from the constitution of the Body for as that is restored to its former health the mind frequently returns to its composure. This seems to have been the Psalmists case and is the case of others to this day. But our ministers Opinion is that for the most part truly pious persons who are thus harassed for wicked men trouble not themselves in any such case. My case at this time is deplorable enough for the vain thoughts that fill my mind find far too quiet reception.[15]

In this single entry in a journal of nearly thirteen thousand others, Ryder's Reformed roots (and fear of his own hypocrisy) already appear in his reference to struggles between external "lips" and internal "hearts," the "seemingly clean" outside set against his apprehension of an "inside . . . full of dead bones." Ambivalence about business successes lurks in his complaints about crowding himself with worldly things. Even the apparently simple connection he makes between God and the "earthly prince" can be read in 1741, and confirmed by other entries, as evidence of his Hanoverian loyalties in a political atmosphere still haunted by the threat of Jacobitism. This passage also suggests what more explicit entries bear out, that Ryder too could be pitied for melancholy thoughts and the bodily afflictions he ascribed to mental unease and spiritual inadequacy. "They that are whole have no need of the Physician," the reverend Whitaker on more than one occasion quoted from Mark 2:17. The minister was nevertheless gentler on his congregation than Ryder was on himself. Whitaker offered the potentially hopeful message that it is precisely because the wicked go unbothered by inner struggles or the intrusion of blasphemous thoughts that spiritual harassment can actually signal piety. Ryder, evidently unappreciative of the irony that he was already eight years under way in writing what would become a nearly thirty-five-year-long documentation of these very sorts of struggles, so often chose to decline offers of spiritual relief, counting himself among the wicked men whose vanity met with too little resistance.

The governing line in this passage came, however, from the 113th verse of the 119th psalm, which in Ryder's King James Bible read, "I hate vain thoughts, but thy law do I love." As Ryder had written the previous Sunday, the vain thoughts that plagued him were "Prophane Blasphemous & Atheisticall . . . Murmuring Discontented & uneasy Thoughts." At the end of that entry, as at the end of many others, and always those written on the Sabbath, he summarized his sense of the day in verse. "Swarms of Vain Thoughts do greatly me Infest / By approbation Guilt is much Increast."[16]

Such self-recriminating language was typical enough in the sermons and diaries of godly Protestants, where "vain" regularly appears as the qualifier of any thought or imagination lacking spiritual content. In an even larger sense vanity was antithetical to the teleology that dominated early modern Britain and had roots in Aristotle's axiom that nature didn't—and by implication humans shouldn't—make anything in vain. But however formulaic the language, a simple word like "vain" could take on multilayered meaning in the right context. Like a pilgrim on the road to the Celestial City, Ryder had daily bouts with a living version of Vanity Fair. "He that lives in such a place has need of an item to caution him to take heed, every moment of the day," John Bunyan warned about the town of Vanity, and for Bunyan's avid reader Ryder, about commercial Leeds. Throughout his life Ryder took the warning to heart. On the day the Mixed Cloth Hall opened in Leeds in August 1758, replacing the smaller cloth market at Briggate that left Defoe awestruck, Ryder reported on a sight in which he had a vested economic interest: "This day there was the first Publick markett in the new cloth hall, and a procession of persons Occupied in Severall branches of the trade bearing Severall Flaggs, and a Considerable Sum of money given to the persons, but this transaction as well as others mett with a different approbation. Some commended the Contrivance, Others sett light by it, as a piece of Vanity. Spectators were very numerous, but we may Say of it, and very truly, All here below is Vanity."[17]

Had they had the opportunity, the paragons of the British Enlightenment no doubt would have told Ryder he was getting it exactly wrong. Joseph Addison swooned over the Royal Exchange in 1711: "There is no place in the town which I so much love to frequent. It gives me a secret satisfaction, and, in some measure, gratifies my vanity." Bernard Mandeville promoted a personified "Vanity" to the "Ministry of Industry" in an early version of his ever-expanding capitalist epic *The Fable of the Bees*. More famously, it was by inverting the meaning of words godly people like Ryder routinely used that Adam Smith identified self-interested and externally unregulated men and women as the source of the nation's wealth. Smith saw the approbation we receive from one another—the very same approbation that "much increast" Ryder's guilt—as built upon our shared and socially beneficial sense of fellow feeling: "To be observed . . . to be taken notice of with sympathy, complacency, and approbation, are all the advantages which we can propose to derive from [bettering our condition]. It is the vanity, not the ease, or the pleasure, which interests us." It was, moreover, the "great secret of education," Smith explained in an era whose luminaries routinely linked education to enlightenment, "to direct vanity to proper objects." If kept in check, vanity could be a motive force for the socially productive improvement of our material condition. "The rich man glories in his riches," Smith argued, "because he feels that they naturally draw upon him the attention of the world. . . . The poor man, on the contrary, is ashamed of his poverty." "Notwithstanding all its groundless pretentions . . . vanity is almost always a sprightly and a gay, and very often a good-natured passion."[18]

Ryder was clearly of a different view, which comes forth not just in his prose, but in his thousands of verses:

> On that I more & more may take delight
> To act what is well pleasing in Gods Sight
> Not with a View of mortall's approbation
> But with the hopes of Sharing Gods Salvation

Yet this is the larger point: he was no simple critic of capitalism or its supportive psychology. His industriousness put him firmly in a middling sort that was largely defined by material aspiration. He may have worried about the surplus wealth that offered access to worldly distractions and social approval and thus reflected his vain ambition, but he consistently identified the alternatives to that success as idleness and apathy, both of which led one as quickly as greed down the multilane highway to Hell. If he could identify material acquisitiveness *for its own sake* as the impulse to resist while trying to balance ambition for this world with that for the next, he still expressed sentiment after sentiment like that captured in the title of one of his earliest verses, "Poverty the Product of Sloth."[19]

It is in the broader context of cultural and economic life in eighteenth-century Britain that the first line of Psalm 119:113 therefore gives such apt expression to Ryder's double-mindedness. At least since the fourteenth century, the word "vain" meant something worthless, unprofitable, unavailing, or devoid of *real* value. By the seventeenth century it had also come to characterize someone enamored of his or her attainments, appearance, or social approval. Ryder's uses of the word throughout the diary indicate that he hated the kinds of thoughts that conformed to either definition—high self-regard *was* spiritually worthless. Vain thoughts and things were not simply missing spiritual value, nor were they only distractions from the effort to honor God. They also stood for the "deadly sin" of vanity: vanity as overvalued self-worth; "vanity," as he put it with reference to a biblical episode meant to tie together the commercial and spiritual, that embraced "all admiring Thoughts of our Selves & Despising of Others as the Pharisee Who when He came to the Temple to Pray Began to Bless God for his own attainments above the Publicans." To a man with a disavowed, resisted, repressed, but persistent desire to acquire increasingly more wealth in a town and nation that had become conspicuously prosperous, hatred of vain thoughts thinly veiled the paradox we considered earlier. If vanity is excessive self-admiration, then to hate one's vain thoughts, as the psalm recommends, is to hate oneself for loving oneself. Self-admiration can lead nowhere by such logic but back to self-loathing.[20]

The King James translation of the Bible that Ryder read rendered the first line of verse 113—the negative line Whitaker chose to quote, or Ryder chose to emphasize—as "I hate *vain* thoughts." "Vain" was italicized to indicate the obscurity of the Hebrew word it came from, סעפים (Se'aphim), a hapax legomenon that had no unambiguous translation. Jean Calvin, who memorably called the Psalms "an anatomy of the soul," had recommended a phrase that in English literally means "crooked thoughts." He explained "that since God acknowledges as the disciples of his law those only who are well purified from all contrary imaginations, which corrupt our understanding, the prophet here [in the psalm] protests that he is an enemy to all crooked thoughts, which are wont to draw men hither and thither." The operative meaning behind the phrase for Calvin was "contrary imaginations," and so in a more explicitly self-oriented choice of words it has been in most post–King James English translations of the Bible, which almost all render the first part of the psalm not "I hate vain thoughts," but "I hate double-minded men."[21]

Ryder could not have known about the biblical exegesis undertaken after his death (though we can wonder what a minister more familiar with meanings lost in translation might have said in a sermon), nor could he tell us everything we might want to know about the making of modern capitalism. But he can tell us as well as any ordinary person we have on record about how difficult and agonizing that process could feel for a man committed as much to his ascetic, self-focused Protestantism as to his commercial life. As we continue to try to understand the cultural roots of industrialization, what it meant (and means) in local and global terms, how it was linked to religion, and how the tensions present at its making persist, we now need to consider the image of this no-name at the productive center of it all, condemning himself as the less bridled pursuit of self-interest increasingly educed virtues from vanity. Once we have gotten to know Ryder and his diary we can also consider what his case tells us about how such ambivalence could be stabilized: by a new religious mode and a valorization of a middle class that offered spiritual protection from the extremes of poverty and excess. But that is where his story ends. This is where it begins: Call Lane chapel on an average day; a Dissenter and clothier; a godly, industrious, self-loathing version of everyman; double-mindedness embodied, sitting in his pew, listening to his minister, and thinking to himself, in so many words, I hate double-minded men.

# 2. "My Character & Conduct"

Opening a diary can be like "walking into a room full of strangers," or so the historian Laurel Ulrich wrote about her first encounter with the diary of Martha Ballard, an early American who recorded, yet said little else about, the names of countless people she came across as a midwife.[1] Opening Joseph Ryder's diary, where the names so often go unmentioned and events are alluded to in indecipherable fragments, is more like walking into a room full of strangers who speak a mostly foreign language. Half-comprehended phrases hint at interesting stories, but most everything is initially inscrutable. Even if thousands of hours spent in such a place eventually yields a measure of fluency, so much in this diary, like subtle inflections in a second language, remains elusive.

For a taste of Ryder's vagueness, which will become familiar over the course of this book, consider a typical short entry, taken from the diary's first pages: "This Day as I remember In the morning I was much affected in reading the Word of God & in Prayer but In want of Watchfulness a prevailing Indifferency Seem'd to Overtake me in the Day Time & Towards Evening I found some rising of Discontent and uneasiness about One Thing or Another, and I found the Stirrings of Corruption Towards Objects of Sense, Tho at the Same Time These words Came Into my mind. Abstain from all appearance of Evil."[2] The image that emerges here of a vigilant Bible reader, praying and worrying about wavering commitments and temptation while effortlessly quoting scripture, is clear enough from virtually every other entry in the diary. What the prose obscures—and in this sense the typicality of this passage can't be overstated—are answers to countless other questions about the themes of the daily and interior life that Ryder hints at: who or what exactly his senses perceived, the source of his discontent, why he failed to watch fully, what in particular was so evil, why exactly the scripture (in this case 1 Thessalonians 5:22) was apposite to the experience—and the list could go on.

One practical outcome of Ryder's obscurity is that, despite his prolixity, much of his biography is unwritable. He was no head of state or celebrated author. Outside of his diary, his equally obscure trade notebook, his will, and a posthumous ad in the newspaper for his real estate, he appears in the archives only on the day he was born, the day he was married, and the day he was buried. Almost all of the allusions in the diary to the personal affairs of his unnoticed life are referenced nowhere else, and this may be one of the longest diaries ever written that so frequently says something about, for all practical purposes, nothing.[3]

If we hold a modern definition of the diary, Ryder is a contradiction in terms. As the literary critic Louis Menand writes, "diaries are composed under the fiction that the day is in control, that you are simply a passive recorder of circumstance, and so everything has to go in whether it mattered or not. . . . In a diary, the trivial and inconsequential . . . are not trivial and inconsequential at all; they are defining features of the genre." Hence the potential of so many diaries to be loaded repositories of material and domestic life: to the delight of historians, they often express the mundane as a matter of habit, even occasionally in the earliest years in which they were written. It probably was not Samuel Pepys's intention to write as lastingly about life in the bedroom as work in naval administration. But it has been the details Pepys gave about seventeenth-century sex and marriage—details absent from most other contemporary sources—that give historians of these subjects something tangible to talk about.[4]

Authors of early modern spiritual diaries in the Puritan tradition were, however, far from passive recorders of circumstance. Unlinked to providence, details vainly consumed paper and ink. What these pious writers sought was evidence of "life *sub specie aeternitatis*," as Paul Seaver once wrote, and in pursuit of life lived under the gaze of the eternal, the artifacts of mere reality were beside the point. Details might still be given, or differences in the concrete still examined, as a godly author found religious meaning in daily experience. Ryder suggests as much in an early passage where "considering about the making and keeping of this diary, and the seeming difficulty at first entrance, and considering that to the best of my remembrance there was not two daily observations exactly alike, but, as I was ready to believe, differed in either matter or stile, from hence I concluded that God's mercies to them that fear him are new every morning." Nehemiah Wallington, in many ways Ryder's counterpart from the 1600s, thought as well that naming the particular "may be for the good of others when it hits upon the same particular sorrow or affliction which they may be in." And probably no diarist pushed the limits of this logic as fully as Cotton Mather, who found himself in the grips of providence while "emptying the cistern of nature" against a wall. As a dog walked up beside him to attend to the same physical need, Mather felt his spirit rising and soaring because of the very fact that "natural necessities debase me into the condition of the beast." But the practical consequence of the hermeneutics that justified spiritual diary keeping is that details typically didn't find written expression when God, the Devil, or salvational meaning couldn't be found to reside in them. Closer to home, this means that the evidence that might allow us to savor the texture of Ryder's material and social experience, or confirm what instead have to remain more tentative generalizations, is buried deeply, if it exists at all, in his self-account.[5]

The problem is admittedly strange: Ryder wrote a massive amount of words that were at least in part intended to be about himself; we can legitimately call this *self* writing. And yet we never have any idea what he looked like; we hardly ever know who, or what things, occupied his house; his sex life is a virtual mystery; he never tells us what he ate or drank or what clothes he wore; where he traveled for work has to be inferred from where other Leeds clothiers went; the books he read are as obscure as the meanings he drew from them ("This day . . . I read a considerable part of a book wherein severall cases were answered, and found many things Instructive and entertaining"—and that's it).[6] We will eventually see that the paradox of prolixity plus vagueness is more apparent than real when we turn to the intended meaning of Ryder's watchfulness. Before we do that, however, we need a descriptive sense, as much as possible, of his life. This might seem like a relatively easy task, but straightforward biography has to give way to something more qualified and nuanced. Diaries often rescue historical figures from obscurity. Ryder has to be rescued from the obscurity of his diary.

The first entry in his journal reads as if the record he was beginning, like the day he was ending, was nothing out of the ordinary. He opened, on May 25,

1733, two months past his thirty-eighth birthday, with what would become habitual introductory words, "this day"; alluded to a journey from which he was glad to return home safely; prayed that "grace may abound" in his life; and closed with self-advice to keep in mind Christ's warning to be watchful.

Beginning in media res was slightly unusual for someone writing in this tradition. It was probably more typical to fill the first pages with an "autobiographical abstract" of pre-diary years to bring the reader up to speed before starting the blow-by-blow account. But Ryder showed no interest in that technique, which may also explain his "difficulty at first entrance" if such abstracts were also useful for getting started. In fact, he virtually never looked in any detail more than a day or two into his past. All we know with certainty about his unrecorded life is that he was born an only child to a widowed mother in Leeds on March 25, 1695, and was baptized in Mill Hill Chapel. Other things we can infer: the education suggested by his literacy and religious background, or the apprenticeship through which any clothier would have needed to pass. Probably at some point in that education he would have encountered the staple Dissenter authors whose names or unattributed words often appear elsewhere in the diary and whose spiritual advice his adult outlook reflected: Philip Doddridge, Isaac Watts, Richard Baxter, Matthew Henry, John Flavel, Elizabeth Rowe, and John Bunyan, among others. We could as easily imagine an apprenticeship exposing young Ryder to the cloth-making techniques if not also the discipline, efficiency, and numeracy that an artisan was unlikely to pick up without some kind of formal training. But what sort of apprentice or student Ryder was, how as a young man he might have read these authors, whether or not he ever cared about them until he was much older, how much he initially wanted to be a clothier, not to mention how much early encounters with trauma, crisis, loss, sex, injury, love, abuse, and countless other experiences may have shaped his psyche—answers to these and so many other questions we might want to ask about his early life remain out of reach.[7]

There is one thing about his pre-diary years that he does tell us, regularly and deliberately: he had sinfully misspent them. As vividly as he was ever willing to say this was to compare himself to the subject of Bunyan's dialogic and fictional biography *The Life and Death of Mr Badman*, Bunyan's downer companion piece to the enormously popular *Pilgrim's Progress*. More than once Ryder declared that his own youthful sins exceeded those of Badman. This was a big claim. If *Pilgrim's Progress* offered the pious reliable directions to Heaven, *The Life and Death of Mr Badman* mapped the beeline to Hell. Badman the child swore and lied compulsively; the teenager read romances and other books that "set all fleshly lusts on fire," stole, drank too much, and slept with prostitutes; and the young man found a hapless, innocent, and wealthy wife and then drained her of her money to fend off his creditors. It is hard to imagine that Ryder could have been or done all these things; at the very least, there is no evidence of a marriage before Elisabeth. For that matter, Ryder makes clear his distance from "scandalous" sins, a word he tended to associate with sex. The temptation is to dismiss his comparison as rhetorical self-incrimination, part and parcel of the self-persecutory imagination of the puritanical, including Bunyan himself, who made his own youthful sinfulness superlative in his spiritual autobiography, *Grace Abounding to the Chief of Sinners,* a book Ryder was no doubt alluding to with the "grace may abound" of his opening entry.[8]

Given the unlikelihood of Ryder having written so much merely to be rhetorical, he nevertheless may have meant something specific by saying something apparently vague and formulaic. *Mr Badman,* as Roger Sharrock rightly noted, is "a cautionary tale of middle-class commercial life in a provincial town." Badman's most socially far-reaching and ingenious spiritual crimes stemmed from greed, corruption, and pride, the last of which was built on the success of his economic manipulation. The more naive of the interlocutors in the dialogue, "Attentive," goes so far as to call Badman a "stinking atheist" when Attentive learns that Badman's mounting debt encouraged him to secure still more credit by learning how "to suit himself to any company." If he were surrounded by honest men who could lend him resources, Badman won their approval by praising religion and denouncing debauchery; if he found himself in unsavory yet solvent company, he as effortlessly and profitably railed against religion, talked "beastly, vainly, idlely," and drank, swore, and whored. By the ironic marginal note alone that Bunyan appended to the paragraph explaining all this mendacious sociability—"Mr Badmans perfection"— middling sort readers like Ryder easily could have drawn the conclusion that economic corruption was the height of wrongdoing, while at the same time wondering exactly how to distinguish mixing with company affectively from angling for a loan. Bunyan's cautionary tale never encourages poverty; the vice is never industry itself. But as "Wiseman" puts it plainly in a text in which moderation in economic matters may be implied as a solution to extremes but is never given a precise quantity in the calculus of social and economic ambition, "The poor, because they are poor, are not capable of sinning against God as the rich man does." Ryder may have been indicating with the comparison, in other words, that the big sin of his youth, the sin that made him worse than ultimate badness, and the sin he much more clearly felt guilty of once he began recording his life, was the hustling—what could so easily be seen as the manip- ulation—needed to bring a self-made man material surplus.[9]

Whatever exactly had happened in his early years, Ryder had found a place in the middling sort at the moment we meet him in his late thirties. He had done so by way of laboring in the "putting-out" system, a relatively elabo- rate mode of early modern manufacturing in which entrepreneurs commis- sioned various tasks in the production process to specialized wage laborers. Few regions in Britain or Europe saw this system flourish as it did in Leeds. The town was the most important part of Yorkshire's economy, and in a century during which wool manufacturing made up the bulk of overall British exports, at least until Ryder's death, Yorkshire saw its share of the national production of wool cloth rise threefold. Much of this success was owing to the receptiveness of the town's economy to small-scale, entrepreneurial clothiers, men who possessed minimal fixed capital (hand looms, spinning wheels, and other basic tools), access to relatively small amounts of credit, and overall worth that hovered around £75 on average. These clothiers were typically only modestly prosperous, but even as they limited their capital investments to what was necessary to sell one cloth at a time, they still ran profitable businesses.[10]

Ryder held a still more prominent and specialized place within this occupational group by virtue of being a dyer. Like other cloth finishers, dyers had to land more credit for heavier investment in the tools needed for their more specialized work. They also typically amassed twice the wealth of the smaller-scale clothiers. And in Ryder's particular case this image needs further and more impressive refinement. His final will and an ad for his prop- erty that appeared in the newspaper months after his death indicate he had £250 in addition to "a Freehold Estate . . . consisting of several Messuages, a Dye-House with a Dying Lead fixed therein, a Tenter Garth, containing half an acre of land, and Tenters." Even at the time of his death he had retained a fair amount of wealth, and this was after years of charitable giving and semiretirement from active trade for more than a decade, living on and diminishing the assets he had accumulated earlier in life.[11]

Making his way to the middle didn't happen accidentally anymore than economic surplus could be maintained without diligence and industriousness, and it is telling of Ryder's busyness and success that his very first words—

"this day I have been upon a journey, tho not a great one"—referred to travel into the nearby countryside to pick up cloth from his spinners. If Ryder begins his self-account in media res, what he was most immediately and conspicuously in the middle of was *work*. In a basic sense this was, of course, a good thing. Few ideas in the corpus of early modern British opinion making get expressed as regularly as the notion that industry is a virtue and idleness a vice. God gave the Earth "to the use of the industrious and rational," John Locke laid out as a major premise of his political thought. David Hume thought "encrease of industry" would transform society as it solved the problem of the poor and dispossessed. Maintain "Church and Commonwealth" not "by idleness," Richard Baxter wrote with an eye on the spiritual value of work, "but by Labour." And in case literacy was a barrier, visual artists could pound home the same message, as William Hogarth did with his industrious hero Francis Goodchild, who was nothing if not a spiritually watchful clothier. But all this advice notwithstanding, holding a pious outlook while undertaking work in

The first plate from William Hogarth's *Industry and Idleness* (1747). Francis Goodchild works diligently on the back shuttle and will eventually be Lord Mayor of London. Tom Idle dozes off, foretelling a woeful life that will end on the gallows. Reproduced by courtesy of The Trustees of the British Museum/Art Resource, NY.

which constant oversight and efficient administration might easily devour earthly time could render industry excessive and sinful. It is not surprising, then, that from the moment we meet Ryder he was not just working; he was worried about the dangers of working in the wrong spirit. "Some have their hearts in their Marketts," he noted one of his ministers preaching in the summer of 1733 to a chapel heavily populated with clothiers and merchants. "Tho they sit as Gods people Sit Yet their heart is Going after their covetousness, and so the word becomes unprofitable to them." "This"—he finished the entry leaving his paraphrase voice—"I frequently find too applicable to my own Case. From Such a frame May the Lord in mercy Deliver me."[12]

Worry about material excess nevertheless did not mean that Ryder accumulated enough to join the ranks of the most prosperous men in the clothing industry. These were the cloth merchants, who sold directly to foreign markets, frequently traveled to London, employed dozens of workers, and were rarely worth less than £2,000. Occasionally their fortunes were extraordinary: the patriarch of Leeds's Denison family had amassed as much as £700,000 by his death in 1782, an amount bigger than the pile of money that the era's much more famously wealthy entrepreneur, Josiah Wedgwood, had to part with on his deathbed. These merchants were not just economically influential; they set the ideal for countless social emulators, and the Dissenters among them made up the trustees of Mill Hill and Call Lane chapels. At the same time that Ryder worked for them by delivering them cloth, they were his social betters and his religious elders. And from the beginning of his recorded life, as at the end, he naturally felt an ambivalence about them that ran parallel to his ambivalence about wealth more generally. One of the first events recounted in the diary was the "splendid funeral of Mr Denisons daughter." Ryder realized this would be something of a spectacle, but he "endeavoured to find if it might be of use to me further than the Curiosity of it, And when they were about to Lay her in the Grave, I considered She was but Laid in Common Dust no more than the poorest, Tho it was in a finer Coffin." Ryder was saying at least two things here reflective of his broader opinion of the town's elite. The spiritual meaning he derived from the event was not simply, as he put it, that "God was no respecter of persons." Social distinctions may have been worthless at the end of the day, but wealth did not necessarily condemn. The "Rich dyed . . . Safe if they were Interested in Christ." Ryder's conditional conclusion after witnessing the event was therefore that it was "not worth desiring to be rich if it is but to Descend with

Pomp into the pit." And yet Ryder was saying that nothing *necessarily* prevented one from being both wealthy and pious.[13]

What sounded doable in the theory—admire but don't envy, be content, don't desire yourself into damnation—could nonetheless be elusive in practice. A month before the Denison funeral Ryder found himself "Reflecting upon a Neighbours profits and Incomes by business far to Exceed mine." His spiritual discipline kicked in: "I Immediately thus reason'd with my Self That if I had the favour of God & a Competency" there was "good reason to be Sweetly Satisfy'd. And again tho Some Others Seem far to Exceed me this way yet Thousands in the World Come far Short of my Enjoyments."[14]

Discipline against envy was never easy. A few pages beyond this entry we find Ryder explaining that on a different day he had caught himself "beholding a man with Superior accomodations for the World to my Self. At first was ready rather to admire them, But by the blessing of God I hope this thought was Quasht." The right lesson to draw was, again, and as always in the diary, to be grateful for "Comfortable Competency." Here, however, Ryder needed assistance muting his ambition and followed his prose summary of the sermon with a self-disciplinary verse he titled "A Contempt of the World." "Raise now my Soul Thine Aspirations high / Dote not on things which Canns't Satisfy," he began the rhymed self-advice before going on for several lines to drive home a theme handed to him by a minister whose very sermon could be taken to reflect the pervasiveness of social envy in his congregation.[15] The advice—don't dote, don't be excessive, keep your eye on Heaven—should already sound familiar. But the fact that Ryder felt a need to repeat it ad nauseam—a need that gives the diary a remarkably static feel over the course of the three and a half decades it covers—arose from an ongoing dilemma. Models for living didn't come exclusively from the pulpit. Daily experience made clear the message projected by the merchants or anyone else profiting from commerce: the acquisitiveness that could lead one astray could also bring visible and impressive economic success. To make matters more complicated, that success, for all its incipient dangers, promised spiritual security against inauspicious poverty as it offered social security against disgrace.

These recurrent worries about materialism, which appear for only the first time in Ryder's opening pages, were nevertheless bound in the beginning of his recorded life to two other preoccupations that do fade over time. The first was maintaining order in his "family," by which he meant his householders. Some of these people were children and teenagers who helped him finish his cloth; some must have helped with other domestic tasks, as occasionally indicated by markers such as "housekeeper" and "manservant"; some were also orphans; and at least some must have come from the workhouse. As we will later see, we never quite know exactly who these obscure figures were—they almost always go unnamed, and those he does identify are missing elsewhere in the archives. But they are there in the diary in the very beginning, with Ryder, as much for the sake of his salvation as theirs, worrying about keeping them spiritually and materially in order.[16]

Ryder's other and connected early preoccupation was to find a wife. Succeeding in this in one sense meant finding a solution to the problem of sexual lust—a solution theoretically found in the prosaic advice of a vast early modern moral literature to marry. In fact, the only time Ryder ever expressed anything like unfulfilled sexual desire in the diary was in the two years before his eventual marriage; in one sense marriage seems to have done the trick. But in this age in which husbands often valued their wives for their accounting skills as much as for their fertility or sexuality, a wife could help manage the household as she tried to help fill it out with her own children. Ryder found someone to multitask in almost all these ways when he married Elisabeth Wheelhouse on June 9, 1735, not long after his fortieth and her thirtieth birthdays. The wedding day was a sullen affair for Ryder, who first saw Elisabeth more as a moral and domestic remedy than as a loving partner. His attitude would nevertheless change as they became more spiritually aligned. It would also become clear over the next few years that the Ryders' marriage would fail to fulfill the cultural mandate to procreate. But even without children of their biological making, by the second half of the 1730s the Ryders' home began filling up with householders. Ryder was never more precise about their number than he was one night as a much older man, writing on the eve of losing his last housekeeper and marveling that he was now being "reduced from a family of eleven or twelve to liv[ing] alone."[17]

During the two decades beyond the diary's first entry Ryder continued to prosper. A regular but vague indicator of this is the anxiety he felt about increase. More useful for us is that these worried expressions occasionally encouraged references to his material life. In 1735, for example, he mentioned owning "a shop," some token of success although it could mean anything from a wooden shack to a separate building to the front room of his house. True to form, the reference appears only because a break-in to the shop carried spiritual meaning. "If I had suffered loss or Damage It was by Gods permission and so was very easy," he wrote toying with the premise that spiritual insolvency meant he deserved material loss, even by way of theft. Two years later, Ryder again reflected his upward mobility by buying a bigger house in Mabgate, a neighborhood in northwest Leeds, half a mile from Mill Hill, a shorter distance to Call Lane and the cloth markets, and still close to the Timble Beck, the water source that the town's dyers used to finish their cloth. For so many people in Georgian England, decorating the home could be a way to show off just how far they had advanced in the world; a century later home decoration had become a way for even evangelical Christians to advertise their piety. But for Ryder the signs of material advancement offered a much more mixed message. As he registered the move he worried about "exceeding the bonds of decency or ability" and hoped he would not make the mistake of investing "any such part of my substance in any thing gay or ornamental." "Furniture in our house more than we used to have," he nevertheless revealingly wrote with his self-reproachful pen. The spacious new interior also sat on a parcel of land large enough for a garden, the existence of which Ryder seemed to mention only because his wife, attuned as he was to the parabolic signifiers of providence, was given a reminder on a spring walk through the yard that "every rose has its thorn."[18]

The Ryders did not stay long at this address. In 1740 they purchased what Ryder called a "small estate" in the same neighborhood and on which he and several workers made improvements for the next ten months. They moved in the day before his forty-sixth birthday, and Ryder's caution remained mixed with his proudest assessments of his economic success. "This Day," he admitted shortly after settling in, "we have had severall acquaintance about us who now seem greatly to approve of our convenient habitation. I seem greatly pleased with it if it may please God to Spare it to me, or me to it. Yet I consider the Great uncertainty of Every worldly comfort." Ryder was no doubt exaggerating to suggest that he actually had access to *every* worldly comfort, but the material life he was coming to know could still easily remind him that he was living beyond basic need. If the home of his good friend and fellow clothier William Arey is any indication, those actual comforts might have included a dozen or so chairs (useful for spiritual or commercial socializing); several tables and some china dispersed in two or three parlors; an "easy chair"; a kitchen with brass pans, a tea kettle, a coffee can, and other iron and wooden vessels; and three or four bedrooms with beds and chests of drawers. This was no minimalist material life in the

1740s; with roughly £50 worth of goods and capital, if we throw in the basic outbuildings and livestock (and in Ryder's case we have to add probably dozens of books), a home like this put one squarely among the middling sort. And yet even without these details on Ryder's own pages, signs of increasing wealth are detectable. To minimize the blow of an untimely death, and to prearrange the distribution of assets that were now great enough to formally consider, he also made out his will weeks after moving into the new home. A few months later a friend told him he should be "fixt" financially, a comment Ryder dutifully deflected with another reference to the "Great uncertainty."[19]

Although Ryder was cautious of his relative wealth, he and Elisabeth nevertheless took advantage of some of the opportunities it afforded them. In 1744 they made their only trip that we know of to London, almost certainly to see friends and family, including Elisabeth's sister, if not also to do business. The trip lasted a month, including a journey down from Leeds that took eight days and a trek back of undisclosed but presumably similar length. We may not know the details of the travel itself, but it is in any case much more of missed opportunity that Ryder was almost completely silent about his spiritual encounter with the metropolis. The entire month he was away he wrote only one entry, which sits in by far the biggest lacuna in the diary. It was tossed off the day he and Elisabeth arrived and tells us only two general things: that on the road south they "found Good treatment at some places" (while at others it was "Indifferent"), and that London "Satisfy'd me that this was not my home." The second line is Ryder verging on comedy. And maybe in a massive personal record in which provincial Leeds supplied more worldly temptations than a watchful soul could handle, this was all he needed to say about London: thank God I don't live there. But whatever the source of the silence, they were traveling to London in the first place because they could afford it. Nor was this their only major vacation. In the summer of 1750 they ventured to an unnamed spa, where Joseph left Elisabeth to take the waters for her health and rode back to Leeds to lament her absence. The fact that it took five days for the Ryders to arrive at their destination is suggestive. There were springs on Quarry Hill and elsewhere along the River Aire just a few miles from their home; a five-day journey suggests that they may have ridden to the much more fashionable spa at Scarborough, nearly seventy miles away. It is no less curious that several years later as a widower and less involved in business, Ryder was sent by his doctor to take the waters himself but went only fifteen miles north to Harrogate. Yet any implications that might be drawn from slim evidence like this should also be set alongside Ryder's more explicit verdict about mixing with the world. As he wrote in the fall of 1747 after a day trip, "my Wife & I were Invited abroad & went to a feast, a feast of Great Variety, there was also music and Dancing, Very disagreeable to my taste upon reflection & trial of the relish of it. I thought I much rather chose to go to the house of mourning than to the house of mirth."[20]

Being festive was one thing; being social another. Ryder constantly alludes to meetings with coreligionists in town—meetings that were meaningful only if spiritually focused—while he kept in touch with brethren farther afield by correspondence. He offers a small gift of details in an unusually vivid mode late in life when, at age seventy-one, he found himself in "a tolerable degree of health" on a day in which he "only followed business in the forenoon, it being a time of leisure for working people in the afternoon. So I sat quietly at my fire side, and went very little further. I writ a letter for my friends to be sent at a convenient season, wherein I gave them some account of my suffering circumstances, as they had done to me in theirs. We are at a great distance from one another but it is a great priviledge that we can by letters so readily hear from one another." It is hard to be more specific about this distance between friends that Ryder found great. At least one of the relatives he bequeathed some money to in his will lived in Ireland; others, like his brother-in-law William Woolgar, lived in London. But we should notice, in any case, that however quaint the moment Ryder evokes of sitting by the fire on a leisurely early spring afternoon, the point of letter writing was to express "suffering circumstances." And not just for Ryder. This is one of many times when we can read the diary obliquely indicating others feeling and behaving as he did, and the social meaning here is clear enough: expressing adversity was a binding agent of this dispersed godly network.[21]

Life outside also enters the diary by way of Ryder's awareness of politics. Even though Leeds did not formally return a member of Parliament, the town's more prominent citizens still traveled to the hustings at York to vote. Since he actually expressed some interest in the election from afar, the fact that Ryder didn't make this trip for the elections in 1734 might mean that he still failed to meet the property qualification to vote: "hearing much of the Talk of the town to be about the choice of a man for a member of Parliament, I found my affections very desirous that God would Incline the hearts of the People to such a One as might prove a happy instrument for the promotion of the Publick peace and Tranquility of the Nation, and that God would make our great Men Good men." But such bland and naive hope for peace and tranquility, and that the new MP would be spared the vanities of power, is also evidence that Ryder's interest in politics ran only so deep. Even in the following days we hear nothing about his response to the Whig victory he wanted. He brought only a little more specificity to his account of voting in early 1742, the one time he did actually travel to York for the occasion, in this case to take part in the election forced by Robert Walpole's opposition. Yet he later told his diary that he was concerned about the act of voting itself consuming his time, and he was only appeased by the thought of God's own participation in the election; voting, he intimated, was less an act of human than divine agency. When the Whig Cholmley Turner was chosen yet again for the seat on January 22, 1742, Ryder was "thankful, because it is agreeable to my Inclination, yet would I rejoyce with Trembling not knowing how soon Men of his character may be out of Favour." As guarded as his gratitude already was, it turned to regret as Turner's victory directly preceded "some Disturbance in the Town. . . . It troubles me to Think that We are so Divided, Oh that God would heal Our Unhappy Divisions, and make us a Holy People, tho may We Comfortably hope to be a Happy People."[22]

The Catholic Jacobites were on the extreme end of the threat to religious freedom posed by a Tory majority, and, as we will see, Ryder was understandably more concerned about the Jacobite march through the north of England in late 1745 and early 1746 than about any election outcome. But political events didn't have to be in front of Ryder's face for him to care enough to register details in the diary, as long as those details also carried providential meaning. When John Byng was accused of treachery for failing to relieve his troops at Minorca in 1756, for example, Ryder made a note of the event. Not only was he willing to give Byng the benefit of the doubt, but the event itself offered an occasion for Ryder to point out the vanity of any sort of politics that were spiritually uninvested. Britons, so Ryder implied by calling to mind a biblical episode, were like the Israelites in the book of Joshua: a people capable of sweeping victories in foreign wars and yet vulnerably culpable because of their inherent sin and divided attention to God. "This day many are ready to mourn, others perhaps to murmur, and it not unlikely but that many are inraged at publick affairs while they look only at Second causes, looking no further than the misconduct or treachery of Admirall Byng, which the Generality thinks he is guilty of. But was there not a cause when Israell fled before the men of Ai?" Byng's execution half a year later led Voltaire to satirical remark in *Candide* that in England it is good to put an admiral to death now and then to encourage the others. But not all Englishmen were so heartened. Voltaire's unexpected ally in Leeds tellingly found comment unnecessary and merely alluded days after the execution to "talk about publick affairs" that were needlessly preoccupying a town he thought would be better focused on its collective sin and piety.[23]

The empathy aroused by the major events Ryder tuned in to also had clear limits. He implicitly recognized the existence of the empire in his expressions of gratitude for British soldiers winning battles abroad or his expressions of remorse when they lost, but nowhere does he recognize that the empire rendered human casualties. Nowhere, for that matter, does he condemn the slave trade, a practice that at least one contemporary spiritual diarist, Pentecost Barker, found morally repugnant, though the restocking of slave ships at Plymouth necessarily brought Barker closer to a reality that landlocked Leeds could more easily ignore. If the Lisbon earthquake in 1755 made Ryder mournful for others who lived at a geographical and cultural distance—he was shocked to learn that, in his estimation, seventy thousand souls had perished on that tragic Sunday in the Portuguese capital—in the same breath in which he calls the earthquake an "awfull providence" he also could not help but express concern about "the very great losses of temporall things which our English merchants will sustain."[24]

The limits of his empathy can be more pronounced in his perception of his social or moral inferiors. "Great . . . it is to attain a sweet contentment in such depressed circumstances," he once presumed after an encounter with an impoverished man: grin and bear it, in other words, because you may very well be rewarded in the afterlife. In the same vein, he had little affection for crowd activity, especially when it threatened his personal safety. But this image needs nuance before we swing too far in the other direction. Ryder fairly consistently avoided casting the first stone. On hearing about a woman "accused of a scandalous sin," he assured himself that if the accusation was false, God would give her "patience in suffering and a happy deliverance"; if true, Ryder promised he would himself "give her true and unfeigned repentance." He dared not insult "but would pity and [be] compassionate [to] any fallen brother or sister knowing that I am yet in the body. I have been tempted, and am tempted, and if God is pleased to keep me from such sins as some others have fallen into, I would desire to ascribe the glory to God." Nowhere, for that matter, does Ryder suggest that women were more liable to sin than men. If any occasion to do so might have presented itself, it would have been late one night during his early widowhood, when a poor woman came to his house in a "sad and sorrowfull frame." Ryder was at first standoffish because he had heard "that at times she has been too free with Strong drink till she had been somewhat intoxicated." But the more he listened to her, the more he grew convinced of her sincerity, and he "endeavored to give her the best directions I was capable of." Nowhere did he connect her mental and emotional state to her gender. He simply lamented the fact that, after his best efforts to offer her spiritual comfort, "she still remain'd Sorrowfull."[25]

By the same token, he could feel more understanding for crowds driven by what he saw as legitimate grievances. On April 28, 1740, he learned of a mob that "Either through Wickedness or want or both plundered severall Mills for provision." If the mob were in fact wickedly motivated, he prayed God would not be too wrathful; but if the plundering were driven by need, then he hoped God would "hear the Cry of the humble poor & Satisfy the Soul of the afflicted & needy & in his own Good Time Send Seasonable relief." A similar logic governed his scattered observations of rioters protesting the expansion of the toll-driven turnpikes in 1753: they "fill'd many spectators with great amazement and fear. . . . A very numerous mobb went by my house in order to pull down the Turnpike at Halton dyal, & accomplished their wicked and rebellious design. Pull'd down and burnt the Turnpikes & laid a dwelling house adjoining in ruins." "Wicked" and "rebellious" indicate clear displeasure with the mob. Yet a week later "tumults of the people still continue. One crying one thing, others another & seem much enraged about the turnpikes. If any of our great men should be prov'd for the Love of money to oppress the poor Inhabitants, it is a Sad case as to their account. But if not, It affords but a melancholy prospect to see such rebellious deed in such a nation who profess Christianity." In the end, Ryder never makes clear whether he thought rebellion was anymore unchristian than the rich oppressing the poor, and that ambiguity is itself indicative of his willingness to hear the full story before passing judgment.[26]

The same measured empathy is implicit in another major theme in his life, charity, which we will turn to in greater detail at the end of this book. Details about how and how much he gave away are, not surprisingly, sparse. Like any action that Ryder glosses in the diary, charity held spiritual meaning, but the act was far less important than the spirit behind it—a spirit that could worrisomely turn up missing as Ryder examined himself. In fact, he references the importance of charity from almost the very beginning of the diary.

But his involvement in doling out Call Lane's relief funds, in particular, is also more apparent at the end of his life, at which point, and in the absence of a family of any size beyond his housekeeper, giving to others gave him personal fulfillment.[27]

Charity also offered Ryder a reason to keep working as he reached his sixties. In practice, retirement was a relatively rare experience for Ryder's generation. Pension plans were uncommon before the nineteenth century, and individually saving up enough money to cease working before death was a less likely possibility than merely inhabiting the middle class, which itself made up a minority of the overall population in the mid-eighteenth century. Here, however, Ryder was exceptional. After vague expressions of uncertainty about whether or not to end his relationship with one of his major, although unfortunately never-named, trading partners throughout the winter of 1755 and 1756, he made what he took to be his "last journey to my spinners upon business of trade" on March 10. A few weeks later (curiously on May 1) he emancipated himself from labor: "This day for any thing that I know at present I delivered my last cloth, and so giving up trading with a gentleman whom I have served for many years, perhaps if I was to join the years I served his Father together with those of his son, there is scarce such an instance in Town, and to the Praise of my Good God I would own it, have been preserved from Losses and disappointments very wonderfully." For someone with a work ethic that could suggest salvation as well as sin, retirement was nevertheless a mixed blessing. And even if freedom from labor brought some psychological relief—"Oh how delightfull 'tis to find/A growing calm upon our mind," he wrote four weeks into his new condition—it was probably inevitable that neither the retirement nor the calmness lasted. By late 1756 he was back in business and would continue to pick up and deliver pieces of cloth throughout the 1760s with a frequency that also suggests something like semiretirement. He never offers a reason for returning to work in entries from the late 1750s, but in 1760, a month before his sixty-fifth birthday, he explained that he did not have "absolute need to hard Labour" but was still "very busy, and was Strengthened to do beyond what many of my age can do." The reason: he found "severall commands in the rule of Gods word by which we are to Govern our Selves." The one that "particularly . . . came to my mind [was] Not Slothfull in business . . . let him labour working with his hands the thing which is good that he may have to give to him that needeth." Not only was Ryder able to undertake at least partly physical labor at a comparatively late stage in life, and not only did he feel a spiritual mandate to do so; now, during these later years in which work and life were no less conflated but necessity no longer a major concern, the ultimate outcome of labor was the benefit of others.[28]

Interspersed with Ryder's impressionistic moral reflections on commerce, religion, his family, the state of the world, and other people is a constant concern with death. The diary is effectively an alternative burial register of Dissenter Leeds, thanks to Ryder's morbid obsession (see Appendix 2). The most relevant death in town that his diary does not directly record was his own. Few diarists are so prescient. But in a text written so faithfully for so long, the final entry is graphically ominous. It is inscribed in shaky handwriting on January 3, 1768, after months of complaints of general weariness, and it is the only entry in the interior of a diary volume written opposite the abyss of a blank page on the right side of the book. Five days later the parish register tells us that Joseph Ryder died of "old age" and was buried on the 11th. For someone who had thought so constantly about death, who had made out several wills beginning in his forties, and who was convinced that countless illnesses were the beginning of a quick end, he had lived a long and productive life.

"I find great cause for humiliation and Self abasement whatever the world thinks of me." This was Ryder confiding a secret to his diary in his early sixties, but the cause was nothing that we would recognize as social disgrace. "I was ready to believe that many persons have a very good opinion of me as to my Character & Conduct," he explained more fully earlier in life, still following the same line of reasoning. "Yet I saw much more of my Own frame & temper than any one Eye could. I lookt upon my Self a Vile Sinner before God (tho I was still ready to hope I was in part sanctify'd) because of my Vile & Sinfull thoughts."[29]

One of the happy accidents of these socially provoked occasions to self-berate is that they suggest how much Ryder was actually admired by others. Some of this admiration may have arisen from his relative success. Upward class movers could so often be driven by emulation, and middling types like Ryder could be exemplary by virtue of having attained some of the material conditions others were after. Yet there is much clearer evidence that what made him likable was his conciliatoriness. Early in the diary, in a lament over his failure to find a wife, he comforted himself with the thought that at least God had blessed him not only with "moderate Labour, and moderate

Increase," but with "a Communicative Spirit." "Communicative" has more than one possible meaning for a prodigious diarist, but context suggests it was a reference to Ryder's capacity to interact well with others. This was implied, for example, when he was sought out to resolve business disputes, or when he occasionally led religious meetings in the absence of his ministers, or why, on at least one occasion, he was called on to help a floundering married couple. "Reconciling offenders oft proves difficult but very delight-full when it proves successful," he proudly wrote days after being asked to prevent "two Persons who profess the Gospell and are members of Society" from taking what he called the "uncommon" step toward getting a divorce (a divorce later entries indicate he failed to stop).[30]

It is ironic that Ryder was so irenic given all the evidence of his internal conflict. But when it came to others, he may have practiced what he was preached. Like Richard Baxter and Philip Doddridge, Thomas Whitaker stressed theological reconciliation. "I very much dislike to hear Gospell truths & Gospell doctrines run down or set at nought, and I long to hear more and more of Gospell doctrines as well as Gospell duties preacht up," Ryder wrote in the wake of heterodox sermons at Mill Hill in the 1750s. Methodists, for that matter, could occasionally be counted among his friends. It may also be that his double-mindedness exposed him to at least two perspectives, the regular accommodation of which may have conditioned him to see alternative views. In this sense there may be yet another parallel with Nehemiah Wallington, who was sought out as a spiritual counselor because the community, as Paul Seaver reasoned, knew that Wallington "had such a long experience of coping with his own morbid scrupulosity." Was Ryder known for his capacity to see multiple perspectives? His ambivalence may in this sense have been a social virtue. He tells us often enough that others failed to see just how riddled he was with vain thoughts on the inside. But that's not the same as saying that others knew nothing at all about his inner conflict, which may have made him an experienced spiritual counselor.[31]

If we can only glimpse what others thought of Ryder, we often get a much more direct sense of what he thought of them. More visibly than by business, his social circle was delineated by godliness. He once described himself as "much delighted In the Company I there Enjoy'd" while spending the evening in a meeting with Whitaker and some fellow congregants and as he "lookt upon the Saints as the Excellent of the Earth in whom I desire more & more to place my principall delight." If the saints were the best people on

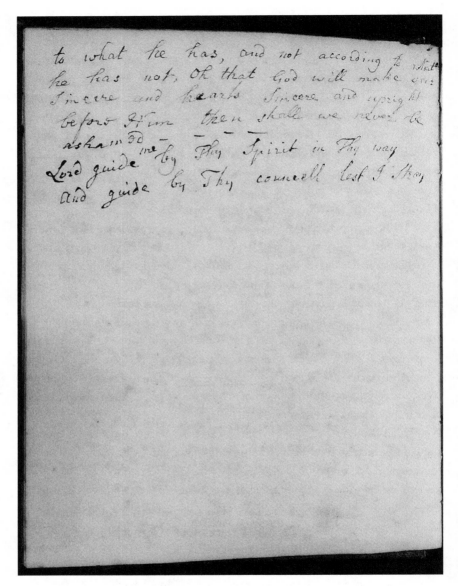

Ryder's final entry from January 3, 1768. The empty page on the right is an ominous sign in a diary of someone so committed to daily writing. Reproduced by courtesy of the University Librarian and Director, The John Rylands University Library, The University of Manchester.

earth, that also means that others necessarily fell short, a perception borne out by Ryder's paternalism not just in his family life, as we will see, but in relationships with others, both real and imagined. On a fall evening in 1749 he found himself wandering through a book auction, "*not being weary* at

seeing or hearing something I might still gett to know," he explained as if the litotes in his formulation (emphasis added) could lessen the consumer desire behind his intellectual curiosity. But he *was* there looking to buy things, and when he handed over "several books" to the auctioneer to pay for them, the auctioneer "said something degrading" about one of his choices. Nothing

Lord bow my will to every Dispensation
at last Display Thy power in my Salvation

January 4: 1768

This day has been as I was informed a
very Cold and Stormy, Day but I was so
confind by Disorder of body that I felt
but little of it; There was a Lecture
at Mill hill preparatory for y Sacrament
on the Ensuing Lords day. I was told that
M Dawson went through the work of
prayer and preaching, but of that
opportunity I was also deprived by
bodily indisposition but God can cause
those that thus tarry at home to divide
the Spoil. Oh that y opportunities of a
religious nature may be blast to those
that enjoy them, and those Satisfied with
y riches of Gods house who are not
able to attend them,
Lord shine upon us by Thy gracious word
And in each case Thy needfull help afford

The shakiness of Ryder's handwriting in the final days of his life is especially evident in his penultimate entry. Reproduced by courtesy of the University Librarian and Director, The John Rylands University Library, The University of Manchester.

indicates the nature or title of the book in question, nor does anything clearly tell us whether or not Ryder had ever actually read it (he refers to it in the conditional—"if it was a bad book"—which might mean he hadn't read it but also that he had not fully considered its moral value). What he does explicitly tell us is that he initially felt "uneasiness" in the face of the auction-eer's response. And yet he still ended up buying the book because, however "bad" it might be, he "might prove the Instrument of concealing it from doing others hurt or destroying it."[32]

Both justifications Ryder gave for his actions are telling. By an insidious mode of spiritual paternalism he was keeping a dangerous work out of the hands of others whom he imagined to be less capable than he was of distinguishing truth from error. In fact, Ryder would also on occasion lend books to readers. But here at the book auction, as he was buying a text more dangerous than anything that other scattered references to authors in the diary suggest would hold a place on his bookshelves, he was taking on the role of censor and justifying his actions with recourse to his moral superiority. "Sad it is that any should publish anything. .. hurtful to mankind," he concluded toward the end of the entry, implicitly separating himself from the bulk of humanity who needed protection from dangerous ideas.[33]

Paternalism was, at the same time, only part of Ryder's outlook. As the scene at the auction makes clear, just as entrenched in his character and conduct was his deep affection for books. Here, for example, he was evidently willing at his own financial and possibly spiritual expense to keep a bad book from being destroyed—destruction too was a means of impromptu censorship, and he never seems to have considered it. Nor is this the only moment when Ryder hints at his relative open-mindedness about reading. Not quite a year earlier he vaguely invoked a scene "at an acquaintance's house . . . who put . . . into my hand a book which appears at first to contain some things contrary to our revealed religion as declared by the mouths of the apostles and prophets." What is striking is less that Ryder was at the house of someone who would read controversial works than that he then makes clear a willingness to go ahead and read the book anyway as he admits that "what I may find upon further perusall I cannot tell."[34]

The same affection for reading books is also apparent in what he claimed was excessive consumption: "This Day having Laid out something more than Common in Books, I Begun to reason a little with my self whether or no my layings out this way was not Rather more than I could well spare out of my stock and Increase."[35] This was Ryder speaking as a young man, and the reference was likely not to his blank diary books, but to the works of other authors. The materiality of his diary, for example, offers a few clues that he often purchased memorandum books one at a time, and that hardly would have been an excessive habit since it would have meant, on average, a new blank book every ten months. In one very rare spot in the diary, for example, he skipped a few days. This was at the beginning of his nineteenth volume (in February 1751), when he was stricken with an unnamed illness that must have come on quickly because he says nothing about being sick at the end of volume eighteen, the last entry for which is February 5. At the top of the new book the date entry reads "Feb the 6th: 7th: 8th: 9th: 10th: 11th: 12th," followed by the explanation, "In these above mentioned days I have endured a great fight of afflictions." Ryder was presumably not too sick to write in his journal—it was common for him to write at other times while citing failing health. It seems rather that he was too sick to venture out to go buy the blank book that would become volume 19. For that matter, the diminishing size of his handwriting toward the end of certain volumes is a graphic clue that he was conserving space for the simple reason that he had not yet purchased the next unwritten tome. If Ryder was buying books in excess, these were almost certainly the works of others.[36]

Some of these authors we learn about from passing references. But as the above example illustrates, Ryder was not always willing to admit what he had read. A glimpse of the range of possibilities appears in the bookplate advertisements in two of his own volumes, which reveal that he bought at least some of his blank books from Samuel Howgate, whose store lay in the commercial center of the city. The fact that the bookplate ad for Howgate's Kirkgate bookshop grew more elaborate between the two volumes in which it was affixed indicates some measure of the store's prosperity. But judging by the content of both plates, this already seems to have been a place with varied consumer possibilities, selling "books in all faculties and sciences," maps, prints, parchment, paper, and at least one doctor's "elixir." Historians of the book have taught us that being in a bookstore in the eighteenth century could offer an experience like that of being in a public library, which was not yet a cultural option in Ryder's Britain. One could browse there or converse with other readers, and that raises questions that are worth asking even if they can't be answered. What ideas might Ryder have encountered while in Howgate's store? Or what books might he have owned temporarily before selling them back to Howgate, who offered "ready money for any library or parcel of old books"?[37]

At the very least, add up these possibilities—the book he bought at the auction to protect the spiritually innocent or the one he borrowed from a friend, the time spent in a bookstore with untold unorthodox possibilities, his comments about being an excessive consumer, and even a vague reference he makes to reading a history of the Duke of Wharton (of which there are multiple possibilities)—and there is reason to believe that Ryder's reading habits were broader than those suggested by the deeply pious authors he does

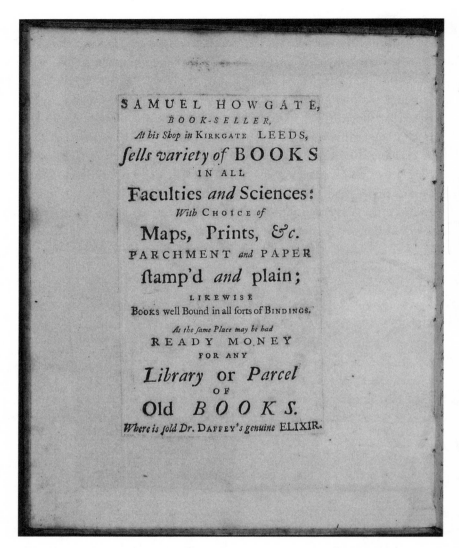

The ad for Howgate's store, a place of varied intellectual opportunity where Ryder bought some of his books. The bookplate ad was affixed to Ryder's tenth volume, written in 1742. Reproduced by courtesy of the University Librarian and Director, The John Rylands University Library, The University of Manchester.

mention or allude to in the diary's pages. The glimmer of intellectual curiosity implicit in his book buying and reading may reflect a spirit of openness built into his Dissenter education. It may also reflect the deeper need for godly learning. "Some considerable acquaintance with many Books is now

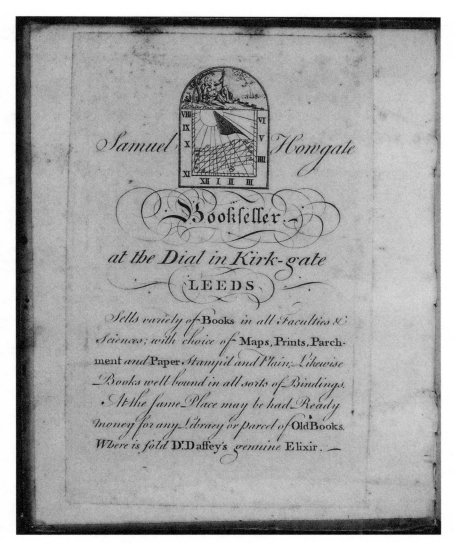

The bookplate at the front of Ryder's thirteenth volume from 1745—1746. The text of the ad had not changed. But the more elaborate image (with the sundial referencing the name of the store's location) may say something about the store's prosperity. Reproduced by courtesy of the University Librarian and Director, The John Rylands University Library, The University of Manchester.

become by accident necessary to a Divine," Richard Baxter counseled in an age when there were fewer books and controversies that one needed to get to know. Ryder wasn't a divine like Baxter, nor did he probably have anything like Baxter's immense and surprisingly diverse library. Yet Ryder was also no ordinary parishioner, and he clearly valued being a learned godly layman, even if, thanks to his vagueness and the absence of any detailed probate inventory accompanying his will, we hardly ever know exactly which books curiosity may have led him to open.[38]

But if the point that Ryder liked books needs to be more tangible, we don't need to speculate further about how he bought or read them. In the story of who he was, the most remarkable thing he did was write them. Whether or not he was willing to admit it (in the diary itself he wasn't), this was his achievement of a lifetime. Along with the religious motive to write so incredibly, his diary also demands a chapter of its own.

# 3. "That Single Word Watch"

And what I say unto you, I say unto all, watch.
—Mark 13:37

*Watchfulness* is the first and principle help to all exercises of Religion; it is the eye to
see them all well done and used, and therefore we set it in the front of all *Duties*.
—Isaac Ambrose, *Media* (1649)

Watching is a duty of general concernment for all Christians and times, but in trying
times a Christian must double his watch, must look out sharp, must be specially intent.
—John Oxenbridge, *A Double Watch-word* (1661)

Let us seriously weigh, how great an offence, how great a dishonour to
God our unwatchfulness is, and this will engage us to watch.
—William Dyer, *Christ's Famous Titles* (1663)

Watching is as needful to the soul as breathing is to the body. . . .
—John Bellers, *Watch unto Prayer* (1703)

Be watchful or vigilant, lest you be too *much entangled with the Affairs of this Life* . . .
—Isaac Watts, *An Humble Attempt* (1731)

I find no Liberty for One that professes to be a Christian to Let down his Watch.
—Joseph Ryder's diary, April 11, 1748

I called these words *Keywords* in two connected senses. . . . Certain uses
bound together certain ways of seeing culture and society. . . . Certain other
uses seemed to me to open up issues and problems, in the same general
area, of which we all needed to be very much more conscious.
—Raymond Williams, *Keywords: A Vocabulary of Culture and Society* (1976)

Ryder's first entry may begin in the middle of things, but it doesn't lack in dramatic foreshadowing. After using the adjective "watchful" and the noun "watchfulness," he forcefully ended the passage with a word he hoped would prefigure the rest of the diary as much as the rest of his life: "May the Lord help me to keep in mind that Solemn Warning which Christ Left his Disciples

May 4 25 1733

This Day I have been upon a Journey, tho
not a Great one Yet would I acknowledge
Gods great Goodness in my preservation, & Especially
So When I consider ye failings & Infirmities
of ye Day, It is of ye Lords mercy that I am
not Consumed and because his Compassions
fail not, If I am Still Spared I Desire to be
more Diligently watchfull against Sin for
ye Time to Come, and would Desire if my many
failings may have this Good Effect upon me to
Excite my heart to Watchfullness, but would be far
from Sinning yt Grace may abound. May ye Lord
help me to keep in mind ye Solemn Warning which
Christ Left his Disciples upon record, & Consequently
all his followers in ye Single Word- Watch. ──

May ye 26

This Day I have been abroad again & have
Comfortably Experienced ye Loving Kindness of
ye Lord in my protection & mercifull preservation
and I Comfortably Hope & readily believe I might &
Shale Enjoy Gods protection from Trouble, or Support
under it Were I but faithfull to Covenant Enga-
=gements & more fruitfull in Every Good word &
work, Not of Debt but of Grace

Ryder's first diary entry. Reproduced by courtesy of the University Librarian and Director, The John Rylands University Library, The University of Manchester.

upon record, & Consequently all his followers in that Single Word Watch." It is an obviously revealing sentence. As unequivocally as he ever says anything, Ryder tells us in the final statement of the first of what would be thousands of entries that this one word holds immense spiritual meaning–a meaning whose immensity the massiveness of the diary would eventually represent. But his usage here is also more subtly telling. He didn't write *the* "Single Word" but rather *that* "Single Word." The demonstrative adjective implies a referent, and yet this is the first entry at the top of the first page of the first volume. To make full sense of his word choice requires imagining an ongoing cultural conversation in which the antecedent for "that" made an appearance and held enough force to be conjured up with such implied shared understanding.

In part, the force of the word derived from its multivalence. Sailors and night watchmen searching for enemies and criminals, northern English folk waiting vigilantly with the deceased one last time before internment, or anyone awake in the middle of the night, resisting the loss of consciousness between the first and second cycles of "preindustrial slumber"–all very particularly called their sleepless surveillance "watching." For good reason: the word shared roots with the verb "to wake" and in virtually all its uses suggested intense vigilance, the radical inversion of sleep–"Some must watch, while some must sleep: So runs the world away," as Hamlet declared in one of his heaviest pronouncements. It was only natural that the word would eventually come in noun form to describe material attempts to master time itself, first as a clock alarm by the mid-sixteenth century and then as a wearable timepiece a few decades later.[1]

Spiritual users of the word imply these same basic meanings: watching needed to be constant; it was a habit probably only some (not the sleepers) could ever cultivate; and it inevitably demanded maximizing time. In his *Seven Treatises,* an early Jacobean work of practical divinity, Richard Rogers felt "watchfulness" had to be his perennial companion. The contemporary spiritual diarist Samuel Ward hoped "all our night watching . . . ought to tend to this end, to the winning of Christ," while John Brinsley found enough resonance in this signifier to title his godly self-examination manual *True Watch and the Rule of Life.* As the Puritan cause grew more militant, and then more beleaguered, the meaning of the word seemed itself to find more precise and anxious expression. "To watch is to keep from sleep, or security, and carelessness, and to be exercised in a holy fear," the Laudian victim John Oxenbridge explained in his *Double Watch-word,* while also urging subtle perception. The Devil was himself a "watchfull enemy"; it was thus impor-tant to keep an "eye open to Gods eye and Gods hand" and "to eye your own heart . . . and see what evil it is a doing, or like to do. . . . to eye your duty, and see what good you should be doing." Or in the words of the Restoration

Calvinist John Owen—words with additional force in an increasingly commercial age—there was "a hardness, an insensible want of spiritual sense, gathered in prosperity, that if not watched against, will expose the heart to the deceits of sin and baits of Satan: watch and pray in this season . . . but especially in a time of prosperity."[2]

Comments like this suggest that to watch was in one sense the duty to be spiritually observant: it drew on an ocular trope and drew attention to the need for an awareness of religious life that any early modern Protestant, or any Christian for that matter, would recognize. Thus the early-eighteenth-century bishop Thomas Wilson called "watching" a Christian duty "commanded by Christ." "How must a Christian watch over himself?" Wilson asked, before elaborating with advice that any of Calvin's closer ideological kin could have accepted: "You must watch over your heart, from whence all evil proceedeth. . . . You must watch over your conscience, to keep it tender and awake, and resolve at all times to hearken to it. You must watch over your senses, and resolve never to please yourself, at the hazard of your soul. And you must watch over your actions, that when you have done amiss, you may repent, and do so no more." In fact, Wilson seems to be a rarity among Anglicans in his willingness to so fully define the spiritual valence of this particular word. But he shouldn't therefore be dismissed as an exception that proves a rule. As was true of other basic forms of piety—prayer, fasting, sermonizing—the roots and resonance of "watching" in a core meaning of English Protestantism bound together believers beyond narrow denominational limits. Hence the importance given to it by a Quaker, like the cloth merchant John Bellers, quoted in one of the epigraphs; or the civil war Puritan Isaac Ambrose (on which more below); or the Anglican Royal Chaplain Edward Littleton, for whom watching subsumed even prayer; or the fallen Anglican George Whitefield, one of whose earliest works in Methodism was *Watching, the Peculiar Duty of a Christian.*[3]

And yet, if there was wide recognition of the need for spiritual vigilance, there was also reason that some believers would have watched with particular intensity. In a nearly tautological sense, this was partly because some were of a "hotter" religious temperature than others.[4] Such people may fit in various categories in the three centuries after the Reformation—Puritans, separatists, Dissenters, evangelicals. And not all overlap. But by definition, and by self-perception, these were believers who fervently tried to lead godly lives along lines recommended by the Reformed tradition. They therefore needed to be watchful of themselves and the outside world as various personal, political, economic, social, psychological, natural, and supernatural forces conspired to disrupt their spiritual courses. Spiritual watchfulness needed to be as constant and comprehensive as God's providential interventions.

Just as importantly informing this more intense need for vigilance was one of the legacies of the peculiar case of English Calvinism. The spread of Calvin's ideas had been distinctive in England from the beginning because it happened amid the failure of his followers to institute presbyterian governance of the national church. English Calvinists of the first generation therefore could not wholly reform the faithful by way of the consistory or a steady supply of ministers—the sorts of external forms of power and discipline that transformed places like Geneva, Scotland, or the Netherlands, where Calvinism was made institutional. A number of "experimental Calvinists" in late-sixteenth-century England therefore adopted a novel approach that, among other things, authorized and encouraged the laity to relatively independently scrutinize their experience (hence "experimental") and participate in the search for their salvation. In their earliest form, in other words, the lay "hotter sort" fully accepted Calvin's potentially devastating major premises— that humans are deeply depraved, the Devil insidiously antagonistic, and God wrathful and inscrutable—as they also accepted more individual responsibility to monitor their spiritual course. The laity could still find support in pastors and a vast literature of "practical divinity" that made clear, among other things, the importance of community and collective action. The way to succeed in "fighting the good fight of faith" was, for John Owen, "not only in watching as single professors, but in marching orderly together." But Owen's formulation is telling: the pious still had to watch largely on their own.[5]

The need for regular and methodical vigilance was also rooted in the godly embrace of providentialism. In so many ways, watching was simply the praxis of the doctrine of providence. That doctrine, as Alexandra Walsham has explained, referred both to the immutable "blueprint for human history" that God drew up at the beginning of time and to God's "direct and dynamic government of the terrestrial realm." God may have made the world with absolute foreknowledge of it, but he was nevertheless constantly involved in its day-to-day operations at the microscopic and cosmic levels and everywhere in between. Of course, to some degree providence, like the need to be in some measure observant, was a fact of life that virtually any English Protestant accepted, at least when it came to the obvious divine interventions. Well into the eighteenth century it was a patriotic litmus test to annually articulate the marvelous, moral, and nationalist meaning in the double deliverances of 1588 and 1688 or in the fact that a terrorist and a king both had their popish machinations thwarted on November 5th. For that matter, no less a mainstream religious figure than Thomas Sherlock, bishop of London, could see clear proof of the providential hand in two earthquakes that struck the capital in 1750. This was a special act of God's intervention, Sherlock reasoned, as he took the occasion to sermonize against the "spirit of indolence and idleness." But to the intently watchful, providence worked in far more subtle ways (think here of Cotton Mather sacredly relieving himself against a wall). And just as importantly, it was tied to their ultimately egotistical sense that their "redemption took pride of place in the divine master plan," as Walsham writes: "Every happening, catastrophic or trivial, was held to be relevant to their quest for assurance that one numbered among the 'saints.'"[6]

This also means that watching could be as profoundly difficult as it was critical to the maintenance of the godly self. It involved serious work to be so sleeplessly attentive to the demands of spiritual practice and divine inscrutability. "Be laborious with your hearts in all God's worship to keep them employed on their duty; and be watchful over them, lest they slug or wander," Richard Baxter advised in his *Christian Directory*, an influential compendium not simply of pious habits, but of the many ways in which spiritual duties could be captured by the metaphor of labor. Far beyond being alert, the watchful also had to be aware that, just as busily, "Satan has been watching and labouring for your Destruction," as Philip Doddridge warned. And much as sin and the tendency of unexamined good works could "contract evil," in Ambrose's words, Satan could escape the senses altogether: "Guard we the windows of our soul," Ambrose therefore urged. "It is incredible, what a deal of pollution and ill the Devil conveys insensibly into the heart, through these floodgates of sin, and therefore we had need to watch over the Senses." Just as incredible is what Ambrose was saying here. The senses, by which he meant the faculties of perception (Wilson's use of the same word above invokes something more like sensuality), were, at once, the means of knowing the world, portals to the soul, and the potential floodgates of sin and evil. Watching thus required a secondary level of reflection, the development of a spiritual sense that could help one watch oneself in the very act of watching.[7]

This was pastoral advice at its most dizzying. It engendered a relentless search for salvation, a constant awareness of the impossibility of living up to God's divine mandate or Christ's image, and, with striking frequency, a sense of melancholy and self-loathing. But it was for these reasons that spiritual diaries were thought to be useful, even if they could also unintentionally exacerbate some of the spiritual and psychological problems to which watching, with or without writing, might naturally lead. As Ambrose spelled it out in both an elaborate exploration of pious vigilance and the first detailed guidebook for spiritual diary keepers, these texts were meant to help one catch sins, judge the wicked, identify the saints, endure affliction, and overcome the temptations of Satan, worldliness, lusts, and corruptions while observing signs of providence and evidence of spiritual election. As concrete guidance, Ambrose offered entries from his own spiritual diary, which details providential deliverances; sermons against vanities; divinely guided victories of the parliamentary armies in the civil war; his brief imprisonment; his ministry in Yorkshire; Charles I's beheading, which, despite Ambrose's disaffection for the Cavaliers, prompts a day of observance in his own family; and so on.[8]

It wasn't just the content of godly experience that mattered, however; Ambrose also diagramed the formal technique for bringing biblical answers and advice into diaries in order to cast light on past experience and the path toward salvation. Here, in other words, was advice about the skeletal structure of the daily entry, which was itself an organizing principle for daily living. Ambrose's examples were again taken from his own diary and fitted into a schema of three vertical columns labeled "Experiences," "Texts," and "Dispositions, &c." One entry, for example, lists under "Experiences": "1647 *Decemb.* 11 This day one observed GODS goodness, in supplying fully all his Temporal wants: This he construed as an earnest both of Spiritual and Eternal favors and mercies in Christ." In the next column, "Texts," appears the explanatory scriptural passage: "Mat. 6. 33. *Seek ye first the kingdom of God, and his righteousness, and all these things shall be added unto you.* Pro. 13.4. *The soul of the diligent shall have plenty.*" And in the last column under "Dispositions, &c." Ambrose's reader could then find advice for how to derive a more affective meaning from scripture: "*Psal.* 62.10 If riches encrease, set not your heart upon them. *Prov.* 30.8 Remove far from me vanity and lyes, give me neither poverty nor riches: feed me with food convenient for me."

| Chap.5.Sect.6. | *Experiences.* | 105 |
| --- | --- | --- |
| *Experiences.* | Texts. | *Dispositions,* &c. |
| 1644. *July* 2. This day was a publike Faſt obſerved in *Mancheſter*, and the very ſame day the Lord returned anſwers, by overthrowing Pr. *Ruperts* forces at *York.* | Iſa. 65. 24. *And it ſhall come to paſs, that before they call, I will anſwer; and whiles they are yet ſpeaking, I will hear.* | *Pſa.*66.13,14.I wil pay thee my vows which my lips have uttered,and my mouth hath ſpoken. *Pſa.* 66. 20. Bleſſed be God,which hath not turned away my prayer, nor his mercy from me. |
| 1646. *Sept.*13. The Lord reſtored one to his health, out of a dangerous diſeaſe,and he praiſed God for it in the publike Aſſemblies. | Deut. 7.15. *And the Lord will take away all ſickneſs.* Exod. 23. 25. *And I will take ſickneſs away from the midſt of thee.* | *Pſa.* 30.3. 12. Thou haſt kept me alive, that I ſhould not go down to the pit;-- to the end that my glory may ſing praiſe to thee, and not be ſilent. O Lord my God, I will give thanks to thee for ever. |
| 1647. *Decemb.* 11. This day one obſerved G O D s goodneſs, in ſupplying fully all his Temporal wants: This he conſtrued as an earneſt both of Spiritual and Eternal favors and mercies in Chriſt. | Mat. 6. 33. *Seek ye firſt the kingdom of God, and his righteouſneſs, and all theſe things ſhall be added unto you.* Pro.13.4. *The ſoul of the diligent ſhall have plenty.* | *Pſal.*62.10. If riches encreaſe, ſet not your heart upon them. *Prov.* 30. 8. Remove far from me vanity and lyes, give me neither poverty nor riches: feed me with food convenient for me. |
| 1649. *May* 5.Some Miniſters were convented before the Committee of plundred Miniſters, and examined by them concerning a Book put forth by the Miniſters of Chriſt in the Province of *Lancaſter*; but the Lord ſtood by thoſe Miniſters, and gave them in that hour what to ſpeak for Chriſt and his Cauſe. | Matth.10.18,19,20.*And ye ſhall be brought before Governors and Kings for my ſake.---But take no thought how, or what ye ſhall ſpeak, for it ſhall be given you in that ſame hour what ye ſhall ſpeak: for it is not ye that ſpeak, but the Spirit of your Father which ſpeaketh in you.* | *Matth.*10.16. Be ye wiſe as ſerpents, and harmleſs as doves. *Matth.* 10. 26. Fear them not therefore, for there is nothing covered that ſhall not be revealed, and hid that ſhall not be known. *Matth.*10. 28. But rather fear him, who is able to deſtroy both ſoul and body in hell. |

P

§.5.

Isaac Ambrose's mid-seventeenth-century illustration of the three major elements of a properly composed spiritual diary entry. Reproduced by courtesy of the British Library.

The language could have been lifted from Ryder's diary. Ryder too found occasions to cite Proverbs 30:8, or "Agur's Prayer," which was regularly called on by opinion makers in early modern Britain to valorize the emerging middle class. More particularly, Ryder almost certainly knew Ambrose's work. It was available to eighteenth-century readers; eight editions of the *Media*, in particular, had appeared by the end of Ryder's life, and Ambrose himself had preached in Leeds in the summer of 1643 to congregations in which one would have found Ryder's forebears and possible local readers of his work when it appeared in print. Much more conclusive is that Ryder actually makes a passing reference in the mid-1740s to reading "Mr Ambrose's work"—a reference all the more significant given how infrequently Ryder mentioned authors by name at all.[9]

But whether or not Ryder knew Ambrose page for page, he was undeniably familiar with the pastoral advice and vocabulary that Ambrose borrowed and refined. We, on the other hand, could be much more conscious of the particular meaning of this cultural keyword, which captured so much of the essence of early modern English Protestantism: the constant, anxious, subtle, and complex examination of the self, the outside world, and the depths of religious habit for evidence of God, Satan, and salvation. Becoming more aware of it begins by seeing how much it made Ryder's diary look the way it did as it also shaped his sense of who and what he was writing for. But the diary doesn't simply record Ryder's watchfulness; it resonates with it fully enough for us to think more broadly about the force of this loaded word and the belief and behavior it captured and encouraged. Watching was a defining habit of Puritan culture in the long term, and it lingers in other modes of thought and behavior in which social order is a function of vigilant souls struggling to keep themselves under control.[10]

We can start with the concrete: what did Ryder's diary look like? Its bound octavo volumes came in two sizes: six and a half by eight inches and seven and a half by nine and a half inches. Virtually the only blank pages, besides those in his final volume that his death left unfinished, resulted from two pages apparently having been stuck together. The numbers also suggest that he grew more affectionate for writing over time. In mostly consistently sized handwriting, his first twenty volumes, which contain 5,578 pages, cover nineteen and a half years, while the second twenty volumes, 6,777 pages, cover fifteen years (see Appendix 1). The two and a half million words he wrote (after we throw in thirty-five hundred more for the forty-first volume that he had just begun before he died) amount to twelve times the total words in Melville's *Moby Dick*, more than three times the number in the King James Bible, and just less than three times the word count of Shakespeare's complete works. By quantitative terms alone, this was a breathtaking achievement, especially for someone who offers no indication of ever having written anything else of substance.[11]

The word count is more than an object of curiosity. For a long time historians saw early modern diaries as polished works, intently focused on the interior life of the diarist. This impression came readily from nineteenth- and early-twentieth-century editions of seventeenth- and eighteenth-century diaries that cleared away the marginalia on the manuscripts, edited out any details thought to be trivial, and made messy artifacts look like finished books. As historians have returned to the handwritten sources, they have noticed instead that diaries were all, in some measure, composite works: alongside daily or semi-daily entries, they variously contained marginal notes, sermon summaries, lists of providences, practical matters, prayers, drafts of letters, verses, and so on.[12] Ryder's diary is generally no exception. Thirty of his forty-one volumes have funeral lists on their back pages; and all but two include back, or occasionally front, matter of some kind: a list of sins to be avoided, a cure for the ague, addresses, or other material that Ryder deemed too practical to be included in the main pages of a journal he wrote to stay spiritually observant. Virtually all of the entries written on Sundays contain both prose and verse summations of the morning and afternoon sermons. Short verses also often follow sermons heard on other days; the number of sermons and religious services he recorded, with varying levels of detail, approaches five thousand, with the number of verses trailing relatively close behind. One of his volumes, as we will see, actually began as his wife's diary. In the fall of 1757, three years after her last entry and her death, Ryder picked up the book she had begun as her own in 1752 and, without any explanation of what he was doing, simply started writing what would become his twenty-seventh volume. Leaving his wife's words in his own repository of self-writing, with no explanatory comment whatsoever, is not just an indication of their spousal camaraderie; it is a reminder of the porosity of the private in godly culture.

Some diaries were nevertheless more formally coherent than others. Virtually the entirety of Ryder's written output was, for example, driven by the daily entry, under which all of his verses and sermon summaries were subsumed. His death lists, the occasional draft of a letter, and so on, were by contrast consigned to a mere one or two pages in the front or back of a volume. Not only did he apparently think that practical matters did not belong in the main pages of the diary, where we instead find daily entry after entry; his mundane marginalia—and here we are talking about the furthest margins possible in a book—also form a tiny fraction of his scribbling when the overall word count is considered. Adding up the pages in the diary not specifically tied to diurnal recording—and almost none of these marginal pages possess the number of words of a typical page of entries—yields a mere 250th of the diary as a whole. Just as conspicuous is the absence of marginal notation of any kind in the diary's main pages, a silence that suggests that writing for the sake of devotional practice was more important to him than reading. Among early modern spiritual diaries, Ryder's actually comes closer to looking like a cleaned-up early-twentieth-century edition than the messier artifacts that have been marshaled as evidence to overturn the view that diaries were reflective of individualism tout court.[13]

This relative formal coherence may have an obvious explanation. By the 1730s, the genre had been around for more than a century and a half, long enough to have given diarists of Ryder's generation a relatively standard sense of what a spiritual journal was supposed to look like. But what is still striking is that Ryder's journal took such remarkably consistent expression over the course of nearly thirty-five years of daily entries; entries from 1733 and 1768 and every year in between are virtually interchangeable. So the question isn't simply why Ryder started writing; it is why he wrote a diary of such length that was so unswervingly faithful to form.[14]

He never divulges why he first picked up his pen. His awareness of Ambrose is suggestive. For that matter, the Bible offers similar advice. As John Beadle noted in his own mid-seventeenth-century guidebook for spiritual diarists, keeping a record of oneself "was the practice of David the Servant of the Lord, who made a Psalm and Song in the day that the Lord delivered him from the hand of all his enemies, and from the hand of Saul." This was also why Moses wrote Deuteronomy, Beadle explained, "which is nothing else but a repetition of the Journeys of the people of Israel, and the great things God had done for them, in their goings out to that day." Ryder reasoned using scripture the same way even if he cited different passages. "I took the encouragement to think that mine and others practice in making memorandum's might be comfortable," he explained one morning in a rare moment of authorial self-consciousness after reading God's command to Moses (in Exodus 17:14), to "write it down in a book what he had done for them."[15]

Such advice by itself still does not explain why Ryder actually took it. More instrumental may have been the covenant he made with his church.

Here too, however, ambiguity surrounds the evidence that he made such a covenant close to the diary's beginning. At the back of his second volume and in his own handwriting sits a "Gospel Covenant" followed by a list of eight "Resolutions of Obedience unto God in the Future Course of my Life," signed Friday night, May 18, 1733, not by Ryder but by a mysterious figure, Peter Stansfield, exactly a week before Ryder started his diary. Words like "writing," "diary," "journal," and so on are never mentioned here, but the need for examination more generally pervades the list. The first resolution calls for morning and evening prayer; the second for nightly serious meditation (before prayer) "on What I have been Doing that Day, what sins I have been Guilty of, What Duties I have neglected in order for particular Confession and repentance as well as Caution for the future, but Especially on the Lords Day Evening I resolve to be more particular in Self Examination, that Great Christian Duty"; resolutions three through seven call for the avoidance of sin and fulfillment of pious duties; while the eighth demands "not only often to review but solemnly to renew my covenant with God, & these Resolutions, to the performance of which I sincerely Beg of God his strengthening & Comforting, & Sanctifying Grace, with the comfortable influences of his Blessed Spirit, in & Through my Lord & Redeemer Jesus Christ." Were the words Ryder's or Stansfield's, or did they both get them from someone else? Was Stanfield the witness to Ryder's covenant? Was Ryder's own covenant written in Stansfield's journal, possibly the same week, as if the two men had a relationship, like that between sponsors in modern support groups, predicated on the assistance they offered each other as they sought the same spiritual course? It is never clear. But in whatever case, the appearance of the words in what would become Ryder's second volume suggests his tacit approval of their message, and regular prayer, meditation, and examination are abundantly evidenced in the rest of the diary.[16]

The need to begin writing also may have arisen from trauma or personal difficulty. The Derbyshire minister and physician James Clegg started writing the notes that would become his Dissenter diary during the Tory-Anglican riots ignited by the Sacheverall affair in 1710. Paul Seaver thought that Nehemiah Wallington began his diary, among other reasons, because of professed difficulties in verbal expression. Samuel Ward, who also had a speech impediment, was driven to resume diary writing after a year-and-a-half break by the crisis he faced when one of his students at Cambridge died from a leg infection. Ambrose's own first diary entry notes his mother's death, while the final and implicitly impelling event that John Rutty records in the memoir mode that precedes his first diary entry was God opening his "eyes to see clearly, that this world is not a paradise, but a stage of troubles, even to those we call good men."[17]

But if crisis of some kind provoked Ryder to begin a diary, the only evident problem he would have needed to address was his own success. "O, what a trial is prosperity," Rutty exclaimed in terms that would have been anything but enigmatic to Ryder: "The reins must be held tighter in time of plenty." It is suggestive, for example, that Ryder's worries about backsliding into poverty are especially pronounced during the first years of the diary. This might mean that he had only recently come into financial security, which itself could so easily lead to its own set of spiritual concerns. Also telling here is the example of the Scot Alexander Jaffray, who began to talk about "watching," as his autobiographical abstract shifts to a diary, after first writing of being so "distracted with worldly business, not a word could I get expressed." Like Ryder or Peter Stansfield or both, Jaffray's solution was to write a list of resolutions for himself. The first called for reading before morning prayer; the second for the "labour to watch more over my heart in time of prayer . . . against wandering and vain thoughts"; and the third "to be more watchful between the times of approaching to God by prayer." What is it, he asked himself, "that Christ saith to such a soul, what bids he it do, for the remedy of its dead condition? 'Be Watchful'—this is the duty."[18]

Simply to point out that Ryder's vigilance of his worldliness binds him to others is to run the risk of understating his worries about the dangers latent in prosperity. These worries take some form of expression in thousands of entries—like this one, from the fall of 1733, still near the diary's beginning, where he complains that his "heart has but been cold in duty, and barren in respect of divine meditation, the too frequent effect of incumbrances of Worldly Business especially when in any Measure it Exceeds." Or this one from less than a year later, on a busy July day that had been "a market day for the body; and the many incumbrances of Time that frequently occur too much obstruct the concerns of eternity." Or here, from the next year, where the "again" in the first sentence says as much as anything: "This Day having again much Business upon my hand I was necessarily put upon much Diligence In some part of the Day at Least I thought upon the Words of the Psalmist, who said, In the Multitude of my Thoughts within me thy comforts Delight my Soul, But fear'd I could not Truly Say so, because my Thoughts were so Carried away with my Business, But I hope did in my heart Esteem Communion with God above all the Wealth which was attainable by Diligence & Success."[19]

Whether or not the incipient danger of economic success explains the diary's inception, it underpins the diary's length and duration, both of which are in any case more in need of explanation. Not all spiritual diarists who began journals, after all, actually maintained the habit to write. The Presbyterian minister Oliver Heywood, to take a single but sufficient example, wrote in his diary from 1666 (a suitably traumatic and diabolical year to begin writing) to 1673, stopped for four years, and then wrote for another three before stopping for good twenty-two years before his death in 1702.[20]

We have actually already come across Ryder's positive justification for writing every day: no "two daily observations [are] exactly alike . . . from hence I concluded that God's mercies to them that fear him are new every morning." There was much for a relatively lucky soul like Ryder to be thankful for, and partly his diary expressed that gratitude. But much more constant in his entries is his preoccupation with his sinfulness. As he put it much later in life: "I desire to walk watchfully that I may not provoke God to withdraw from me. Sin is the only thing which God hates, and which was the cause of Christ's death." In fact Ryder may have been thinking here of words from one of the few books he mentions reading by name, a spiritual manual that brought together advice from Richard Baxter and Philip Doddridge: "Be thoroughly acquainted with your corruptions and temptations, and watch against them all the day; especially the most dangerous sort of your corruptions, and those temptations which your company, or business, will unavoidably lay before you."[21]

As this admonition suggests, every spiritual diarist had, in some sense, an individualized preoccupation with sinfulness. Ryder, for example, might have the occasional and mild suicidal thought. Or the late-Stuart spiritual autobiographer George Trosse considered himself to be a de facto "*Self-Murtherer;* for I liv'd in the constant Practice of those Sins which had a *direct Tendency* to the *Hastening my Dissolution:* For by my vile Courses I *destroy'd* my Health, *weaken'd* my Constitution; and so in effect *courted Death*." But these suggestions were tame compared with those of the predestinarian Wallington, who struggled against the urge to do himself in after having attempted suicide nearly a dozen times in his youth, all for the sake of ending the uncertainty that surrounded his spiritual election. An eternity in Hell at least had the virtue of being unambiguous.[22]

Or then there was overindulgence. Ryder occasionally frets after a lively meal with friends. But his concerns pale next to those of James Clegg, who asks for divine aid against drunkenness at least twenty-six times in his relatively short journal, or John Rutty, who was consumed with worries about intemperance and gluttony, the descriptions of which rival any eighteenth-century novel: "O that I may not abuse riches! Certain it is I often have, in guzzling"; "Feasted, not innocently, in not refusing the bumper"; "An hypochondriac obnubilation from wind and indigestion"; "Ate and drank swinishly: nature wants less"; "I rather exceeds in solids at dinner"; "Take care, take care of the fumes of cyder and whiskey, tremble at the mixtures."[23]

By the same token, if worries about worldliness are common in spiritual self-accounts—"It is no argument that the Lord loves a wicked man because he is rich," the debt-ridden turner Wallington wrote with a measure of bitterness that he was in little danger of actually becoming one of the rich men he distrusted—Ryder stands atop the heap here. But before we listen to Ryder's specific concerns here, we should notice that he was not anomalous. The social world we can glimpse in his diary reveals plenty of others who shared his concerns. Less than a month after beginning the diary, he recorded a scene at Mill Hill Chapel in which he heard "one complain my guilt is too great for God to be reconciled to me, another complaining of his corruptions being too many too strong, another complaining that this present world has got too fast hold upon him." There was reason for Ryder to record these concerns of others. Lapses into excess were not just personal. Sins could be committed collectively. John Beadle explained that every diarist had to "consider seriously, and observe very strictly, what the Nationall Epidemicall sin of the time and present generation may be. Where iniquity abounds, it is hard to determine, but questionlesse every age hath a peculiar distemper." Writing during the tumultuous 1650s, Beadle went on to argue that some ages were known for their drunkenness, others for their swearing, pride, ambition, contention, hypocrisy, or apostasy. The problem in his own day, he was clear, was "open opposition of Christs Kingly office," which took expression in "Sectaries and Schismaticks" unleashed by a decade of civil wars: "Antitrinitarians, Antinomians, Antiscripturists, Socinians, Familists, Quakers, etc."[24]

Whether or not Ryder read Beadle, this was common enough advice, and one of the national epidemics Ryder had his eyes peeled for was the decline of piety. We hear his concern in dozens of conversations he alludes to having with Elisabeth about fellow communicants "growing strange to one another." Just as often, we hear him sharing these fears with others. In a random conversation he alluded to early in the diary, he warned a woman about her waning spirituality—already Ryder was playing a spiritually paternalistic role. Who knows exactly what he said to this unnamed woman, but maybe it was something along the lines of what he puts in a draft of a letter—a nearly singular occurrence in the diary—written at the end of his ninth volume to a young friend coming into adulthood: the "Rising Generation that are Towardly in Religion are the Only blooming hopes we have of a Succession of Pious Christian Men and Pious Ministers among us. If a word of advice may but be accepted from your humble Servant & Distant Friend. I would advice that you would allways be upon your guard and Although you are from under your Parents Eye & observation yet My Dear Friend consider you are under the Inspecting Eye of God who knows your heart." But it is again important to stress that worry about others had personal implications. The broader decline in piety could, for example, dampen Ryder's own fervor. During the early weeks of 1740 his affections ebbed low in his soul not because of worldly losses—this was, he admits, a more typical cause if just not in this case—but because of "perplexities by those about me," an obscure reference to diminishing piety by way of the doctrinal transformation of Dissent, which we will later turn to.[25]

The sources of waning godliness were varied. Denominational variety can appear to play a minor role. Ryder was troubled to find friends in a "wavering frame in regard to the practice of Religion not fully determined in their minds among what denomination to fix." But this is not to say that the seventeenth-century differences between Presbyterians and Independents were still significant in Ryder's Leeds. He never distinguished Mill Hill and Call Lane by these terms, for example, and his irenicism underpinned his more consistent view that all denominations of Christians should and can improve themselves. Without any qualification, for that matter, he could read an unnamed text by the bishop of London that "exposes the present vices of the day" (almost surely this was Sherlock's providential gloss on the earthquakes of 1750) and then find evidence of this Anglican authority's point on that evening's walk, which took him by a busy, noisy pub, filled with the activity lacking in his chapels. Even his worries about the Methodists eventually subsided, as we will see. If what was happening within Mill Hill concerned him more than what was happening in Call Lane, this was because the congregation at the former was quicker to embrace the heterodoxy that would eventually take denominational form as Unitarianism in the years right after Ryder's death.[26]

Ryder in any case more persistently found cause for declining piety in the habits of the younger generations, if not in youth itself. However much he described feeling his sinfulness in middle and old age, he acknowledged during his diary-keeping years that God had delivered him from an unholy youth just as he had rescued his chosen people from Israel. But that deliverance did not eradicate memories of misspent years that palpably lingered in the town where he had lived his entire life. His regular pathways might easily turn into lanes of memory, as one did in the mid-1730s when he passed by a "certain place" where he had committed sins as a young man. More than a decade later, in one of the more poignant scenes in the diary, he takes an evening walk in the fields to meditate and escape the things of this world. The walk, like many of his meditational strolls, was a trip in space, time, and the realm of his thoughts of the eternal. His first recorded observation was of the need for new, inspiring preachers, like a young minister he had met a month earlier. Exigency turned to hope as he wondered if he still belonged to a people blessed by God. But no hope, especially not one as fragile as Ryder's, could escape his unhappy memories. A survey of the landscape reminded him of the unnamed, and maybe unnamable, sins he had committed when he was an unrepentant young man in this very place where he had come now to meditate. If he of all people had been so mired in sin during his youth, there was overwhelming reason to be anxious about the next and unmistakably impious generation.[27]

But once again we come back to the major thread of the diary: these countless remarks on the "decay in the life and power of religion" were also intimately connected to his concern with increasing worldliness. "Hurried with business and weary, weary I was in Duty, but would Gladly hope I was not weary of it," as he put it in the early 1740s, in a phrase formally redolent of the hurry. Later in the same decade and from a wider angle, he judged religion and religious things "to be out of fashion in favour of things of the world." And this could be just as bad for the economy as for religion itself. As he saw it as an old man, declining piety mounted a financial cost in a society driven by both material and moral creditworthiness: "This day has been a fine pleasant day, but many unpleasant accounts have I heard of one and another, great extravagancies which have been found too apparent both among professors and prophane, whereby they are become unable to pay their honest debts, which ought to be warnings to us all that think we stand, to take heed lest we fall." But even as a seventy-two-year-old man, Ryder brought the worry back around to himself. "What is further distressing," he continued, expressing himself in biblical allusions, "is that I find my self so cold in religion, and so prone to wander, and to turn with the dog to his vomitt, and with the sow that was washed to her wallowing in the mire. . . . the wages of sin are death" It was a point Whitaker too was still making in the 1760s, as Ryder noted. "Diligent men could be in their worldly affairs from morning to evening," he preached as Leeds's economy was running full throttle toward industrialization, "yet they neglected living Godly which is the first and great commandment."[28]

That such comments can be found in the 1760s as easily as in the 1730s reveals the consistency of the personal and national sin of material excess that Ryder watched and recorded. And it is that consistency that also stands out more obviously than any other cause as the explanation for the constancy of the diary. Ryder watched so regularly because there was so regularly something to watch out for. As Whitaker preached in the diary's middle years (from Matthew 26:41), one must "Watch and pray lest ye Enter Into Temptation." Ryder continued in his own voice: "whence we had the Duties of watchfullness & prayer Explained, & the necessity of them urged from the Consideration of the many Temptations we are Exposed to in Every age of Life, in Every Station, relation & Condition, rich or poor, and were reminded of watchfullness in a more particular manner against such sins as we find ourselves in a more particular manner Inclined." As if his particular inclinations were not already clear, he went straight to the economic subtext in verse lines written to accompany the sermon—lines that point, as do so many, to the value of moderation:

> The Dangers numerous are, Which Every Saint Surround
> Each Worldly pleasure has its snare If riches do abound
> If poverty Oppress, and makes them live obscure
> They're oft uneasy more or less, While hardships they Endure
> What need has Every Saint to watch & always pray
> Lest Whilst he's uttering his Complaint from God he turns away[29]

• • •

Size may be one expression of the form Ryder so faithfully followed, but so was the diary's relative absence of details, the frustrating and incongruous companion of his prolixity. The one piece of clarity in the vagueness, however, was the criterion governing what he did and didn't write down: whatever was worth recording in some detail had some kind of religious meaning.

Thus we get the structure governing the appearance of names of people and places. Daily entries, for example, never actually identify two clothiers and coreligionists we will later meet, Joseph Sigston and John Darnton, despite their involvement in an event Ryder alluded to for weeks. This speaks to the general truth that Ryder virtually never reveals the names of his business contacts. Similarly, we almost never hear about where his business trips took him, despite the fact that he restlessly traveled for work. On the other hand, daily entries do name the countless ministers he heard preach throughout the West Riding, and here almost no name seems to go unmentioned even when he has to strain his memory to summon a lone surname. The same applies to places where he traveled to hear a sermon or attend a religious meeting or funeral. With more precision he made record of deceased members of the Dissenter community on the day they died or were buried, moments with obvious religious meaning that provoke details not just in the daily entry, but in the death lists at the backs of most of his volumes, where he also often included age and cause of death (see Appendix 1). Those back pages were themselves qualitatively different from the daily entry. And it is there, somewhat predictably, that we find the names of Sigston and Darnton, whom we can then connect to vague references in the daily main pages. The logic of much of this seems clear enough: specifically referencing ministers, chapels, and the deceased reflected Ryder's regard for his diary as, in some sense, a record of his Dissenter community that would tell future readers, if nothing else, who belonged to it and who shepherded it. Even in self-writing, there was space for other professors and any specificities that may have had socially spiritual utility. And if here in the back pages we also find other practical matters, though much less frequently, this makes the point another way. These marginal pages were functionally and spatially removed from the thoroughly sacred territory of the rest of the diary.

But the religious meaning that justified writing in those main pages was nevertheless not always so obvious. Writing a proper spiritual diary required more than simply knowing the difference between market and chapel, or minister and merchant. It meant knowing a more elaborate hermeneutic for deriving the divine from the ostensibly ordinary. Not all entries (though thousands do) simply tell us "this day I prayed, watched, worked, heard Whitaker preach a sermon, wrote a poem about it, prayed again and now I'm off to bed." If God was the author of daily differences in "matter or stile," it was up to watchful diarists to open their books daily and explain how that was the case. The trick was that as ubiquitous as the signs of providence potentially were, not all conveyed enough divine relevance to earn inclusion in the diary. The necessary and defining role of a spiritual diarist was to distinguish between the ordinary and the providential, the implicit line between which began to be drawn with the letters of the words on the page that indicated an observation was actually worth writing down.

To put this in terms that might be useful for thinking about the structure of any early modern spiritual diary, providential meaning was read less as straightforward prose than as poetry—as a form of expression made distinctive, that is, by catachresis, an unexpected use of language. The various ways in which poems typically deviate from ordinary modes of communicating— by tropes, symmetry, contradiction, nonsense, ambiguity, rhyme—send perceptive readers on a search for resolution on a level of meaning more unified than the messy reality we know through representational language. In the same way, providentialist watching and writing so often seem to have been stimulated by unusual signals indicating that God, the divine poet, was in the process of signifying.[30]

The point isn't simply analogical. Poetic and providential forms of catachresis overlapped. Ryder's recognition of tropes, for example, could regularly send him on a search for divine meaning that ended with the articulation of details. He bothered to tell us he had a garden only after he noticed that the weeds he had to clear away around his house were like sins that needed to be eradicated before spiritual fruits could take root, or that tilling and watering the ground were like receiving the word and the Holy Spirit. Or then we get a fleeting detail of material life in Leeds when he was struck by a metaphor on one of his daily walks: "I saw two persons hewing a knotty piece of Timber for their work, which reminded me of the Power of God, who can of persons, who are perverse by nature, & prophane by practice, make unto himself a peculiar people by the hewings of his word and spirit and change our nature." Such details need not relate to physical or social experience. Reading about the pharaohs of Egypt, Ryder once explained, provoked the thought that "an Estate here below might be Gain'd Through the Favour of the king or Prince." But, he countered, "if the Prince was

Arbitrary It might Very soon be lost and Gone. Herein I was Led out to see the Excellency of Heavenly Enjoyments above Earthly because they are an Enduring Substance." In the logic of the negative metaphor buried in the conditional, God (like constitutionalist monarchs) is unlike the pharaohs because his divine judgment is not arbitrary; hence heavenly enjoyments, which God bestows, differ from those that an arbitrary earthly prince might grant to his subjects.[31]

Providence was just as likely to appear in symmetry. Like the rhymed words that brought unity of form to his verses, the patterns Ryder observed led to recognition of an active and unifying presence in the world, much as they offered an occasion for bringing spiritual narrative coherence to his own life. Probably at no time was providential meaning more regularly obvious than on the fifth of November, a day on which Ryder recorded Joseph Priestley sermonizing on the remarkable linkage of three events: the Gunpowder Plot of 1605 and William of Orange's landing at Torbay in 1688, which were connected by the fifth itself, and the deliverance from the "Invincible Armada" in 1588 an exact century before the Glorious Revolution. Twenty years earlier, Mill Hill's enlightened minister Thomas Walker made more or less the same point, explaining that the fifth of November was a reminder that God had done "great things" for Britons, giving them good land and a means of education while delivering them from popish tyranny.[32] Symmetry nevertheless did not need to occur on such a grand scale. Just as regularly did Ryder find meaning in the annual occurrence of his birthday, entries for which offer the closest thing we ever have to an autobiographical narrative. On the first birthday he celebrates in the diary he complained of failing to accomplish personal goals. Three years later he wanted the occasion to be "the birth day of some spirituall blessing to my soul, yet while I was thus praying the appearance of some triffling worldly loss seem'd to interrupt me." In fact, his regular practice on these days up until the mid-1750s was to focus on his business. On turning forty-three he thought it auspicious to receive "a sort of promise of continued Trade"; at forty-six a neighbor tells him he seems financially secure; the next year he "lacked nothing," although he felt undeserving.[33]

The occasion gathered additional meaning when Ryder married Elisabeth, whose birthday they chose to celebrate not on the day she was born, but on the day she was baptized, which (by Ryder's reckoning) happened to be March 25, 1705, ten years to the day after Ryder's birth.

Playing up the symmetry, even if it meant slightly playing with the calendar, made a relationship that was by its nature as spiritual as it was emotional or material also *seem* more providential. And if in the happier years of their marriage the birthday entries offer an image of Ryder at his most grateful, the day enlarged his capacity for sad reflection when Elisabeth's health irreversibly declined. For two years after her death he refused to mention the day's relevance at all, and when his annual observations eventually resumed, he at first felt little to be thankful for—"I am but Eight years short of Seventy, and those are often years of little pleasure." But over the course of the next year, as he worked more than he expected, he noticed his labor bolstering his health and offered a few details on turning sixty-four as evidence: "I eat heartlier & sleep more sweetly than I did while I did less. I am at present through the goodness of God in a better state of health than I have sometimes been." His final birthdays were nevertheless mostly unhappy and require characterization as contradictory of the typical nature of things rather than as symmetrical—though they are no less devoid of providential meaning—since he was increasingly amazed to be living beyond the "usuall term of mans life."[34]

Many other signs were like late-life birthdays in holding their divine meaning whether by symmetry or by contradicting typical patterns. If the weather was remarkably providential when it produced nation-saving winds in moments spaced exactly a century apart, it was no less so when unusually disruptive. A late spring snowstorm inspired Ryder to give details that in their vividness convey the presence of the divine hand in the event: "Going to the barn to Give my Cow hay, & Near my own Door I found the Snow Drifted nine Inches Deep—Gods works are upon Observation all wonderfull but going abroad the Same Day I saw Snow Drifted near a Yard & a half thick." Or the next year an odd "mixture of weather Hail, rain & snow" led to "a renewed call for Faith & Patience & Trust in God, who by his Power can, and who in his Goodness will do Every thing for us that is Good . . . If We on our Part Would by all his Dealings & Dispensations be reformed, repent & return unto him." Ryder was also far from unique in expressing these habits. An early summer hailstorm in 1711 brought the minister James Clegg to attention. Clegg saw hailstones "8 or 9 inches about and some larger" killing all manner of birds "in multitudes," stripping trees of their bark, and damaging houses and crops. He was lucky enough to sustain little damage, but he lamented that some of his "hearers had very great Loss. This was a dreadful day and many thought the dissolution of things was at hand. Oh! may it be improved and awaken us to prepare for that great and terrible day of God. Great and marvellous are thy works."[35]

More like the category of nonsense in poetry were "curiosities of Nature and Art," which Ryder thought could be "very pleasant to the eye but upon Cool Consideration [were] a sorry portion for an immortal Soul." He consistently held this negative view when it came to cultural curiosities, even if they could at times be tricky to read. A gentleman's collection of artifacts that he saw in 1737 was obviously vain. Seeing the royal family rendered in wax was, however, "very splendid," until later reflection made Ryder judge it "not very profitable to the heart" and, in essence, a form of idolatry. Nature's curiosities, on the other hand, could send a happier message. On hearing about a woman on Vicar Lane giving birth to "three living children," Ryder took the "wonderfull" event as a sign that he should be ready to relieve her burden with charity; but of course the fact that he had to resort to such a measure, however deserving he found the recipient, meant that even the wonderful could come with the price of responsibility and guilt.[36]

But of all things, nothing shifted in meaning with such polarity as the signs of economic life. Here the distinctively poetic characteristic of the providential was *ambiguity,* but not an ambiguity tied to his belief that economic gains could suggest divine approval while losses signaled disfavor— few beliefs run so consistently through the diary. Ambiguity arose from the fact that the line that separated success from excess and labor from worldliness could so easily be blurred. To make matters more complicated, Ryder could also hope for shifts in meaning in ways that so much modern economic theory dogmatically claims are irrational. If the equilibrium of moderate success could suggest the providential hand, it might also be necessary to embrace economic *loss* in order to restore the balance that excessive success disrupted. In prosperous years he explained that he had "severall times Considered of a Disappointment I mett with about seeking after an Earthly treasure. I lookt upon it to be in much mercy hoping hereby to find my affections more taken of from things below, & more at liberty for the pursuit of a better Inheritance." "The world with its alluring charms," as he put it in one of his thousands of verses (the rhymes of which themselves brought order to divine meaning), "Would tempt me Jesus from thy arms."[37]

The signifiers of providence didn't simply provoke Ryder to write details in prose; they also encouraged him to quantify. When he thought that

14,000 priests died in the Lisbon earthquake, the seduction of British anti-Catholicism palpably overwhelmed his desire to stay tied to reality. But it is also the case that the numbers bolstered parabolic meaning. God was no doubt making a more dramatic point if he killed 14,000 priests rather than a mere 140. Numbers also increasingly appear as Charles Edward Stuart's army marched closer to Leeds in the fall of 1745. "I began to Examine my Self, & lookt on my self greatly adding to the National Guilt," he wrote two weeks after Charles had landed at Eriskay. The nation was on trial in Ryder's mind, everyone was guilty, the fate of Protestantism hung in the balance, and the fact that so few were "complaining of the Sins of the nation or endeavouring to reform them" in favor of trivially focusing on "this or the other officer at court or in the army" was thus "only stupidity." Ensuing days brought out bromides. "In an arm of flesh I would not trust for protection." "Religion is out of fashion." People like him who were unfit for military service needed to pray; people unlike him in pious temper needed to desist from sports and sinful pastimes. The Whiggish Whitaker preached about the "invasion and unnatural Rebellion of a Party in our Land" and prayed that his congregation would come "to a Generous Defense of our King & Country of our Liberty & priviledges, since everything that was valuable to us was now in Danger." And then the specificity appears, as extraordinary in Ryder's generalized prose as the presence of a foreign army on British soil. October 10: "near a thousand soldiers coming towards the north in order to Attack the Rebells which are coming out against us." October 22: "an army of men computed to be nine or ten some say twelve thousand men came to encamp at Clifford Moor being on their Journey towards Scotland in order to attack a number of men Rebelliously risen to give disturbance to our King & Kingdom. My heart is much concerned for another appearance of providence in our favour." October 23: "This day I had an account that there was upon the road for Scotland eighty carriages loaded with powder and ball for the use of our army." When news of Hanoverian victory eventually reached Leeds (the Battle of Culloden was fought on April 16, 1746, but people in Leeds only heard about it a week later), Ryder wrote down the signifiers collectively sent by the town to God—a collective reverse transmission—in gratitude for their providential rewards: "Great rejoycing there was at Leeds. Ringing of bells, & abundance of Illuminations & Great bonfires, as outward Expressions of Joy."[38]

We can find, finally, a similar logic governing Ryder's attention to time. Time is always implied in a diurnal account written to get the most out of a finite life for the sake of the eternal. More mundanely, Ryder also evidently had access to a timepiece. But he never classified time passing by hours or minutes unless an extraordinary occasion called for it. He noted, for example, that his wife died at five o'clock in the morning. Or he once mentioned having to write a daily entry at 11 p.m., a fact worth noting to illustrate that he had been so "lively" throughout the day that he hadn't gotten around to writing until later than usual. And this too was spiritually loaded because he took the day's busyness as evidence that the here and now was steadily vanishing. What is all the more striking about the paucity of such details is that Ryder would have used his watch and his numeracy throughout his business life. His trade notebook, for that matter, offers abundant evidence of a willingness to quantify (although, equally obscurely, no explanatory text accompanies the numbers written there). That he wrote with such consistency, structure, and predictability tells us he was a creature of habit. But his faithfulness to such a functional form also indicates just how much writing was intended for a specific purpose: not to mindlessly collect trivial details, but to record divine meaning, to stay on spiritual course, and to fulfill the spiritual promise of that single loaded word "watch."[39]

Does this therefore mean that he wrote only for himself? Exhibit A in the case for his awareness of audience is the very survival of the diary. The option existed to throw finished volumes in the fire, as might have been done with the artifacts of mere spiritual commonplacing. This was an option Ryder obviously never exercised, at least with any of the surviving volumes (although the possibility exists that he started a diary earlier in life that he destroyed). More than this, he actually selected the beneficiaries for his manuscripts and can very occasionally appear to speak to them, as when he uses a phrase like "what *we* call a catching hay time" (emphasis added), in the process distinguishing between what he and his contemporaries call a harvest period and whatever alternate name posterity might give to it. Ryder even felt literary rivalry on at least one occasion. While he was out walking on a spring day in 1761, a fellow diarist called him into his house to "entertain me with severall of his manuscripts." As Ryder disappointedly found that what the man had written was mostly "Quotation from other Authors," he verged on pride in reminding his diary—and his implicit audience—that he had himself written more than pastiche. This was Ryder in slight denial of reality since he often quoted authors without attribution. And this was also Ryder, for once,

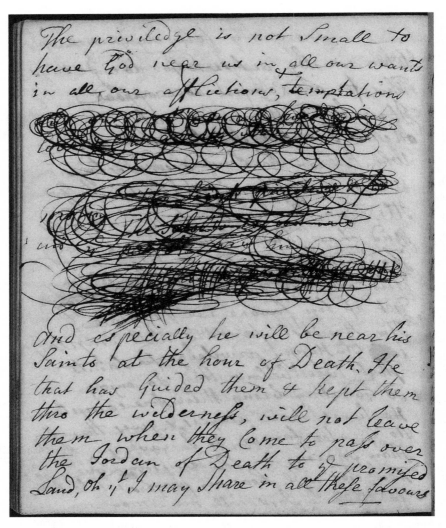

Whatever exactly Ryder wrote under this black cloud of ink was clearly not meant for other readers. For that very reason this is a strong suggestion that he imagined others one day opening his diary. Reproduced by courtesy of the University Librarian and Director, The John Rylands University Library, The University of Manchester.

not checking his sinful feelings, possibly because he tried to sublimate pride into a critique that feels as literary as spiritual: "I have heard or read of other eminent Christians who have spoke or writ of their attainments with a greater degree of humility [than that of the fellow diarist] . . . I allways esteem humility a comely Christian Ornament."[40]

Occasional nonverbal graphic clues can also evince tacit acceptance that other eyes would one day see the diary and therefore shouldn't see some things he had written in it. In one case, he was insistent on keeping his original words hidden. But just as intriguing is an instance where he seemed almost indifferent to a formal blemish. There are at least two ways to read the evidence here. While writing his entry for March 29, 1767, he either turned ahead a page when he reached the end of the prose part of the entry in order to compose a draft for a verse that he then rewrote in its proper place, or he somehow lost sight of the fact that he was on the wrong page and wrote eight lines before he realized his mistake. In either case, he simply drew an "x" over the eight lines with no apparent intent to destroy evidence of their existence and worked around them as he wrote his entry for March 31. If in fact this is evidence of Ryder writing drafts of his poems, then that itself could be taken to mean that he thoughtfully constructed verses in the hope that they might be as useful to others as he himself found the hymns they emulated; at the same time, his ability to assemble an artful collection of spiritually meaningful lines also may have been a skill he needed to show God, his ever present other reader. In whatever case, the fact that he left the crossed-out verse nearly entirely visible and intact suggests that he was unbothered by taking his implied human audience deep enough behind the scenes to steal some of the magic of the diary's performance. The implications of these curious pages are even more varied if showing the reader his mistake in written performance was itself a useful lesson in Christian humility.[41]

The diary holds other evidence about Ryder's sense of his human audience that can be read in contrasting ways. He fretted when his entries were lackluster. After a string of passages that read like lip service, for example, he complained about lapsing into empty ritual and losing his abilities to watch. "There is so much coldness, & So much formality prevailing in me That I can Scarce Tell What Judgment to form of my Self." This concern could lead him to consider "desisting work" on the diary until he felt more "affected." Yet he noted that doing so might look like "weariness in well doing, which through Grace I would not be Guilty of." The audience in front of which he worried about looking weary mostly seems to have been divine in this case, but it is also possible that he was worried about seeming uninspired in the eyes of human readers.[42]

A slightly mixed message about audience also comes forward from one of the most striking features of the diary: his verses. Calvinists of an earlier continues or takes away, life or the enjoyments of life when and from whom He pleases, Oh that I may enjoy life and all the circumstances of it with patience & thankfullness, and have death in daily expectation and be endeavouring by y' Assisting grace of God so to live as that death may be no terror to me, and when the Summons shall come be it at Evening, at midnight, at cockcrowing or in the morning may I not be found Secure and Sleeping but in a watchfull posture, oh that I may find a growing hatred to all Sin and a growing love to God and holyness, a growing purity of heart and life, then will Sight of God be comfortable — — — — Oh that in God I may find sweet delight Then Joys will grow when faith is turn'd to sight

March y' 31

This day Gods goodness appears in Sending us a fine warm day and tolerably dry most of the day, I asked a farmer or Country man how seed time went forward & he answered that y' Season was So wett that in Some land they could neither plow nor Sow, and Said they were late if y' weather

The page where Ryder wrote eight lines of a poem, possibly a draft, and then drew an "x" over them. Whether this represents a draft or a mistake on Ryder's part, the clean "x," set in contrast to the violent crossing out on another diary page (see page 68), is a meager attempt to conceal what he had written. Reproduced by courtesy of the University Librarian and Director, The John Rylands University Library, The University of Manchester.

descended from above
and did Gods holy law fulfill
He suffered on the tree for us
according to Gods Soveraign will
if we on Jesus do believe
and take Him for our Lord and King
and well observe His precepts here
we shall with Him in Glory sing

Should take up, and corn I was Informed was
upon y advance, sore complaints prevail among
both tradesmen and the poor, but y nick of extremity
is Gods chief opportunity, Oh that our prayers
may be more fervent, and our complaints fewe
for shall a living man complain a man for the
punishment of His Sin, We are well assured
that God is righteous in all His ways, & holy
in all His works, and punishes us less than
our iniquities deserve, and is kind to y unthankfull
and to y evil, for it is of His mercies that we
are not consumed, and because His compassions
fail not, Oh that we may experimentally find
that God in His righteous providence, and rich
grace is causing all things to work for our best
good, as Itt can, & has promised to them that love Him
Lord may Thy providence and grace appear
To bring us to Thy Self whose help is near ———

generation, like the late-sixteenth-century clergyman Henoch Clapham, who
castigated himself for an impious youth because of an interest in the "vayne
exercise of Poetrie," easily could have condemned much of Ryder's diary.
Views may have changed a century later. A vision of Ryder's kindred spirit
appears fleetingly in Benjamin Franklin's passing comment in his autobiography about his godly uncle, a London silk dyer who wrote original verse

The previous diary page where the poem appears in full. Reproduced by courtesy of the University Librarian and Director, The John Rylands University Library, The University of Manchester.

and "was a very pious . . . Attender of Sermons of the best Preachers, which he took down in his Shorthand and had with him Many Volumes of them." It is nevertheless difficult to find a spiritual diarist who wrote verses as consistently as Ryder. The most substantial ones–those of eight lines or

Jesus descended from above
and did Gods holy law fullfill
He suffered on the tree for us
according to Gods Sovreign will
If we on Jesus do believe
and take Him for our Lord and King
and well observe His precepts here
We shall with Him in glory Sing
But if our Saviour we should Slight
and all His precepts disregard
What can we then expect to find
But mis'ry as our Sad reward
Oh may we Jesus much esteem
Be our beloved, and our Friend
Then may we hope for comfort here
And Joys above when time Shall end —

March ye 30

This day by the goodness of God I was in
some degree better able to walk and work
than I have been some time past; but to
whom is praise due but to God ye Father
of mercies and God of all comfort & conso-
lation, who can wound, and who can heal
That I should in any measure recover at
this age of life while Such numbers who
are much younger than I do Sicken & dye
is entirely in the hand of God who gives

more–appear after Sunday sermons, of which Ryder heard slightly more than eighteen hundred over the course of the diary. But given that shorter verses–sometimes a mere couplet or quatrain–appear after sermons preached during the middle of the week, and given that some couplets occasionally appear unattached to any sermon at all, there are easily three thousand verses of varying length scattered throughout the diary.[43]

No single function explains these verses. In part they must have been mnemonic. Ryder never directly said this, but he does indicate having trouble remembering. "Poor broken Scraps they are which I can recollect, for my memory is so poor that when two lines of a Psalm are read together for Singing I very often forgett part," he confessed at an age when memory can naturally begin to diminish. In part the verses may have been written to express a talent he admired in hymnists like Isaac Watts or Philip Doddridge, whose simple rhyme schemes Ryder virtually always adopted. But if we are left guessing about where Ryder got the idea to versify, it is much clearer that these rhymed lines nearly invariably mirror the content of the sermons that they follow in sequence. Sermons on the need for scrutiny generated poems with transparent titles like "Self Tryal Necessary," while sermons on the need to be charitable and devout led to poems like that he wrote in the late 1740s, "A Good mans Character," in which he defined the standard of the pious man that he set for himself:

> Unto the needy in Distress,
> He deals with liberall hand
> And as God does his labours bless
> Gives out all Gods Command

His familiar concern with vanity appears in poem form, as "Vanity of Vanities All is Vanity" (with a title borrowed from Ecclesiastes), but it also followed a similarly themed sermon:

> Vanity of Vanities are those Joys below
> To which we do Such Eager Temper Show
> Riches & Honours, Pleasures Profitts too
> All tend to make an Empty Gilded show

Funeral sermons preached for the untimely dead would provoke verses on sudden death; those preached for deceased elderly men and women would lead to poems on old age. Or then there is the revealing case of George II and Caroline. When Ryder heard a preacher sermonize on Caroline's death, he promptly wrote the poem "On the Death of our Queen." In fact, he referenced Caroline only in the title—even within structures, Ryder could improvise. As so often, he saw the occasion in broader spiritual terms, and not without a hint of class-consciousness:

> Behold how all the World must needs Obey
> The Voice of Death that calls them hence away

Princes & Peasants all alike must Go
To Endless Joys, Or Everlasting Wo

But what is especially interesting is that Ryder was more affected by the death of Caroline's husband. News of George II's death on October 25, 1760, arrived in Leeds to Ryder's knowledge two days later, and he not only dedicated several lines in the entry for the twenty-seventh to the event, he wrote an entire page at the end of that entry's volume on George and his various issue. He was, in other words, more than willing to write about the king's death in prose. And yet, that Sunday he recorded no sermon preached specifically on George's death, and he wrote no poem to mark this obviously important event.[44]

Probably nowhere is his sermonic inspiration for verse more obvious than in the case of the Jacobite army's approach to Leeds. As we have seen, the Jacobites had Ryder deeply concerned as they represented a threat to both his religious and political outlooks. At the height of his worries toward the end of November 1745, however, he went to hear Whitaker preach not about the army headed toward the town, but from the Gospel of John: "Love not the World, Neither the things that are in the World . . . whence we heard the inconsistency of the Love of the World with the Love of God, Or of serving two Masters Of Contrary Interests." Whitaker's familiar cautions against worldliness may of course have held implicit political meaning. The problem of serving God and Mammon could correspond to the inconsistency of serving a Hanoverian and a Stuart. The analogy is imperfect, but a similarly possible allusion appears later in the sermon, as Whitaker tells the congregation "that we ought So to Love the World as to take care for necessary Subsistence for our Selves & family, to go to the Ant to Consider her ways & be Wise. To provide things honest in the sight of all men and to be Diligent in the Duties of our Place & Station. We heard that the Danger lies, in Our loving it, So as Violate the peace of a good Conscience to obtain it, by fraud or oppression." How could the words "fraud" and "oppression" have failed to resound with political meaning during these weeks? And yet, however allusive the sermon may have been, however thick the air with the town's collective fear of foreign invasion, Whitaker took the occasion to draw explicit attention to the underlying national epidemic: the sin of worldliness for which Leeds, under imminent siege, was in the midst of being punished. That Whitaker gave such attention to generalized worldliness at a moment like this is by itself striking; it is as if the easiest way to remind his congregation that they were flawed creatures was simply to point to their immersion in their material pursuits. But the larger point here is that there was such *predictability* in the way that Ryder wrote his poem following the sermon on November 24—not on the immediate and dramatic danger the Jacobites posed (a threat that had consumed him all week), nor on his loyalties to George II (a king he admired), nor on his fears of Catholicism (an international threat at which, like so many Britons, he shuddered). Falling perfectly in line with Whitaker's sermon, Ryder's poem for the week bore the self-explanatory title "Of the Danger of Worldlymindedness."[45]

And in case we think Ryder might have been averse to writing a poem with an anti-Jacobite theme, we simply need to turn to a spot where a minister sermonized directly on the subject. The previous month he heard a minister from Morley preach that "Insurrection & Rebellion is on foot in Order to Dethrone our King, & to Strip us of all that is Dear & Valuable to us . . . we might be brought to burn at a Stake as our Friends have Done before us." The sermon thus called for public prayer and Ryder responded with "A Publick Spirit a Christian Spirit":

> Away with Private Interests now
> Let Every Praying person Go
> Into Gods Courts, & Crave transcend
> His Pious prayers to God his Friend
> In Worldly things let's not rejoyce
> While Zion has her mourning Voice
> But with her let us weep and Cry
> That God will to her help draw nigh
> May God prevent Insulting foes
> Who meditate revenge & woes
> Lest they Should overrun our Land
> And have us at their Stern Command
> May God in Love preserve Our King
> And to His house Salvation bring
> That we may still with Chearfull Voice
> With him & Every Saint rejoyce.

The commingled nationalist and economic symbolism is arresting. Britain as Zion calls in her mourning voice for Britons to forego their private interests for the sake of the common good; this is effected and signaled by a collective appeal to God to preserve his king from foreign invasion; only unified prayer can save a sinful people on the receiving end of divine punishment. But what we should also notice is that the verse is written on cue. However vivid its imagery, its catalyst and its justification came from the pulpit.[46]

Passages like this nevertheless both negate and affirm Ryder's individualism: if the placement of the verses was structured, their content can be idiosyncratic. For that matter, Ryder would also occasionally finish entries with a mere couplet that referenced no sermon, as if two rhymed lines stopped short of implying that he didn't require pastoral authorization for aesthetic self-expression.[47] All this said, Ryder could have clearer worries about others seeing what he had written. He once feared that revealing the depths of his doubt and anguish could hurt rather than help a reader. "Some struggles I have had this Day in my mind about persisting in this diary," he wrote in his early years as a diarist. "Sometimes I am afraid it Springs from a weariness in well Doing, on another hand I think so many are my Doubts & fears, that I know not if they should Ever fall in any other hand, whether the reading of them may Do Good or hurt." And if he failed to notice his pride when confronted by the Leeds author of pious pastiche we met earlier, he could be acutely aware of it in even the mildest forms of going public. "I had some concern on my mind about showing something which I write in private, with a jealousy over my self lest there should be anything of pride in it," he admitted in the late 1740s. "I know it is God alone that knows from what principle we act, & to him alone we are accountable, but when I consider that we are commanded to let our light shine before men, & other good authors recommend communicating of Experiences, I took some courage I am afraid of being tricked by a Deceitfull heart. Oh that God will make and keep me humble." One thing he was of course saying here is that he could bracket his pride for long enough to ask himself whether or not his diary held spiritual value for others. There was spiritual utility in letting one's "light shine before men," but he never found an unambiguous answer to the question of just how bright that light should be. Nor did he include anything in the diary meant to advertise his project or assist other readers as obviously as John Rastick's handwritten mimicry of a print title page or Wallington's table of contents.[48]

Add up these examples, and it is clear that sharing one's pious prose and poetry, even among godly readers, wasn't purely innocent in a religious culture that advocated self-denial. Even godly self-writing was inevitably in some measure about the self. For that matter, even speaking publicly with authority was tricky, as Ryder once admitted after giving invited counsel to a church member that made him feel like he was both flattering himself and being a fraud. But this ambivalence about audience was also consistent with Ryder's outlook. He vacillates between public and private possibilities because he had not spiritually decriminalized the self and self-writing any more than his acquisitiveness. And still, much as he acquired despite the fact that it was a morally tricky thing to do, he entertained the possibility throughout the diary that a text in which he was constantly and necessarily featured might have publicly spiritual worth.[49]

To draw too sharp of a line between a godly diarist and his no less godly imagined audience is nonetheless tricky. If the readers Ryder implies were vigilant souls like him, then they were engaged in a collaborative project, as if they were writing a single book, with a providentialist plot, and the same God looking over the shoulders of authors united in their intent to meet the same end by shared means. The structural similarities in watching can make almost interchangeable a diary from late-sixteenth-century Essex, another from seventeenth-century Massachusetts, and another from mid-eighteenth-century Leeds. They can also minimize the size of the ego implicit in a diarist's awareness of other human readers.[50]

The "almost" before "interchangeable" above shouldn't be passed over too quickly. Even a single book, as Roger Chartier once said, changes in a world that changes: compare, for example, Beadle's and Ryder's structured attention to national epidemics. A once political subtext of the objects of surveillance in the mid-seventeenth century—Beadle's major concern was, we may recall, the civil war—had more endemically become economic by Ryder's lifetime. Furthermore, when we actually start to read these diaries for their details, and as agency appears within structure and the habitus eventually begins to take new shape, the coherence of this cultural collaboration—of this "single book" that all spiritual diarists in some sense coauthored—appears to be thinner than thick. If beauty is in the eye of the beholder in the aesthetics of poetry, divine meaning was in the eye of the watcher in the semiotics of providence. Ryder and the contemporary apothecary Arthur Jessop, who lived fewer than thirty miles to the west of Leeds in Lydgate, both noted the frigid weather and strong winds in January 1740. But only Ryder elaborated on the climate's providential significance. The godly Jessop, on the other hand, so routinely made a note of the weather at the beginning of his entries that he seems to have grown inured to the potentially foreboding significance of breaks in normal patterns. Or consider the way James Clegg examined the urine of a pregnant and ailing patient, searched for a diagnosis, failed to save her life, and then, with no recourse whatsoever to divine imagery, recorded the medical encounter and her burial in his diary. Clegg's spiritual commitment is beyond doubt, but in his medical practice the capacity for urine to deliver the sort of divine meaning it held for Cotton Mather was understandably supplanted by its capacity to deliver a diagnosis. For that matter, some whose diaries evade spiritual characterization often show signs of being providentialist. The mostly secular Sussex shopkeeper Thomas Turner linked the ebb and flow of his emotional state to his finances, which he then linked to the divine. "Not that I want to get an estate," Turner wrote; "if it will please the Supreme Being to bless me with only enough to pay everyone their own and to maintain my family in an indifferent manner, I am satisfied."[51]

But following a cultural signifier like "watching" is unlikely in any case to reveal everyone marching in lockstep. It rather helps us grasp, in William Sewell's words, "a sense of the particular shapes and consistencies of worlds of meaning" in order to see how cultures "hang together." And in Ryder's case, the culture that still visibly hangs together in the mid-1700s, even if by threads, isn't simply that of spiritual diarists, it is that of Puritanism more broadly. Puritanism may not be easy to define—it now hardly needs to be said that "Puritan" was a term of abuse that many to whom it was applied were reluctant to use. But the cultural ethos of Puritanism was coherent enough. To paraphrase a recent survey, it expressed a profound belief in human worthlessness set alongside Christ's saving grace; an intense searching for salvation, which might come at a moment of conversion or after decades of agonizing, melancholy, and self-loathing; a singular zeal (often seen as so by the avowedly less zealous); and a deep commitment to prayer, sermons, and, even more conspicuously, the Bible, of which there was need to have a working knowledge typically demonstrated in effortless quoting of scripture. Just as distinctively did this culture reject *adiaphora,* or "things indifferent," to salvation—only what the Bible could back up deserved to belong in spiritual practice. This fed the attempt to ensure that baptism, marriage, funerals, music, liturgy, and so on didn't veer into idolatry as it also informed suitable ways of being social, by fasting, attending sermons, meeting with others to discuss those sermons, and embracing a host of household exercises after public worship on Sunday, which was itself sacrosanct. And since the limits of the socially meaningful were circumscribed by the spiritual, Puritans were no less distinguishable by their efforts to exercise control over others, whether in the community or in the household.[52]

This is an item-by-item description of both the social and personal image Ryder's diary offers. And among other things, this should encourage updating the historiography. There is less agreement about when Puritan culture loses its coherence than there is about when it takes shape.[53] That may be largely because the introduction and overlap of new categories like separatism and Dissent can obscure things. But those categories don't change the culture's basic characteristics. Moreover, the story typically told about Puritanism rarely goes beyond the Stuarts. This isn't simply a problem because the narrative excludes people like Ryder, along with many others, writing all the way until the 1760s, hardly distinguishable in spiritual outlook and behavior from Nehemiah Wallington. Ryder also indicates that the very marginalization often taken to signal the waning of the Puritan ethos stimulated keeping his world intact. By virtue of the regularity with which he watched the national epidemic of declining piety, for example, his intent gaze was meant, in some small way, to stem the tide of cultural dissolution. The fearful and galvanizing perception that godly culture was coming to an end itself suggests its presence and tenacity.

Invoking the Puritan tradition also brings us back to the different degrees of watching. It is true at a general level that this was a word with both intended and discernable resonance far outside the confines of what by the mid-1700s was the demographically puny realm of old Dissent. At a more specific level, however, not every English Protestant actually did embrace the watchfulness that the godly recommended. And certainly no one embraced and embodied this habit as much as spiritual diarists themselves. This was no accident. These were custodians of the Puritan ethos—and not simply because their logocentricism in combination with their journalism meant that they captured everything in sight. The very form of diary keeping was the most strenuous and relentless mode of lay watching for both personal and cultural decay, and it therefore gave durability to the habit of spiritual vigilance as well as to the broader culture that diary keeping reflected and molded. Spiritual diary keeping was designed to last as long as it did, in other words, because of the formalized mechanism that underpinned it: it could easily reinforce itself as the watchfulness of diary writing heightened a sense of anxiety–which included worry about religious change–that only more watchful diary keeping could allay. The spiritual diary could so easily be, if we like, an addictive technology of the self.[54]

The Puritan ethos, at the same time, does eventually lose its coherence–it is not for no reason that Ryder obsessively worries about declining piety. Coherence doesn't simply evaporate, however. Those with Puritan habits could redirect their spiritual energy to other denominations, like Methodism. Or those habits might be transmuted into altogether different cultural forms. Literary historians have long told this story in relation to the novel. It is a poignant image of a torch being passed as the protagonist of arguably the first novel in English begins writing a spiritual diary while ship-wrecked on an island–a diary that, as more than one critic has noticed, spuri-ously antecedes his conversion while saying little of spiritual value. The fictional artifact Robinson Crusoe writes within the novel to tag him as a Restoration Dissenter is so unlike the real thing, not least because it is so *un*spiritual, that it tells us we are slowly entering a different era. Puritan habits may be discernable in Crusoe and his anticipation of a new economic order, but when he "watches," it is for rescue ships, to protect his corn, or as he lies in ambush waiting for his enemies.[55]

While the early English novel may owe something to spiritual self-writing, the resilience of watching, in particular, is evident in at least two other places that more insidiously reflect the conceptual development in English Calvinism that led the faithful to internalize the gaze of others. For the spiritual watcher, those external eyes belonged most potently to God. But this hardly changes the basic correspondence between this spiritual practice and the form of control that Michel Foucault called panopticism. Foucault famously found his perfect image for the modern "automatic functioning of power" in Jeremy Bentham's late-eighteenth-century image of the panop-ticon. Like sixteenth-century English Calvinists facing a scarcity of resources, Bentham had a practical reason for designing a circular prison in which the cells face a central watchtower so prisoners could be observed without knowing whether or not guards were actually in the tower observing them: Bentham wanted to make institutional surveillance cheap and easy for the people who do the primary monitoring. "In an establishment like this," he noted, "a watchman need cost nothing." As was also true of the authorization of the laity to assume some spiritual responsibility, the panopticon wasn't simply about economizing; it was about inculcating an ocular, self-controlling instinct in the prisoners. And Bentham also hoped that his "architectural breakthrough" would extend beyond prisons, leading to the reformation of manners, the invigoration of the economy, and the amelioration of poverty; hence, as he wrote on his title page, the panopticon's applicability to "houses of industry, work-houses, poor-houses, manufactories, mad-houses, hospitals, and schools." Of course, surveillance in general could probably be tied to any institution, religious or not. There is a remarkable image from Puritan New England of a pulpit in a Calvinist meetinghouse that one Congregationalist remembered having "as its sole decoration, an enormous, carefully painted, staring eye, a terrible and suggestive illustration to youthful wrong-doers." This chapel too was obviously about ocularity and in some crude sense panopticism, although in a religious culture where external discipline was easier to find. But what links spiritual watchfulness of the type Ambrose describes and Ryder embodies to the form of surveillance and social control Bentham visualized and Foucault later seized on is the less obvious and more interiorized mechanism of discipline. Bentham and the experimental Calvinists were drinking from the same well. Both wanted discipline to function *automatically*, and they formulated remarkably and curiously similar strategies and images for getting at it.[56]

Ryder's vigilance was, at the same time, not one-sidedly about restraint. It also encouraged the search for God's favor as evidenced in a measure of economic success. Watching made economic life matter spiritually—the spiritual gave incentive to the material, and the material could return the favor. It may be even more curious that with a simple substitution of "social" for "spiritual," we find ourselves talking about another ocular conceptual triumph of the eighteenth century: Adam Smith's "impartial spectator." The secular Smith took his obvious cue from Joseph Addison's cultural archetype, not from Calvin's. Yet what Smith was after, in his most recent biographer's words, was "the consistency of . . . ethical conduct" and "the capacity for self-command" that encourage virtuous behavior in the free market.[57] In basic form these were the goals of Ryder or any of Calvin's true believers. For that matter, a Smithian agent constantly informed by internalized social perceptions, like a spiritual watcher, required careful study of the signifying system of others. Both the social and spiritual habit involved winning the approbation of an internalized onlooker (an amalgam of human eyes for one, mostly God for the other). Both were meant to provide a basis for self-constraint in a world comparatively free of obvious external regulations, whether in the form of the guilds or the consistory. And much as spiritual watching could lead to the psychological equilibrium offered by the middle class, the "impartial spectator" laid the moral psychological basis for a mode of capitalism constitutive of and dependent on an expanding bourgeoisie that, Smith hoped until the very end, should know how to balance personal gratification with social need.

These analogies—though they are surely more than that—are not meant to trivialize differences. What makes the outlook Ryder expresses distinctive is that in the very position in the psychological calculus where modern economics has followed Smith's lead in placing the social, the watchful reserved a space for the spiritual. Too much approbation of the sort that propelled Smith's *Homo economicus* increased Ryder's guilt. At the deepest level, Ryder acquired not by social, but by divine mandate. And unlike social *dis*approval, the divine sanction against excess came at a far greater price. When driven by the old faith, aspiration could thus easily engender spiritual agonizing. But now we are coming to a different way in which Puritan culture took secular expression, to a more familiar argument—to the subject, as one sociologist has written, of "the longest running debate in modern social science."[58]

# 4. "An Active Frame in Courts Below"

If any man all his affairs neglect
His poverty his neighbours soon expect
Whilst he for Slumber is in Craving frame
And Still from Day to Day desires the Same
No wonder that his craving Wants do call
And he for them has no Supply at all
Want unto Some more Leisure steps does take
To Others it does swifter progress make
Am I at any Time in Slothfull frame
The Just attendant ought to be my Shame
Duties neglected Leave but Guilt and grief
None but Our God can Grant us Sweet relief
Rouse up my Drooping Soul O Lord I cry
To all my wants afford a Sweet Supply
All Inclinations of frowns remove
Cause me to feel the Sweetness of thy Love
Give me an active Frame in Courts below
That I the Riches of thy Grace may know
Let me not like the Slothfull servant hide
Thy Talent, and in slothfull frame abide
But make me active while my strength remains
May it Thro Christ prove my perpetuall gains
—"Poverty the product of Sloth," Joseph Ryder's diary, August 26, 1733

With Chearfull heart & Willing hand
To Labour God does me Command
And Worse than Infidells they prove
Who take no Care for those they Love
But here my Greatest Danger lies
When things below to tempt mine Eyes
To take in them forbidden pleasure
Or to Esteem them Chiefest treasure
—"Of the Danger of Worldly mindeness," Joseph Ryder's diary, November 24, 1745

I am concerned that I may be strengthened to every social duty
of life to testify my faith by my works and to be guided & assisted in what lies
before me, but particularly in the great business of Religion.
—Joseph Ryder's diary, October 17, 1751

I am an old man: in man's account, a Dissenter; in God's, I trust, a Christian. I am
also a tradesman, of no small account in this town and neighbourhood; but I trust my
more beloved, because most gainful trade or traffic, lies in a far country . . .
My traffic is to the country beyond Jordan, and my chief correspondence with the
King of Zion, a good friend to merchantmen; he first condescended to traffic with me,
furnished me with the stock, made me many valuable remittances, and hath firmly
assured me of an infinitely great and good inheritance, richer than both Indies, to
which I am to sail and take possession as soon as I shall be ready for it. . . .
—Joseph Williams to Samuel Walker, 1754

Weber is a sort of hero for my purposes, albeit a flawed hero.
—Patrick Collinson, "Religion, Society and the Historian"

It may be the fate of any author of a work as subtle, dense, and complex as *The Protestant Ethic and the Spirit of Capitalism* to be misunderstood. Nowhere in this text did Max Weber claim that only Protestants (or Christians) can be good capitalists, that without Protestantism capitalism cannot happen, that ideas and culture should simply replace materialism in the attempt to understand motive forces, or that the West is somehow superior to the rest of the world. His argument was that the relatively difficult search for salvation that Protestantism made central to the lives of its believers encouraged behavior characteristic and partly formative of the spirit of modern capitalism.[1]

Much that we associate with capitalism in its most basic form—exchanging goods, calculating loss and profit, using money—Weber recognized as having been around for thousands of years. Modern capitalism represents something different. Partly this has to do with its modified economic forms: its freer markets, its more sophisticated bookkeeping, its more systematically organized workplace and dislocation of the household as the locus of production. But what also makes capitalism modern is the ethos or "spirit" that legitimates and sustains these economic forms. Modern capitalists feel duty-bound to methodically increase their wealth. They cherish labor as its own reward. They chase money as an end in itself (even if they avoid spending it when they get it). The question Weber had, and a question still worth asking, is what made this systematic and diligent mode of amassing wealth such a faithful and relentless calling?[2]

In tracing the development of the capitalist spirit, Weber, in essence, was looking for something powerful enough to justify the conflation of work and life, and he found it in a novel religious mode. During the late Middle Ages devotion to Christianity came, he thought, relatively easily. A believer could pray, confess, perform good works, obey the Ten Commandments, and feel reasonable assurance of salvation. Martin Luther first unsettled the clear path to Heaven by making salvation utterly dependent on faith and by conceptualizing work as a sort of spiritual calling. But it was not until Jean Calvin and the advent of ascetic Protestantism that life and work were systematically brought together. Calvin's more wrathful, distant, and inscrutable God was understood, for one thing, to have predetermined souls for Heaven or Hell to such a degree that no amount of good deeds or penance was any longer salvific. For another, Calvin made the world, in the words of one of his sixteenth-century English followers, a "theater of God's judgment." All earthly activity, whether religious or secular, should therefore be performed as if in front of a divine audience and aimed toward a spiritual end.[3]

More than either Calvin himself or his continental followers, it was these same English disciples, the Puritans, who Weber thought firmly brought work and life into a collective project and sanctified economic striving. The Puritan ethos was especially clear to Weber in the writings of Richard Baxter, the seventeenth-century polymath whose readership in early modern England was surpassed only by that for the Bible and John Bunyan. Baxter made piety synonymous with methodical work, even when work was practically unnecessary. Even, that is, for the rich, restless labor usefully dampens self-importance, staves off anxiety and an unclean life, glorifies God, and encourages more serious consideration of the possibility of spiritual election. Hard work is of course liable to produce hard wealth, which, as Baxter well knew, Christians found suspicious long before Luther. But to produce a measure of wealth as an outcome of work was nevertheless more auspicious than to produce nothing. For Baxter the real danger lay in resting upon and enjoying material success. Repose was for the afterlife. Virtue in the here and now depended on avoiding sloth through the maximization of time with labor and for the sake of rewards in this life that were meaningfully profitable only because they signaled rewards in the next.[4]

Already, much of this should sound familiar. The epigraphs to this chapter alone convey commingled godly industriousness and industrious godliness: the spiritual aversion to poverty and indolence, the longing to maximize time, the conflation of worldly and heavenly rewards, or the use of social duties and works to testify faith "in the great business of Religion," as Joseph Ryder put it with his effortless ability to infuse spiritual talk with economic imagery. Ryder was also in the very occupation and transitional mode that Weber highlighted among the destroyers of economic traditionalism. Weber imagined the revolutionary capitalist as "some young man from a family that ran a cottage industry [who] moved out of the city and into the countryside, carefully selected weavers for his particular needs, and increasingly tightened their dependence and his supervision over them. In the process he transformed peasants into workers."[5] The characterization is, at the same time, not an exact match. Ryder was not entirely instrumentally driven in his relationships with his family of workers, as we will see in the next chapter, nor was Leeds exactly the countryside. But Weber captures here the lineaments of the face Ryder wore as an employer and imagines the sort of putting-out clothier that Ryder was by occupation.

The more important qualification is that Weber's protagonist was an "ideal type," not an actual person, generalization, or average, but, as one historian of religion has aptly put it, a "purposeful exaggeration."[6] At the level of generalization, for example, the most that could be said about any "Protestant-capitalist" is that such a person followed, in some way, one of the many Protestant confessions and pursued, successfully or not, one of the many forms of capitalist accumulation. An ideal-typical Protestant-capitalist, in contrast, embraces as many blatantly signifying characteristics as possible: unimpeachable piety, commercial success, masterful efficiency with time and labor, inner-worldly asceticism, and, importantly for Weber, the doctrine of predestination. Ideal types exist not to be proved or disproved, nor are they built inductively from individual examples. They function as maximum case scenarios for the sake of making comparisons. And yet, this is all the more reason that it is remarkable to find in Ryder many of these exaggerated characteristics rolled into one.

It is striking, too, that Ryder occupied the chronological midpoint along the Protestant-capitalist continuum on which Weber placed his principal historical subjects. At an earlier and more clearly spiritual position was Baxter himself, for whose generation the link between spiritual and economic meaning was already evident. "Time is money" had "not yet been expressed by Baxter," Weber wrote, "yet this axiom holds in a certain spiritual sense." Zoom ahead a century in Weber's story, and there is his other protagonist, Benjamin Franklin, the author of the brazenly secular "time is money" axiom, residing at a more vestigially Protestant place on the same continuum. If Baxter was more clearly about God than commerce, then Franklin, a "bland deist" who had rationalized his religion almost beyond recognition, now expressed the modern capitalist spirit of accumulation with no apparent worry about spiritual outcomes. In contrast to both Baxter and Franklin, Ryder had equally clear links to the economic and religious themes Weber simultaneously tried to follow.[7]

What do we make of all this? Someone about whose particular existence Weber gives us no evidence of awareness lines up with the characteristics of his ideal type and the contours of his narrative better than anyone else we have so extensively on record.

Part of the explanation has to be that in describing Baxter's outlook, Weber was also inevitably touching on the outlook of Baxter's countless avid readers, like Ryder, not to mention the Puritan culture Baxter influenced and promoted. It also wasn't by blind luck that Weber chose a putting-out clothier to illustrate the transition to modern capitalism at the ground level. Producing textiles was the most common and important mode of protoindustrial manufacturing. Picking someone who deals in some way with computers to illustrate the dynamics of early twenty-first-century capitalism would be similarly obvious.[8] But the correspondence goes beyond happy accident or good guesswork. Ryder emphatically supports the more lasting insights of Weber's thesis. The broadest of these concerns Weber's general view of causality. Weber was not out to offer, as he put it in the essay's closing words, "a one-sided spiritualistic analysis of the causes of culture and history in place of an equally one-sided 'materialistic' analysis. *Both* are *equally possible*." It can be useful to start out emphasizing one part of the equation over the other, but understanding the past will be "served equally little if either of these analyses claims to be the conclusion of an investigation rather than its preparatory stage." The causal mechanism Weber was after was, in effect, a feedback loop between the cultural and the material, the sort of flow of causation that Ryder demonstrates when he is driven to acquire profits in part by religious mandate and is constantly watchful in part because his economic success teeters so regularly on sinful excess. This is the sort of causation, moreover, that economic historians, once the great proponents of materialist explanations, increasingly take seriously.[9]

Yet Weber wanted this dynamic view of causality to be taken just as seriously by religious historians. And his insight into the mechanism of religious change lies in his notion of "elective affinity." He assumed that the origins of religious ideas were obscure enough to be considered autonomous; Marx was wrong to treat religion as epiphenomenal. Weber also made clear, however, that the religious ideas that survive over time, or define a group, or resemble in some way a vocational ethic, are those relevant to individual and social interests. The obvious elective affinity for Weber was the one that existed between "the virtues cultivated by Calvinism . . . [and] the restrained, strict, and active posture of capitalist employers of the middle class." But the concept is especially useful because it also points to the conflicts that arise between religious and social concerns in the long process by which a better fit between them develops. Ryder, for example, constantly complains about declining piety among Calvinist Independents and Presbyterians, and as we will later see, by the last decades of the eighteenth century the wealthiest of these Dissenters had begun to abandon traditional Christianity and embrace a heterodox set of beliefs that were relevant to their material needs and interests and that would eventually come together as doctrinal Unitarianism.[10]

None of this means that Ryder simply proves the Weber thesis in all its detail, as if a single case could ever do that. On the one hand, and like Weber's ideal type, Ryder is useful to think with—in this sense he is *ideal* because he was so perfectly poised between the religious and economic outlooks he helps us to understand. On the other hand, Ryder was not confined to the realm of an informed sociological imagination—and in this sense he was anything *but* ideal. He was a flesh-and-blood human being, filled with unpredictability and emotion, and thus a complication of the image we have grown accustomed to seeing from a more abstract angle of vision.

For one thing, and as others have pointed out, Weber overemphasized the doctrine of predestination. Even Richard Baxter was so disturbed by the prospect of this doctrine encouraging antinomianism—the view that preordained salvation exempted one from traditional moral behavior and, as Baxter and others saw it, encouraged political radicalism—that he came to a theological position on salvation that was closer to the antideterministic doctrine of Arminianism (this via media was, in fact, known in Ryder's lifetime as "Baxterianism"). We should be careful here, however, not to swing too far in the other direction. Lingering predestinarianism, alongside providentialism, lay behind Ryder's watchfulness, and the two had long been connected. The early-sixteenth-century Swiss reformer Huldrych Zwingli thought they amounted to the same basic doctrine. As Alexandra Walsham has explained, providentialists assumed that God had the sort of foreknowledge that could underpin predestination even if that foreknowledge was also linked to active divine intervention. In doctrinal terms, in other words, Weber may not have been completely off the mark. But this was because he also effectively seized on the religious habit to watch, which was cultivated for more than simply the search for evidence of predetermined election.[11]

Related to this, Weber paid overwhelming attention to prescriptive literature and official culture. When we turn to lay expressions of piety and belief, we discover varied theological positions that in their variety correspond to the complex nature of lived experience and arise from the unpredictability of the individual interpretation of doctrine. To give a single example, Ryder, much like Baxter a century earlier, could be disturbed by predestination when he found it tied to the antinomian position that the comfortably elect could test the irrevocability of God's preselection of souls by outwardly living sinfully. Ryder (like Baxter) could therefore sound Arminian, when, for example, he claimed that the key to salvation was balancing good works with faith, the latter of which was attainable by way of freely given grace. The repudiation of the doctrine of predestination could, however, be just as troubling. Ryder balked when a minister he identified only as "Smith" made the case that "to preach that man was universally corrupted, and that God had chosen a certain number to Salvation and left the rest in a state of reprobation was repugnant to the Gospell." The sermon "gave some of us great sadness of heart and it is to be feared helpt greatly to disrelish all the rest of his discourse[,] but wherein this sentiment agree not with what appears plain to others may the Lord be pleased to direct him aright." Ryder, in other words, was inconsistently predestinarian to a degree that is hard to find matched in the writings of theologians or authors of practical divinity.[12]

By contrast to the specific determinism that captured Weber's attention, watching, like the providentialism that helped underpin it, was general enough to remain intact amid variations in theological thinking, lay or official. This might explain why one historian has noticed that early modern

English spiritual diaries and autobiographies are ultimately more providentialist than predestinarian in their assumption that God maintains an active presence in daily life. Especially by the late seventeenth century, spiritual journalists also placed much less importance on the moment of conversion (a moment Ryder never emphasized, whether or not it anticipated his first entry). "What seemed to count far more than highlighting the special but singular experience of God's favor through conversion was the daily record of godly conduct," an examination, writes Kasper Von Greyerz, that brought about both "rigorous self-control" and striving for "collective sanctification in order to avoid God's displeasure as to gain His grace." None of this should surprise us. Watching was neither uncomplicated nor monolithic, as we have seen; it was supple enough that its objects need not be restricted to signs of predetermined election or reprobation.[13]

This leads to the second point, which we considered in the last chapter. In their authorization of the laity to assume some of their own spiritual oversight, the godly also encouraged more individual religious practice alongside the communal. Some of these men and women, even within the most pious categories, therefore inevitably watched more intently than others. The hotter sort got their heat from a daily intake of spiritual advice, pious upbringing, and the cumulative effects of watching itself. As that intake varied, so, surely, did its consequences, both material and spiritual.

There is another way in which Weber's thesis needs modification. Probably because he considered ordinary people only in the abstract, he inadequately accounted for the psychic anguish wrought by double-mindedness. In Ryder's industriousness lay prospects for salvation: here was the positive encouragement religion could give to economic striving. But in his avoidance of poverty lay the prospect of striving so well that he entered the morally suspect realm of inordinate accumulation, "the too frequent effects of Incumbrances of Worldly business especially," Ryder was careful to add, "when in any Measure it Exceeds."[14] Some of this anguish we will consider below; some will be dealt with when we turn to the question of whether or not he was melancholic.[15]

Adding up these arguments for and against Weber's thesis calls not for a rejection of Weber's basic argument or its spirit of multidimensional inquiry. It calls, rather, for modification of a thesis whose depth and subtlety are attested to by the way in which Ryder almost squarely falls into a mold designed without any awareness of his existence. The qualifications, nevertheless, are important. For one thing, there is no necessary link between watching and the capitalist ethos, much as there is no inevitable relationship between Calvinism and capitalism. It goes without saying that, even in more commercial eighteenth-century Britain, not every Protestant was a practicing capitalist or every capitalist a practicing Protestant. Protestants were themselves varied (in eighteenth-century England alone there were self-identifying Presbyterians, Independents, Anglicans, Particular Baptists, General Baptists, Quakers, Wesleyan Methodists, Arminian Methodists, Calvinist Methodists, Arians, Unitarians, Muggletonians, and the list could go on before moving north to Scotland). Even more, among those who felt pulled by both God and Mammon, the surviving evidence offers no one among protoindustrialists who as copiously described being pulled as equally and tortuously in both directions as did Ryder, though of course that may indicate as much about the ephemeral nature of historical source material as anything else.[16]

All that said, instead of fleeing from the significance of the evidence Ryder presents for addressing Weber's thesis, we might ask a modified overarching question about the connection between culture and capitalism. How did spiritual watchfulness and the capitalist ethos shape one another when they were fated to come into contact, as they were for decades in Ryder's life in pious and increasingly commercial Leeds, and as the diary and other evidence indicate they did in the lives of countless other men and women of whose work and worship we may only have suggestive record? Put more abstractly, what were the consequences of the interaction between English Protestantism in one of its most distinctive and strenuous forms and capitalism as it was taking modern shape? The previous chapter got us part of the way toward an answer. The following examination of Ryder's relationship to his labor and capital, like much else presented in this book, suggests that the interplay between watching and working both enlivened and agonizingly threatened the soul. What distinguished this eighteenth-century Protestant capitalist so evenly pulled by the worldly and the spiritual was both a compulsion to succeed in the here and now in preparation for Heaven and a lifetime of ambivalence and anguish spent trying to avoid the excess that led to Hell.

The woolen and worsted industries in Yorkshire and the West Riding have been a preoccupation of historians of Britain's early industrialization. After relative stagnation in the late seventeenth century in the wake of expansion in western and central European countries where England had previously found a substantial cloth market, making woolen and worsted cloth, a process that already dominated manufacturing in the national economy by 1700, became ever more dynamic over the course of the eighteenth century. Nowhere was this growth more pronounced and transformative than in Leeds. The town was the most urbanized, specialized, and capitalized area in the West Riding by 1750, and its merchants were connected to a vast network of markets stretching to cloth houses in Holland, Germany, Switzerland, Italy, Portugal, and Spain, with steadily increasing traffic to London.[17]

The West Riding's economic growth still meant a difficult life for the independent clothier and his employees. This was arduous, time-consuming, and dangerous work, and people like Ryder didn't enter into it by chance. From his diary we admittedly hear only the spiritual echo of labor in protoindustrial Leeds, but for details we can turn to other sources, like the anonymously written "Poem Descriptive of the Manners of the Clothiers, Written About the Year 1730," which takes us directly into Ryder's world. "Seated some hundred yards from Leeds, / Crowded with those industrious breeds," the clothiers we first meet in the poem may be "merry," but they also rush in silence through their "hard oaten cakes," beer, and some mutton for their midday meal before resuming their fifteen-hour workday. When "the clock gives warning," under what are already now time-mechanized working conditions, the workers in their wooden shoes wash off a day's acquired filth around a "savoury wash-tub" and dress for supper with "Master and Dame." Supper ends, and the master, Hall, and his wife, Mary, go to their friend "Joe's / To talk and hear how matters goes," while the workers retire to the coal fire to entertain themselves with a story about a former worker, Sammy Shorty.[18]

"Sammy"—a slang name for simple-mindedness—tragicomically illustrates by his pitfalls the myriad health hazards of work in the domestic industries.[19] When a rock on which he has rested his foot takes flight, he is thrown off balance and into a tub of "swine-muck." He cries out for help and catches the attention of Hall, who rushes over to help the fallen worker. But in the process Hall sets down a bag of sandalwood onto a truss with too much force and inadvertently releases hartshorn, an ammonia-like substance, into the air. The hartshorn flies into Sammy's eyes, "Which caus'd great pain, spite of resistance," and in a state of blind panic Sammy gropes his way from the tub into the truss, "Which made the poor man's head turn round / And threw him flat upon the ground." The combination of chemicals that this collision releases into the air changes his "mucky hue to red" and in temporarily blinding him also sends him into a pile of coal, "Which showering down, like hail, so thick / Had not our Maister Hall been quick, / He sure enough had there been slain." Sammy's painful series of pitfalls finally comes to an end, and he retreats home, still carrying "the savoury wash-tub scent" and having been brought by fire, or more accurately by chemical burn, into the profession.

The poem is cartoonish for dark comic effect, but the eighteenth-century toxic materials site it depicts is simply part of the understood background. We typically determine the protoindustrial nature of worksites with reference to growth-related concepts like market expansion and their potential for capitalization. But another characteristic of the material landscape that would only intensify after full-fledged industrialization was environmental toxicity. The "savoury wash-tub scent" of the poem is, for example, facetious because the main ingredient of dyes was often manure. Because Ryder never even mentions the word "wool" in any but a brief metaphorical sense until years into the journal, it is not surprising that he would not actually draw attention to this toxic, or at least noxious, aspect of his daily life. But in his dirty business, in which boiling vats of dyes and charcoal stoves were part of the backdrop—literally inside or in the backyards of the cottages that made up the misleadingly bucolic-sounding "cottage industry"—the "savoury" was constantly within range of his senses and may have physically and viscerally compounded the sinfulness he felt when immersed in work.[20]

None of this is to suggest that bad odors posed the threats to respiratory health that we associate with industrial Britain of the nineteenth century—at least if they did we do not possess the biological indicators to know. The greatest danger Ryder faced came from his regular travel. There was no shortage of reasons why he so frequently thanked God for a safe return from a trip. Horseback riding could be dangerous, as evidenced by the deaths of several riders reported in local newspapers. But the mishaps were probably less a consequence of being a bad rider—which would be unbelievably ironic in the case of a man named Ryder from the West Riding—than of guiding his horses down bumpy roads while balancing folded packs of cloth on the horses' backs and making, at times, journeys as long as the fifty-mile roundtrip from Leeds to York in a single day.[21]

Manmade dangers, robbers roaming the countryside, and other frustrations also must have made many trips as miserable as hazardous. A man

An idyllic image of Yorkshire clothiers from the early nineteenth century that nostalgically captures the way they traveled with their cloth through the countryside. Reproduced by courtesy of the Yale Center for British Art, Paul Mellon Collection.

Ryder met on the road in the early 1750s told him that only the "swiftness of his horse" saved his life as he was violently struck and shot at by highwaymen. A more detailed account singled out the poor quality of the Yorkshire roads even after the arrival in the 1740s of the better-funded turnpikes, which not only aroused resentment and rioting because of their costs, but were clearly far from perfect even for the people who could afford them. Henry Crooke, an Anglican curate from Hunslet, just a few miles from Leeds, traveled Ryder's roads and regularly complained about them. He described in his own diary, for example, that the passage "from Homesly to Kippax was the worst Road I ever went in all my Life . . . We were about 3 hours tho' not above 8 miles." Typically bad weather only made things worse. The detail-obsessed Crooke once had to cut short a visit with a friend's mother because "the Rain had been so violent and so sudden as to overflow the Turnpike Road almost to my Mare's Belly near 100 yards together." In December of the same year he saw water running "1/2 Yard over the Causeway so that We were obliged to turn back to the Waggon-way, from there to the Causeway in the Midst of the Moor and down the Causeway

Home which took me near an Hour and 1/2 in walking for I did not get Home till near 11." Crooke was not alone. Ralph Thoresby and Defoe singled out the poor condition of Yorkshire's roads earlier in the century. As the century closed, the hardened traveler Arthur Young grew frustrated enough to call the road through Wakefield bad enough "to be indicted." And none of these men traveled with Ryder's sense of necessity. An early historian of the Yorkshire economy once wrote that "from the time when [a clothier] travelled into the wool-producing areas to the time when he deposited his cloth on the stall in the market he was constantly on the road, and hence the making of good highways was to him a veritable blessing." Unfortunately for Ryder, good highways from Leeds to the towns of the West Riding to and from which he constantly traveled seem to have been few and far between. He could understandably feel grateful to God for surviving so many dangerous journeys, but the danger itself was a regular reminder that work was a mixed blessing.[22]

Ambivalence about success came just as readily from experience closer to home in Leeds. In the late summer of 1737 Ryder found himself "in the markett place . . . considering with what pains & difficulty I see many persons Obtains the means of Livelihood." We should imagine this scene alongside Defoe's marvelous depiction of the Leeds market, of the £10,000 or £20,000 in cloth traded in an hour, and the clothiers who conduct their business in silence because they "stand so near to one another; and 'tis always reasonable that one should not know what another does, for that would be discovering their Business, and exposing it to one another." Ryder makes us wonder if such silence was as useful for spiritually meditating on the precariousness of his wealth as for concealing any economic machination. On the same market day in 1737 he would later tell his diary what had earlier been on his mind. The sight of the less successful trying to obtain their livelihood "help'd to raise my heart in thankfullness for that easy & comfortable way wherein I was provided for, & tho I considered many persons had superiour advantages in a way of business for improvement, yet was ready to conclude the far greater number had less priviledge, which help'd forward my thankfullness. Lord help me to Improve Every Talent Spiritual & Temporall to thy glory."[23]

No less was there a social facet to Ryder's ambivalence about economic activity. On the one hand, the positive comparison to others that led to gratitude could also feed pride. When he saw a "Neighbour who had formerly been in advanc'd circumstances to what I was but now seemingly much

Lower," he grew "much afraid that the Least Pride of ambition should find room in my Heart being Very sensible that I have nothing but what I have received." Aversion to sinful pride was in turn linked, on the other hand, to worry about being divinely punished by a *lack* of material success: "This Day I met a man who I Imagined was at some considerable distance from Home & Habitation Exposing woolen Goods to sale I began to consider his case a Little. I was afraid In any case to despise or undervalue him as an underling as we call them in Trade not knowing how soon his circumstances might be mine, but took occasion from hence I hope thankfully to acknowledge God's goodness." Virtually nothing that made Ryder's frame so usefully active came without the fear of excess.[24]

Finding success did not just mean traveling, enduring hazardous conditions, and putting in long days. It also meant securing credit, which a number of recent economic historians have shown was both indispensable for capital growth and a function of social reputation. In what could be called the "credit as a currency of reputation" thesis, Craig Muldrew has forcefully stressed the importance of the full range of creditworthiness in the English economy from the sixteenth to early eighteenth centuries. English society was cash poor and thus ran on credit partly by necessity. And the establishment and maintenance of credit relationships depended so heavily on good social standing that people therefore strove for social credibility—and hence became disciplined and self-controlled—as a means of building an often vast web of financial relationships.[25]

Parts of this innovative and influential thesis are beyond dispute in the local environment of Yorkshire. As Pat Hudson and John Smail have shown, the cash-poor mid-eighteenth-century wool economy, like the economy in general, depended on extensive forms of credit on which clothiers drew to buy their raw materials and to pay for various postmanufacturing procedures, such as fulling, a process of washing and beating wool to clean and thicken it, or scribbling and carding, which brushed out more impurities and straightened the wool so that it could then be saturated with dye. Reputation and trust were crucial for securing credit for which the repayment period, however comparatively short it was, could still stretch up to half a year. But here the relevant question Muldrew raises is less about the technical terms of credit than about the way that the attempt to remain creditworthy influenced behavior.[26]

Ryder could very occasionally worry about credit in economic rather than moral terms. We saw this in the last chapter in his concern about extravagance leading to debt. But he hardly ever frets about his own debt obligations, and not because he completely restrained from pushing the limits of his capital and credit resources. Given the nature of the economy and the fact that his business was growing, he could not have operated as a clothier without accruing at least temporary debts. This is of course not to say that Ryder was indifferent to his social reputation; it is rather that what consumes page after page of the diary is worry about the way God perceived him.[27]

It is nevertheless complicated to suggest that simply because Ryder doesn't talk much about credit it therefore mattered little. He doesn't talk about many things. But the subject was also not off-limits in the main pages of the diary. In the entry from June 27, 1749, he makes clear that to lose credit was disgraceful (as he also suggests that, at this point in life, he was all paid up). At the same time, not only were passages like this exceedingly rare, but here credit is only one item in a long list of earthly occurrences of spiritual consequence:

> This Day I have somewhat of a hurry of business and sadly am I afraid lest anything here below should ever have any unhappy tendency to prevent my warmest pursuits after a better world. Now I am in health, my earnest desire is to be preparing for sickness. Now I am in prosperity, I desire to be well prepared for adversity in whatever shape it may be sent, whether by providentiall losses, persecution or whatever God the ruler & righteous Judge may see meet to send it. Now I am in credit, I desire to be prepared for disgrace, if it may not be brought upon me for sin, I desire in every case to behave as a child of God that I may live & that I may dye under the Smiles of Gods Countenance through faith in a mediator whom I would love above all.[28]

To better assess the degree to which the social reputation that was built on Ryder's business life molded his behavior, we need to step outside of the diary and into that actual business life. But this can almost never be done since Ryder doesn't meaningfully exist in history outside of his diary. A single note written at the back of his twenty-seventh volume, however, offers one chance to supplement his moral commentary in the diary's main pages with some actual details. The note references a trip Ryder took to nearby

Dalton to be a witness for John Darnton, a Call Lane congregant and kinsman by marriage, who tried to repay £25 to Joseph Sigston, another Call Lane parishioner. Ryder explains that he bore witness to a transaction in which Darnton tendered £15 in specie and a £10 note, but Sigston refused the latter, saying "he would not allow a penny of it, tho He oen'd he had received it. We Came away without having the receipt Signed, we Came a part of the way homward, & turned back. Mr Darnton offered a twenty pound bill upon Mr Sigston paying ten pound back," but Sigston still "refused the bill because he would have nothing but specie."[29] A few things are immediately clear: Ryder had acquired trust from Darnton; neither of these men had an abundance of social credit with Sigston; and the mysterious Sigston, like many in the eighteenth century, was still deeply suspicious of paper money and unconvinced that the reputation of either Darnton or Ryder could secure the piece of paper credit being offered.[30]

In that day's entry in the main body of the volume matters are slightly confusing, which is itself worth noting as it indicates the virtual impossibility of knowing what had occurred at all without having recourse to the uncommonly detailed note; this is what we otherwise almost always face in the diary—we never know the details as much as the feelings that surround them. On November 30, the day he and Darnton traveled to meet Sigston, Ryder wrote that "after some business in the forenoon . . . I heard both Good and Evil. I was desired into company upon a speciall occasion a little out of town with a man who had made a profession, and some part of life behaved somewhat plausibly, but this afternoon I thought he both talked & acted very strangely, I could scarcely have Imagined to have heard & seen so much in any man, at least in any man who professed the Gospell." Such is the vague nature of Ryder's entries that at first it is unclear whether Darnton or Sigston is the "man who had made a profession"—only elsewhere does Ryder reveal that Sigston had behaved like a "troublesome Brother." A few days later Ryder and some members of the community meet to discuss "a very different piece of work" and to "make alterations with many . . . upon the most equitable terms." The matter at hand is clearly the dispute between Sigston and Darnton, which now verges on becoming a lawsuit. Ryder cannot help but notice the connection between breaches of "unity in nation, country, house or family"; he hopefully records a sermon delivered "very apt to the purpose," which must have targeted both Sigston and Darnton since both sat in Call Lane's pews. But despite Whitaker's attempts at reconciliation,

Darnton tells Ryder that his encounters that day seem to make a lawsuit inevitable.[31]

Much about this triangular relationship remains obscure; what is nonetheless clear is that, however much Ryder was in the preeminent position of trust with respect to the Darntons, he was facing a challenge to that trust, his reputation, and ultimately his creditworthiness by Sigston. Something else is clear. As Ryder introduces Sigston's claim against him with "I suppose," and considers his guilt with a conditional "if I have done amiss," he suggests incredulity if not nonchalance about the event. And then the most telling indication that the episode was not a major preoccupation is that it simply disappears from the journal—even as a discernibly allusive theme—after this last entry from December 3, 1757. Rather than the social and financial implications of the challenge Sigston posed to Ryder's reputation, what mattered—what always ultimately mattered to Ryder—was how God saw the event. Credit and social trust were important, to be sure, but their importance was swallowed in the diary by spiritual concerns.

Quoting Weber quoting Franklin's famous "time is money" passage, Muldrew contends in totalizing terms that, contra Weber, Franklin's advice "was not about the creation of a 'capitalist spirit': all the advice about diligence and frugality was concerned with reputation. Its aim was outward into the community, not inwards, concerning belief." Of course, credit was the most important financial mechanism of the early modern economy, and securing it required projecting creditworthy behavior. But Ryder's diary indicates that concern with the attributes by which one's reputation was cemented came less from secular communal values or from striving to seem creditable in the eyes of others than from belief. Diligence and frugality were of supreme inward importance precisely because of their salvational consequences. "This Day I have had my hands much busied in the World," he wrote in the early summer of 1741. "Yet in some part of the Day was cast among the Great Ones. . . . These words came into my mind. Seest thou a man Diligent in his business, he shall stand before princes, he shall not stand before mean men. But I consider what will it avail me in any Case to have the favour of any Great one, or many Great ones upon Earth, If I want the favour of God."[32]

It is not the case, it should be added, that Ryder was unaware that there was a more secular way to justify the behavior that the pursuit of credit could be taken to encourage. Thomas Whitaker preached a sermon on "the middle clause of the 47th verse" of Matthew 5. The full verse reads: "And if you greet your brethren only, what do you do more than others? Do not even the tax collectors do so?" But that middle clause in particular—"what do you do more than others"—offered an occasion for Whitaker and Ryder to think about the difference between those who sublimated their work spiritually, and those who didn't. "We who profess our Selves the followers of Christ, & especially Such as do it more publickly, Should do more than others," Ryder understood Whitaker to be saying. "Be sober, and honest"—here Ryder begins to sound like Poor Richard, but only for a second—"not only Sober for the preservation of health, & honest [to] preserve our reputation. [T]hese things others may do, from Selfish principles, But we must do them from a principle of Love to God . . . because we have a better rule, A better example, & more precious promises." It is as if Ryder (and Whitaker) were tuning in to a conversation that the secular opinion makers were having in the mid-eighteenth century about the value of the behavior that might earn one credit. Some, namely the "selfish," clearly thought that value was social. Ryder agreed in part—he needed financial credit too. But without a spiritual end, sobriety, honesty, and reputation hardly made one morally and materially different from the tax collector.[33]

The spiritual implications of economic behavior and self-control in the face of material achievements are not trivial. Nothing could make getting right the balance between success and excess more serious than the fate of one's soul. At the same time, divine approval could be so much more inscrutable than social approbation. As a young man making his way in the world, Ryder knew that the balance was critical. During a busy July in the mid-1730s, he hoped that "if Riches Should Encrease upon me, I might not set my heart upon them, & thought withal they were a sorry portion unless I or any Other have the Comfortable & Additional blessing of the Grace of God . . . a market Day for the Body, too often makes but small addition to the benefit of the Soul." The same need for balance was foremost in his thoughts when he returned to the theme nearly two weeks later, in much the same language, lamenting another "market day for the body and the many incumbrances of Time that frequently occur too much obstruct the concerns of eternity." He could clearly state the solution—"the things of time may and must be minded in their place"—while finding "somewhat of comfort upon this or the like reflection, that if these things here below encroach not upon my religious hours nor upon sabbath time, then by the blessing of God I might be enabled to go on my way with comfort and notwithstanding many frailties, failings, and infirmities by the blessing and grace of God through Jesus Christ die in peace."[34]

A solution that was simple to state in the abstract turned out to be elusive in practice. That elusiveness engendered depression and amplified Ryder's fears of death—both subjects we will turn to in greater detail. And if he could increasingly find refuge in a middling mindset that embodied equilibrium, as we will also see, the quest for that golden mean was lifelong. In his early seventies, well after he had ceased to be so active in his trade, he still struggled over how to allocate his hours: "I endeavoured to mind my business and finds it necessary while I follow trade, but finding so little or nothing of profit arising it is apt to damp a little, for I always think that this is the greatest motive to industry whether it be in things relating to this world or a better, next to Obedience to Gods comment. But then I do not think a prosperous condition without its snares, & great ones too . . . God knows what is for the best, for if riches Increase much, we often set our hearts too much upon them." The operative phrase here as so often elsewhere is "if riches Increase much," not if they simply increase. At the risk of stating what may now be the obvious, Ryder was not a leveling critic of the business practices forged in the clothing industry; he consistently thought that not to labor was no solution to the conflict between commerce and morality. Too old to work in his last year of life, he wrote "that being quite without business is no friend to piety . . . for vain thoughts are very apt to gain the ascendant in the want of employment."[35]

This was always the danger at a secondary level: it was easy to overdose on the antidote to spiritual and material impoverishment. And if Ryder's ministers could help with this dilemma by prescribing moderation, they could also encourage self-doubt. Imagine the setting of a sermon delivered in the late 1740s: a congregation filled with industrious clothiers, who, after all, were in the business of helping to dress a society that was becoming increasingly fashionable. A minister rose to preach from I Corinthians 7:29 that "time is short." In his explication of the text, he "came to show us how to improve time, namely in watching against an Inordinate care about the World, neither must we bestow too much of it in dress nor pampering the body." Too much attention to clothes was "as it were sowing fig leaves together which must shortly perish." Moreover, it was "sin that brought dress into the world." And it was a pity, he concluded, that dress should therefore be "abused to sin." To potentially confuse matters, though, the sermon ended with a final warning against lapsing industry. What the clothiers sitting in the congregation were doing with their labors teetered dangerously on the verge of being sinful, and yet not to labor with diligence was to commit the no less dreadful sin of idleness.[36]

Moments like this reveal how much more there is to the history of economic change than practical concerns, rational expectations, or social pressure. In keeping with a general disinclination among spiritual diarists to provide details, Ryder may reveal less of his buying, selling, supervising, and pulling his own weight among his workers than he does the spiritual reflection of those activities. Recovering the practical aspects of his life requires turning to other sources. But when we access only those other sources—account books, business memoranda, debt litigation, or the practical back pages in his own diary—religious belief comes misleadingly to seem like a mere symptom of economic change rather than one of its agents.[37]

Hanging over this discussion of Ryder's spiritual perception of wealth is nevertheless the possibility that he was exceptional even among diarists of this era who paid careful attention to both their economic and spiritual lives. So much surviving personal writing about economic life was heavily quantified and practical, like Ryder's own trade notebook, which would offer a radically different picture of him—a portrait painted entirely in numbers—were it the only piece of his writing to have survived. So much spiritual self-writing, in contrast, was either unmoored from the concrete or produced by authors whose worldly interests had little to do with commerce or manufacturing. There is one glaring exception among Ryder's contemporaries: the spiritual diary of Joseph Williams, which was published in an excerpted edition in the eighteenth century and more recently anatomized by Isabel Rivers. Williams, the author of the remarkable allegorical letter quoted as an epigraph to this chapter that effortlessly smears together trade, empire, and Christianity, was a deeply pious Dissenter, born in 1692, just three years before Ryder. He was also a successful clothier from an economically similar region, Kidderminster, fifteen miles from Birmingham and home not only to Richard Baxter's ministry for two decades in the seventeenth century, but to a thriving clothing industry as early as the 1500s. With forty looms and as many workers at one point, Williams ran by all indications a bigger operation than Ryder's. He also did not write with the same regularity or prolixity—he produced one three-hundred-page handwritten volume, as opposed to

Ryder's forty-one. For that matter he had a slightly broader range of interests as an author and a comparatively muted sense of self-doubt. Probably the most interesting difference is that in the 1750s Williams reached a tipping point with the increasing rationalism of the old Dissent and embraced Methodism. But the similarities are far more striking: both of these Josephs were tied to the same Puritan tradition; they read the same authors; they wrote journals with the intent to watch the self and the outside world and methodically meditate on sermons; they composed rhymed verses; they cautioned anyone who would listen against leisure and spiritually vacuous socializing. Most importantly here, like Ryder, Williams linked both his gains and losses to providence: he had a spiritual mandate to acquire and a moral ceiling on the limits of his acquisitiveness.[38]

The other thing each diarist does is remind us how much sermons themselves reflect the cultural reach of the ethos of tempered materialism. In 1747 Williams recorded a minister

> discoursing on our Lord's saying, *Make to yourselves friends of the Mammon of unrighteousness.* Thus we are taught true wisdom, even by iniquitous example, and to consider all worldly riches as of a deceitful nature. Indeed, all created enjoyments are vain and dissatisfying; our happiness does not consist in the abundance of them; their abundance rather increases the miseries of life; they can do nothing for us in the hour of death, and will make our future account the more awful and difficult. O my soul, wisely improve these hints. Sit loose to the world. Catch not at riches too eagerly, nor grasp them too closely. Use them for the end for which they were given. Use them as not abusing them. Be solicitious to make thyself a friend in heaven, by a right distribution of this mammon of unrighteousness.

Williams's minister was alluding heavily to the Bible—to 1 Corinthians and 1 Timothy in particular. But the exact phrase "sit loose to the world" also appears in Matthew Henry's popular biblical commentary: "Sit loose to the world, and to all your Possessions in it," Henry explained in his influential work. "Sell that which you have *superfluous*, all that you can spare from the Support of yourselves and Families, and give it *to the Poor*."[39]

Williams in turn administered the same advice he got from the pulpit and authors of works of practical piety. In a letter to a friend from 1751, he opened ebulliently, linking providence to success: "I rejoice to hear of your prosperity. I trust God is building you a house." But the main point of the letter was to offer "a word of caution." Williams's own prosperity had been dangerous, he explained: "Riches increased, and the love of riches increased as fast. I made an idol of that which should have enlarged my heart in gratitude to the bountiful Giver. . . . I had been sensible how inordinately my heart went after my covetousness, and that my spiritual interests were in a declining state; yea, I prayed against it often . . . yet still it prevailed, till it pleased God in great mercy to cast me into deep adversity." The danger for Williams was the same as it was for Ryder: *excessive* attachment to the material. "The Love of the world is downright idolatry," Williams wrote. "We cry out against the jews for selling the Lord of glory for money; but every covetous worldling plays the same game over again, and crucifies him afresh."[40]

And yet, just as clear in Williams's diary, as in the opening of his letter to a friend, is his more positive association of providence with temporal gains. In a bittersweet moment early in his widowerhood, he explained that his household business had recently "had flowing prosperity in trade. Were my wife now alive, I should tell her, with an air of pleasure, if not thankfulness, as I formerly have on like occasions, of the bounty of Providence to us." Or just as easily could he express both thanks to providence for granting him wealth and concern that he might fail to keep those successes in perspective: "He hath given me great worldly prosperity, and is still making it to grow; yet, through the riches of his grace, though earthly riches increase, hitherto I have not set my heart upon them."[41]

Such worries over worldliness pervade the Puritan tradition, both in the vast official literature and in these rare expressions of lay piety. But in Britain's more commercial age, the equation of providence with success in trade is more pronounced and elaborate, at least in those lay spiritual diaries that give us a chance to compare. The later writers seem much more emphatic and elaborate, that is, in saying that the spiritual could be materially productive: if God was looking down favorably on his flock when businesses prospered, it only followed that one would be encouraged to do what it took to prosper in business in order to win that divine approval. At the same time, these two eighteenth-century men of commerce have an angle of vision wildly different from the more secular economic theorists of the era who redefined self-interest as a rational ameliorator of the passions. It was clearly by way of Ryder's and Williams's providentialist interpretation of the meaning of success that God incentivized them to be productive. The fact that material ambition was morally limited does not preclude the spiritual motive behind it—the economic manifestation of this spiritual balancing act is the very definition of worldly asceticism.[42]

The two-way street running between practical and spiritual articulations of economic life need not be found in diaries or sermonic literature alone. Years ago, Douglas Reid documented the way in which mechanization and entrepreneurs in the Midlands eroded the weekly labor holiday "Saint Monday" in the late eighteenth and nineteenth centuries. Decades before this moment in the West Riding, however, industry was threatening even the sanctity of the Sabbath. Quarter Sessions records from the town of Pontefract in 1739 report that clothiers were so concerned to maximize their time "that they even contrive to bring more cloths to be milled upon the Sunday than any other day." The Justices of the Peace complained that "both Masters and Servants" were guilty of this "public Neglect" of the day's "Holy Duties." In moral language not unlike Ryder's, they were "insensibly drawn into the Commission of all manner of Sin and Wickedness, To the great displeasure of Almighty God, the Scandal of the Kingdom, the Evil Example of their Neighbours, and the Breach of all Laws, both divine and human." This concern about business crowding out time for religion did not belong solely to the court. The ruling was inspired by a petition signed by nearly a dozen millmen on behalf of themselves and their area co-workers. "It now is and for many years last past has been a very prophane and bad custom to mill cloth on the Lords day," the petitioners wrote. Because so much cloth was brought in on Saturdays, the mills were "clogg'd with cloth on Sundays," and workers were "forced to work the whole day," leading to "wickedness, immorality and vice" and keeping petitioners and their servants "from resorting to church or any other place of Divine Worship." Complaints like this about being too busy to attend church may have been partly rhetorical. The clothing industry was still firmly under government oversight, and the millmen may have hoped a religious appeal would persuade the court to regulate their workweek more firmly and help prevent end-of-the-week pileups. But simply to discount professions of piety is excessively cynical. If Ryder's overwhelmingly spiritual account benefits from the supplement of practical details, the motives behind the sources in which those more social and economic details can be found may be only partly intelligible until we read into them the spiritual earnestness that Ryder demands we take seriously.[43]

The point is not that uneasiness about changing work habits only or inevitably came from religion. Tensions can be found in everything from novels and advice manuals to crowd acts, resistance to time-mechanization, and condemnations of masturbation. For that matter, it is relatively easy to find Hanoverians—the fashionistas who kept clothiers in business, for example—celebrating consumerism. Ryder can't capture every Briton's behavior or outlook, nor should he be made to. But as someone deeply anxious about economic changes that he was himself bringing about, he can nevertheless be the basis—a different sort of "ideal" type—for questioning a number of assumptions about capitalism as it became modern. The notion that a thriving economy inevitably brings happiness to those who materially benefit from it—a central assumption of economic theory born in the eighteenth century and nearly unassailable in the twenty-first—did not apply to a budding capitalist whose salvation prosperity threatened as much as suggested. The premise that profit maximization was an unquestioned goal even for entrepreneurs throughout the eighteenth century, never mind for ordinary people, cannot be sustained for Ryder unless we add a resoundingly spiritual meaning to "profit." Even the more banal assumption that everyone wants financial security fails to account for Ryder's persistent concerns about security becoming sinful excess.[44]

Above all, Ryder's record of his working life tells us that the capitalist spirit could settle uncomfortably into the lives of the very godly people who pushed economic change forward on the eve of industrialization. The confluence of Protestantism and capitalism comes forth not in the composed, prescriptive pages of Baxter or Franklin, but in the life visible in the private diary of this obscure layman and clothier. Here he is, one last time, thinking about God and Mammon:

> This Day or in Some part of it I was Somewhat encouraging my self in hopes to raise my self by Industry & Diligence to somewhat of Greatness (not that I thought to do it without Gods Blessing) but Immediately these words came into my mind: Labour not for the meat which perisheth but for that which endureth to everlasting Life. But when I consider well upon this Prohibition I do only understand it to forbid an Inordinate Care about the Things of this present Life & Time, for Elsewhere the word Declares that if any

> man provide not for his own Especially for those of his own house,
> he hath decried the faith & is worse than an Infidell.[45]

This is self-encouragement by way of industry and diligence, which quickly leads to a parenthetical qualification, which itself leads to a scriptural qualification, which for its own part requires a qualification based on another scriptural prescription for family provisioning that only then finally justifies surplus over poverty; rather than some straightforward material sublimation of religion, the defining habit of this flesh-and-blood godly Protestant watchfully becoming a modern capitalist is uneasy shifting back and forth between encouragement and concern, ambition and reluctance, and needs and desires both spiritual and worldly.

# 5. "The Sparks That Fly Upward"

Every Parent & Master of a Family is both a Prince & a Priest in his own
House. God hath invested him with a sovereignty over his little Society, a Priesthood
over his little Flock. And this Dominion is founded in Nature & Reason, & in all those
Texts of Scripture, where Children & Servants are enjoin'd Honour & Obedience
towards their Parents & Masters, to whom God has committed the Guidance &
Government of 'em, & intrusted the Care both of their Bodies & Souls.
—"Rules for the Religious Conduct of a Family" (c. 1705–1750)

Thus an anonymously written manuscript defined the early-eighteenth-century paternalist: master of the house (and the basic unit of the economy); spiritual mentor; sanctioned by scripture, nature, and reason to guide and govern the bodies and souls of wives, children, and other domestics. A more concise anatomy of the basic structure of the early-eighteenth-century household and its governance would be difficult to find. But if asked to describe his own family, Ryder would have needed to tell a more elaborate story. The spiritual paternalism of this particular manuscript may have captured the basic structure of life at home, but two other linked and recurrent keywords in his diary point to a commingling of instrumentality and affect and to tensions brought on by trying to raise his household's economic and spiritual productivity.[1]

The first was "adoption." Ryder's house was filled with children, although none were his biologically. Some were likely paupers with living parents, and others Ryder more clearly identifies as orphans; neither instance, in fact, made his family all that far from ordinary. Apprenticing children was a pervasive form of early modern poor relief, and as late as the last half of the century, one in six people lacked a mother at age eleven, while one in five lacked a father (in modern Britain the rates are nearly ten times lower). The history of orphans is deeply obscure, but their relative abundance alone must have meant that they composed a significant portion of the eighteenth-century workforce, especially in the domestic industries.[2]

Matters grew slightly more unusual when Ryder's need to sustain and expand his household led him to marry, for the first and only time at the late age of forty, Elisabeth Wheelhouse, a woman younger by ten years. In the sense that initially mattered most to him, his marriage failed: he and Elisabeth were never able to have children.[3] The young people the Ryders brought into their home to help them make cloth came, then, to represent both unfulfilled expectations and the means of building the kind of family Joseph as a young man, and presumably Elisabeth as a young woman, imagined marriage would engender. It was clearly difficult for Ryder to instill diligence and piety in his family, and no doubt molding his orphans in his own image was partly his way to try to overcome his failure to fill the church pews with his own children. But the struggle was compensated for by the spiritual camaraderie he increasingly found in his wife. In this sense, and over time, his marriage was more successful: oversight of the household did not have to be under-taken alone.

"Trouble" was the second of the multivalent keywords that often accompany references in the diary to family. Paternal responsibility so heavily invested with spiritual, emotional, and economic meaning demanded endless and frustrating oversight. If Psalm 119:113 ("I hate vain thoughts") regularly expressed Ryder's vanity and self-hatred, and Matthew 16:26 ("For what is a man profited, if he shall gain the whole world, and lose his own soul") reminded him that profit meant nothing if the soul was lost, Job 5:7 captured his feelings about his family relationships. As he put it in the diary's opening months for the first of many times, "perturbation and commotion from one in my family who is often vexing my heart and ears with one argu-ment or another caused me to sit down in sorrowful manner and cry out"—as Job did—"man is born to Trouble as the sparks that fly upward."[4] "Trouble," Job's calamities made painfully clear, was inevitable. Being born with it only preceded being thrust into it for the remainder of life. But inevitability didn't entail passivity. Much as Ryder actively sought to persevere amid his own trials, he tried to offset the tendency for upheaval in his family with prayer, watchfulness, and discipline, which were all aimed at increasing economic productivity, spiritual rigor, and emotional connection.

Ryder's household should sound familiar to anyone who knows the early industrial-age nostalgia for the eighteenth-century domestic industry. An 1839 Yorkshire Hand-loom Commissioners' Report claims, for example, that the crowning achievement of the bygone domestic industry had been the way it "concentrates the family under one roof, gives to each member of it a common interest, and leaves the children under the watchful eye of the parent."[5] Ryder was, in fact, driven to make his house something like the bucolic panopticon that later industrialists imagined and admired, and much of our concern here will be to examine how his watchfulness could discipline others. But to fully understand Ryder's domestic life we also need to follow his watchful eye as it looked to make emotional and spiritual connection part of the completion of material goals. Much like stable marriage and household management, successful adoption—making the children of other people his own—meant internalization of his economic and spiritual values and authority. Here as elsewhere, the spiritual, material, and emotional were inseparable.

When the diary begins, the first of Ryder's family relationships we encounter is not, however, that with Elisabeth or his children, but the troubling one he had with his live-in mother, Mary. Ryder's regard for his mother is intriguing and obscure. His most unqualified affection comes forth on her death at age seventy-seven. "I look in one place, and she is not there, I come into another place where she was wont to be, and this is also empty. The eyes that used to see her, must now see her no more," Ryder mourned in the diary. But there were clear signs of tension between Joseph and Mary during her life. One of his earliest complaints—about anything—comes from an "aversion to do something or another about or for my mother." The indefinite "something or another about or for" tells us there was only so much detail he was willing to give, but in any case he immediately checked himself with a biblical proverb— "despise not thy mother when she is old"—while cryptically citing a memory of something that "had sometime ago passed among us which rather still tended to carry on resentment." We can only guess at what he meant, but one likely possibility is that he resented her for pushing him to do well in business. In an only slightly clearer entry from the following year he referenced his "many Thoughts of heart with respect to my Condition in the World." This was a characteristic allusion to economic ambition, but here he followed it with the thought, "My mother Desires one Thing, & in my Apprehension

God Commands another. In this Doubtfull Case to know whether my apprehensions be right or hers is the thing that causes so many Doubts in my mind." By setting her desires for his condition in the world against God's, Ryder may have meant that she pushed for the sort of success God would judge excessive. Then as now, mothers could encourage their sons in vocational calling. The late-seventeenth-century spiritual autobiographer George Trosse explained that in youth he "was still bent upon Merchandize; presuming I should be a more successful Trader, & a richer Merchant, beyond the Seas, than I could be at Home." Trosse therefore noted he "desir'd to visit some other Country again, and my Mother was also very willing of it, for my Worldly Advantage: For she could have a Prospect of nothing else by my Going in Foreign Parts." If Mary Ryder similarly encouraged her son, she may have been a surrogate for his economic misgivings.[6]

Interspersed between cryptic mother references in the early pages of the diary run equally obscure but undeniable indicators of unfulfilled sexual desire. As the spring of 1734 was regenerating life in the West Riding, Whitaker preached against the "vile sin" and "vicious habit" of masturbation, adultery, fornication, and "obscenity in the Imagination," which could lead to "poverty, disgrace, loss of reputation (tho valuable) and many loathsome diseases, and if unrepented of, eternall death." Moral and medical authorities in the mid-eighteenth century were working overtime to criminalize a form of self-pleasure that had been viewed with less explicit suspicion in the more puritanical seventeenth century. This new attentiveness to the moral meaning of masturbation, in particular, may explain why Ryder summarized the sermon in uncharacteristic detail: "We were cautioned against lascivious pictures, unclean songs and books, the effects whereof has been of bad consequence filling the world so with this vile sin against all intemperance, which tends greatly to lead the soul aside." But he never admitted to any actual transgression: "many and great have been my temptations to this vile sin . . . would earnestly desire to be more and more armed against it, not only against the outward acts of uncleanness, but against the vicious habit [and] against every unclean fancy and affection."[7]

Ryder's frustrations worsened when he turned his attention outward. Traveling a month after Whitaker's admonition, he encountered "a lovely young girl," at which sight "I was ready to desire such a gift from the Lord, and thought if such a gift might be bestow'd my great delight would be to pray for the welfare of such a child's soul." Ryder's leverage with God in asking for a mate was the very promise that he would merge sexual desire with spiritual paternalism—it was by bundling spiritual paternalism with virtually any other motive for engagement with others that he found solid ground for relationships. But spiritual meaning was also invested in his failures. Not having "such a blessing," he told his diary, might itself be a "tryall of my faith and patience." And whatever divine message he was supposed to decode, sexual frustration is palpable in his final assessment of the encounter as he finds his "corrupt affections much unsubdued."[8]

Whoever he was lusting after goes unnamed, but it is hard not to wonder whether she continues to haunt the diary a few months later in an entry written November 28, 1734, the day "a Young Woman whom I dearly Lov'd & with whom I had raised Expectations of spending a few days Comfortably here upon Earth in preparation for heaven was to be married to another man." "Not in the Least," he reassured himself, did he "have hard Thoughts upon the Wisdom & Providence of God who in this Case Seems to Cross my Intentions." In a remarkable spiritual rationalization, he claimed that remaining linked to her via Christ could in any case prevent estrangement if not preserve affection: "If we were members of one mysticall Body of which Christ is the Head, it would no way Tend to Dissolve the Union betwixt us & our Dearest Lord & Redeemer, and was Desirous It might not in the Least tend to Occasion any Disaffection betwixt us who are I hope particular members."[9]

If losing his love interest led Ryder to call to mind union with Christ, the inspiration for the imagery he invoked may have been the only surviving text he owned: a manuscript copy of the elder Thomas Whitaker's "Spiritual Marriage, or The Union of Christ to Believers set forth and explained in Twenty-two Sermons," which Ryder acquired in his late twenties. Christ's spiritual marriage to his believers promised enormous, eternal benefits for "the bride," Whitaker explained in a common enough metaphor from the book of Jeremiah. But Whitaker drew the metaphor further into the language of seduction and sensuality. "Jesus makes love to the soul" in seven different ways, he explained: "1st by kind invitations, 2 by affectionate Intreaty 3 by urgent Expostulations 4 by Importunate knocking 5 by Gracious allurements 6 by pathetick lamentations 7 by long waiting patience." This could as easily outline the forty-year-old Ryder's apparently unsuccessful strategy for attracting a mate. Set against his unwanted bachelorhood, an erotically conceptualized connection to Jesus would also have to substitute for being alone:

If we Sincerely on our Lord rely
And when he has his pleasure in us wrought
In this Low region Then shall we be brought
To him unto his Bridall chamber where
We shall behold him Not as we do here
But face to face as Do the Saints above
And be for Ever Ravisht with his Love
Then shall we taste those precious fruits which flow
from Marriage union with our Lord below[10]

. . .

With an overbearing mother, amid sexual and emotional rejection, and reluctant to pursue whatever relief from frustration that masturbation offered,
Ryder not surprisingly found his wife in a woman in whom he initially had
little interest. In the weeks before his wedding day he had to ask a friend to
lecture him on the need for conviction in the face of what he was about to do.
Only days after their marriage he complained of feeling sick (with no stated
cause) and before two weeks had passed found death more appealing than his
new marital conflicts: "I have had somewhat of a renewed Trouble Even in
my new Relationship which well teaches me the Truth of that Scripture That
man who is born of a woman is of few Days, & full of trouble, and was ready
hereupon to begin somewhat more earnestly to Desire after that happy state,
where peace is enjoy'd without disturbance, and Quietness without end."
The new bride was such a letdown that in order of importance she initially
ranked second to his diary. Still just two months into their marriage he found
himself "prevented by one thing or Other from Doing any thing in this
Book, In the Evening I found an Inclination or Temptation to Omitt . . .
these words Coming Into my mind as my Excuse, I have married a wife and
therefore Cannot Come. But Lord prevent me from Excusing any that is
vicious." It is telling that he chose not to omit the words. His snide remark
may have occasioned regulatory self-disciplining, but his confession also
feels like assurance of his affection to and for his beloved journal.[11]

The woman on the receiving end of this disappointment is much more
elusive in the archives than her husband, who in his thousands of diary
entries never mentioned her by name. She was born on March 18, 1705,
although she and her husband, as we have noted, would celebrate her birthday
on the twenty-fifth, the day of her baptism and of Joseph's own birthday.

Local records of births, burials, and marriages mostly offer a glimpse of the personally catastrophic. At the beginning of her life, her family included her father, Joseph, her mother, Debora, and one sister. Two years later her mother had died shortly after the birth of another sister who herself survived only a few days. Her father remarried in 1710 and had at least two more children, one of whom failed to outlive infancy.[12]

Ryder never explained why he did not care about Elisabeth in the beginning—the sad realization that they would fail to have children could not be the cause because it unfolded only gradually. The disappointment, in any case, subsides in the diary as the evidence appears of their outlooks coalescing. "One Make & mould" was the expression he used in a draft of a letter to a friend meant to capture the merging of personality and goals that married couples should pursue. Contrary to "ye more witty & polite part of mankind" who call it "confinement" (or those, he might have added with better self-recollection, who call it a distraction from diary keeping), he had come to view marriage as a happy "social state" whose value was deeply tied to its utility. Marriage made people "more Extensively usefull in the World, Because rendered Capable of acting in Different Relations, and without which the Bonds of Society must be Entirely Broke, or at Least Labour under manifold Disadvantages, which I have neither Time at present nor Indeed Occasion to Insist on, Only I beg Leave to say that I think it Extremely Happy where two persons are pretty much of One Make & mould not only as to naturall Temper But as to the Spirituall & Divine Life."[13]

Ryder was echoing popular godly attitudes toward marriage, but as time passed the evidence mounts that his own marriage was becoming more emotionally and spiritually meaningful as he and Elisabeth came into alignment. He began to call her his "Dear Wife" as they talked more often about spiritual matters. They traveled together on working trips, short vacations, and to London in the late summer of 1744. We discover little beyond his disaffection for the city in his single entry recorded while there, but in the summer of 1737 he indicates that much of what they witnessed when encountering the world beyond Leeds was seen with the same eyes. In August of that year, for example, they took a two-day trip to "Squire Arolby's curiositys" to experience "a little worldly pleasure & poor pleasure it is." Their joint assessment? Solomon was right: "all is vanity."[14]

Where it is audible, Elisabeth's voice is often deferential, which at times may have satisfied her husband. Even relatively late in their marriage he called to mind his enjoyment of friendly company until his "pleasure [was] damped by an unguarded word which dropt from my wife." But it is facile to assume that Ryder simply guarded Elisabeth's words. He could also feel uncomfortable with his customary authority. When by her own admission she misspoke on another occasion while giving advice to a distressed neighbor, he quickly stopped her apology. In no way, he told his diary that evening, could he be offended if God made either him or her instrumental in helping someone along the path toward salvation.[15]

Elisabeth clearly emulated her husband, but not inevitably. They could, in fact, alternate their roles as spiritual guide. "My Dear Wife . . . was describing a Hypocrite," he explained in the late 1740s, "& Said a hypocrite could not delight in the holyness of God, nor In the Justice of God, but a believer could triumph in the Justice of God." Ryder took her comments seriously. "I call'd it over in my mind, and was ready to hope that I could do so, by the Law I count my Self a condemned creature but hence arose my comfort: although God be Just Yet he is the Justifier of them that believe in Jesus." His record of their conversations of religious matters also depicts two-sided engagement. She had become his chief conversation partner and confidant by the 1740s, "a pillar of wisdom and worth," as one historian aptly called the middle-class housewife of the era. What they shared as they noticed declining piety in their town or dwindling numbers in their church was often despair. But that they shared it is still telling.[16]

Affection continued to grow with spiritual compatibility in the later years of their marriage. A decade after their wedding, Ryder finally began to include Elisabeth in his entries written on their birthday. The day he reached fifty and she forty was spent "in Chearfullness one with another." But Ryder's overriding concern was "that if God shall add another year to our Days . . . he will well Enable us to the performance of Every Conjugall Duty, and help us to the Conscientious Discharge of every Duty & trust we may be engag'd in, & so prepar'd for Dying *well.*" What brought happiness on this particular day was the confluence of their spiritual paths. The next birthday he even more hopefully prayed that they would be productive "in whatever work & Duty (as members of Civil & Religious Society)" God had incumbent on them. Elisabeth too suggests that merging their spiritual outlooks created a happier marriage. On the following birthday she expressed (through her husband) her most cheerful statement in his diary: "My Wife declares it to be the best year as She apprehends she has ever yet spent." There were several

reasons to celebrate: her health was relatively stable; the family was prosperous; her husband, judging by his comments in the diary, was increasingly
showing her signs of affection; and the goal of the godly household was in
sight. As Ryder put it in a verse from early 1747:

> Blest is the Pious house Indeed
> Where Graces in their Beauty Shine
> Where Man and Wife their Interests twist
> In Labouring after things Divine

Not only were the material interests of husband and wife bound together; the
metaphor of labor, the recurring trope in Ryder's poetry, tells us it was as
important for the pious house as for the couple who ran it to direct domestic
industry toward a spiritual end.[17]

Almost everything we know about how Ryder shaped and reflected other
people comes, in the absence of other sources, from him, and this inevitably
leaves us with a one-sided impression of how he dealt with what were at least
two-sided relationships. But there is one place where Ryder's mediation is less
immediate. Elisabeth too, it turns out, kept a spiritual diary, and it survives as
a cryptic collection of entries at the beginning of a book that Ryder finished
as one of his own volumes a few years after her death. Her self-account was a
relatively modest undertaking. She wrote only nineteen entries, all composed
in 1752 except for the final entry, which was written much later, on December
1, 1753, a day that justified recording because it brought her so close to death,
although she would live for another five months. It is also impossible to tell
whether these entries, most of which are no more than two or three lines,
constitute all that she ever wrote. But as chance would have it, three of her
longest entries, put down on days that she and Joseph spent together, cover
shared experiences. What we therefore possess, by chance, is an opportunity
to listen to a husband and a wife in an unintended dialogue.[18]

> This is what he had to say on May 3, 1752:
> May 3 Sacrament Day
>
> This Day Mr Whitaker preacht Rom 5: 1 Therefore being justify'd
> by faith we have peace with God. From the words he has treated of
> the nature of Justification and of the means by faith and of the fruit,
> namely peace with God, and of the means or medium whereby, that

A page from Elisabeth Ryder's diary in a book her husband would continue as his twenty-seventh volume. Reproduced by courtesy of the University Librarian and Director, The John Rylands University Library, The University of Manchester.

is, Through our Lord Jesus Christ who is the propitiation for our sins through faith in his blood, the fruits of Justification he has this day been enlarging upon, and these are pardon of sins past, a freedom from the gross abuse of our comforts, adoption into the family of the children of God, and a participation at last of eternal glory. It was after sermon of the sacrament & when I had got sett I began to recollect I was come to sitt with Christ if I belong to his family and so at the table to send up requests for pardon of sin for the mortification of my corruptions and the quickening of my graces and finds longing about Increase, but memory fails.

Here Ryder ran through his usual practice: he quoted his minister and the relevant passage from the Bible, explained the sermon, and found a way to connect Whitaker's message to personal experience. In passing we should also notice his use of the word "adoption" in the broader context of his spiritual family, on which more below, and of course his typical linkage of grace to "increase."

> Here is Elisabeth on the same day:
> this being our Sacrament Day I waited in on god in publicke worshep but found my heart but Littel afected Til we came to the Table & then my Soule was melted, for a Long Time hearing so meny Desputs I have been almost Tempted to Athezare [atheism?] but I am Resoveled through grace Strenghten me never to Qutt [quit] my faith in a Redemer & was incorredg [encouraged] his grace would be Sofisiant [sufficient] for me as it was for paul when he had a thoarn in the flesh the mesege of Satan to buffit [buffet] him[.] mr whit preached from Romans chap 5 ver 1

Some differences between husband and wife immediately stand out: Elisabeth's handwriting and spelling indicate that her formal education, like that of many other early modern women, fell short of her husband's. If Elisabeth meant "atheism" where "Athezare" appears—at least this would fit both the context of the sentence and the first four clearly visible letters of the word—then she used a word that hardly occurs in her husband's thousands of pages. For that matter, nowhere does her husband use the evocative metaphor of a soul melting. Maybe more surprising is that while Joseph seemed content with Whitaker's interpretation of the concept of justification by faith, Elisabeth's encounter with disputes, presumably theological ones, led her to articulate the possibility—even if rhetorically—of abandoning her religion until she was encouraged by the thought that receiving grace might allay her doubts. This is a microscopic moment, but it nevertheless tells us important things: Elisabeth was no simple reflection of her husband, her doubts may have run deeper than his, and she wrote her handful of diary entries to some degree in her own voice.[19]

When we turn to their other entries that line up, however, the operative phrase is "to some degree." Her entry from May 30, 1752, more glaringly reflects her husband's habit. Here, first, is Joseph:

This day Mr Whitaker preacht from Psalm 127: 1: 2: Except the Lord build the house, they labour in vain that build it; except the Lord keep the city, the watchman waketh but in Vain. It is vain for you to rise up early to sit up late to eat the bread of Sorrows, for so he giveth his beloved sleep, from which words [Whitaker] undertook to prove a generall providence, and to show of how little avail all our best laid projects and all our toil, tho soon and late, without gods blessing, not that he excluded either care or labour, but both must be done with an eye to Gods Glory, and in dependance upon his provi- dence, and under this view recommended daily prayers for daily blessings, he showd that many had outward things who did not pray but showd when we had them in answer to prayer we were most likely to have a blessing with them, & if God did deny it was because he saw they were not good for us, & hereupon taught us resignation to his will, what I heard I approved, & I hope endeavours after the practice recommended.

As we have come to expect, Ryder made note of the biblical passage on which Whitaker built his sermon before explaining the minister's providentialist gloss, one part of which was, typically, that material rewards could betoken God's favor. Elisabeth, on the same day, wrote:

this day I have been in poor heath & Dul mr whit preached from psalm 137 [127] we Except the Lord buelt the hous thay Labour in vaine that build it & wherin he showed that & nither our diligeance nor care would avade evel in the thing of this world without god blising our indevers & that his provideance entends to all thing & persons. which should [sic] our Dependance on him & not on our selves & give him the glory of all our succes & to pray to him for ablesing as all so to submit to his will under afflective prove- diances

The discrepancies in formal education are still evident, but here the similari- ties stand out. She too made note of Whitaker's biblical reference before explaining its providential meaning, part of which is the now very familiar notion that God should be given "the glory of all our succes." Her diary reads, in other words, as if Ryder—or Ryder's spiritual mentor Whitaker—had told her how, if not more or less what, to write.

Stronger parallels appear when their final matching entries are overlain (this was also Elisabeth's final entry from December 1753). Both use virtually the same phrase to describe Elisabeth's illness. Joseph says that providence should be thanked for sparing his wife, who "both in her own apprehension, and in the apprehension of others, was upon the very confines of Eternity ready for taking flight into an unseen world." She too thanks providence as she "Lay in my own happrention [apprehension] and the happrention of my frinds Ready to take my fl lauch [launch] into a Eternal world." Intriguingly, she appears to have started to write the word "flight," as he had in his entry from the same day, before writing "launch." That she chose her own word when she had his at her disposal could certainly be read as a deliberate deviation from his words—or maybe she was remembering correctly a ready-made phrase that they both knew and that Ryder recalled with less precision. But in either case this reads as scripted. Even her phonetic spelling of "apprehension" suggests that this word was less likely one she had seen in print than one she had heard spoken, possibly in the very phrase that Joseph wrote in his diary and she echoed in hers. Elisabeth may not merely have been an echo of her husband, but she had, to a large degree, become very much like him (and the people he himself mirrored). And this is of course also evident in the fact that she was keeping a diary, if this was her only one, only after nearly two decades of cohabitation that must have made clear his expectation of pious practice in a marriage partner. Ryder had a religious mandate to keep the sparks from going astray, and that meant bringing others into line with the model of piety he worked so hard to internalize and presumably couldn't help but to reflect in others.[20]

If comparison of their diaries at the very least shows that spiritual compatibility underpinned Ryder's affections, then that affection also seems to have taken on a life of its own, especially as Elisabeth languished from unspecified illnesses. Disease that Ryder found in his own flesh was a sign of spiritual impoverishment. As Elisabeth verged on "taking fitts" before he could confirm that she still enjoyed her "reasonable faculties," there was tellingly no trace of the diabolical. He simply and worryingly called her "my Loving wife." When they made the trip noted earlier for her to take the waters, he returned home alone to find "a very affectionate concern for my absent wife, being in the representation of a widdowed state." Days later, he excitedly received her first letter from abroad and afterwards, in "ye Company of Severall of my Friends and acquaintances," lost himself in thoughts about her "absence long."[21]

This affection only intensified amid an unnamed illness that struck her during the months before her death. Alan Macfarlane once wrote that one sign of the insecurity of early modern life "was an inability to judge the severity of an illness." As true as that must have been in countless cases, it did not exactly apply to Ryder. He may have lacked diagnostic sophistication, but his pessimism and preoccupation with death led him to mostly correctly assume that serious illnesses were fatal. It is a testament to his growing concern for Elisabeth, however, that he broke from this habit in the final months of her life. As hopelessly sick as she became throughout late 1753 and early 1754, his expectations for her recovery could flow as much as ebb, much like God's apparent willingness to keep someone alive: "God says to his diseases to One go and it Goeth, to another come and it cometh." Ryder's hopefulness makes it all the more heart wrenching when Elisabeth finally succumbed to an illness about which the most specific thing Ryder ever mentions are intermittent pains. "This day in the morning about five o clock my Dear wife departed this life," he wrote on April 25, 1754, with detailed attention to time that in its very rarity in the diary adds weight to the event. "I was always ready to entertain hopes of her recovery," he confided to his diary, once again in the absence of a human confidant. "But alas I now see all my hopes of her stay here in Vain."[22]

Ryder poured forth expressions of affection as he struggled to accept the death of his wife, whom he now referred to as a "dear friend" or "my Dear & Delightfull companion of Life." Two weeks after her burial, Whitaker quoted lines from the Gospel of John that Elisabeth "in her life time had desired might be insisted on after her death." After his summation of Whitaker's sermon, Ryder composed a full two-page, forty-four line poem, the longest of his many verses. He touched on the biblical passage but mainly used the occasion to recall, in language so unlike that he had used when he and Elisabeth had met, the "sweet seasons of her life." "With her I'll hail the happy Day / That I by Death am call'd away," he wrote with readiness to spend eternity with the woman who years earlier had frustratingly eaten up the time he wanted to spend with his diary.[23]

It is just as revealing of this shift in feeling that in later years Ryder painfully noted her absence. On arriving back at his house after a business trip in the hectic summer of 1754, he was relieved, as usual, that God brought him home safely, "yet at my coming home I found my wife was not here who used to receive me at my return home at any time with much pleasure." Months later he continued to struggle—as he boxed up her clothes to send off to her sister in London or as he read through her diary and noted her "conflicts with one trouble or another she met with." His silence on their birthday in the years right after her death is no less telling. Death had ruptured the providential symmetry. There was no apparent memory trigger at all on December 16, 1758, when being "at labour and consider[ing] about the time that I had spend in the wilderness of this world in my widdowed state since the death of my dear wife, I had a sweet transport of Joy in hoping to meet her again in another, & a better world." None of this, however, changed the fact that Ryder was now widowed, at age fifty-nine, and would remain so for the rest of his life despite the occasional advice of friends to remarry.[24]

Ryder had long before accepted the fact that he would never produce children of his own, but he did so sullenly. Countless eighteenth-century men and women, after all, continued to be guided by the *Book of Common Prayer*, which gave a role in marriage to love and honor but also made clear that finding a husband or wife meant protection against unlawful sex, assistance in sickness and in health, and, not least, the possibility of legitimate procreation. In fact, Ryder was ready to have children almost at the moment we meet him. The unlikeliness of this ever happening nevertheless steadily unfolds in the diary. "Inordinately desirous of an offspring," he wrote while immersed in self-pity within ten days of commencing his first book. "Children this Day I thought . . . were delights & Comforts to their Parents and I have none." In the months before he married, he was "ashamed" of his "unfruitfulness" in relation to children. Six months after his wedding he recorded "affections as to a Posterity to keep up my name. I appear'd in a very resigned way. I thought if my name might but be found written amongst the Living In Jerusalem It was a Blessing Infinitely beyond my Desert." But he was careful to define what children would ultimately be for. "If God was pleased to Give me Son or Daughter that might Live to be any way Instrumentall to bring Glory to his Holy name . . . I would Desire to be very thankfull. If not I Desire to arrive to full Contentment with Such Things as I have." Less than half a year into his marriage on a trip in the countryside his wandering mind once again began to long for offspring, though his conscience cautioned him not to be greedy in the desire. More and more he thanked providence for making him trustee for fatherless children, as if this were compensation for his unfruitfulness. And by 1740, he seemed accepting of reality. In his entry of June 9, his fifth wedding anniversary (the first he actually mentions), he cryptically wrote that "I have been Five Years married yet tho I have a very agreable companion Such a mixture of Troubles from one hand or another have attended us, which helps to embitter the Dearest, comforts & relation of Life . . . if we seek comfort & satisfaction meerly in things below. They must all make this reply: it is not in me." What was not in him was in fact many things: the kind of affection he longed to have for God, a sense of equilibrium between the spiritual and material, and now, it appeared clearly, the capacity to bring children into the world.[25]

In every sense that would ultimately matter to him, however, Ryder already had a large family in which he could instill spiritual values. Details about the children are remarkably rare. Some must have come from the workhouses. Some he calls "fatherless," others he doesn't, but we are still left guessing if in fact all were—or if only some were, how many? There were enough of them in any case to make for "troublesome differences" at home, and "enough" differences, as he once complained, "to make one . . . weary of Life." His family had grown large enough by the early 1740s to occasion a move into a bigger house as well as regular worry about his abilities to provide for everyone living under his roof. And those worries were as spiritual as they were material. The manuscript regarding rules for the religious conduct of the family that opened this chapter called every parent a prince and priest, a sovereign of his "little Society" and a pastor "over his little Flock." Children and servants alike were enjoined to honor and obey their parents, by whom they were governed and guided and in whom they should entrust "the Care both of their Bodies & Souls." Thomas Whitaker could deliver the same message. He once preached that the children of the deceased have a duty to worship the God of their father. But that duty ran as much in the other direction. Ryder routinely reminded himself that failing as a prince and priest deterred his own salvation.[26]

But unless it implies economic management, "prince" is also an incomplete metaphor for the secular role Ryder assumed in his family. Salvation, he makes clear over and over, was suggested by his family's continued economic success as much as by filial piety, which of course also undergirded household order and productivity. "The Comfort and Happiness of *your Religious*

*Parents* does, in a great Measure, depend on your Seriousness and Piety," one of Ryder's treasured authors, Philip Doddridge, preached in *Sermons to Young Persons*. "If they meet with Prosperity in their worldly Affairs, and have a Prospect of leaving you in plentiful Circumstances, it will be a Satisfaction to them to think, that they shall not consign their Estates to those who will meanly hoard up the Income of them, or throw it away in foolish and hurtful Lusts." The same mix of piety, industriousness, and craving for order permeated the diary. In his patently titled "Family Order Beautiful," Ryder explained that

> Husbands and wives do well agree
> When they with Joynt delight
> Talk of Gods wondrous Grace and Love
> With Pleasure day and night
> Masters and Servants harmonize
> When each fullfill their place
> Neglect on Either Side does leave
> But Sorrow and Disgrace

More seamlessly if less consciously Ryder joined the spiritual and material when he described the "behaviour of an ungovernable boy who breaks through commands, & is to me a great Burden. I daily Long to see a better Servant of God and if I might have the happiness to see him a true Servant of God I then never doubt of the pleasure of his Service to me." So linked were spiritual and worldly duties that adherence to the former seemed to make the latter naturally fall into place.[27]

Converting idleness to industry was a cultural preoccupation of early modern Britain, as we have noted, and much of the "trouble" Ryder regularly complained about must have arisen from tension between his attempts to make children industrious and their resistance to his efforts. There could also be a deeply complex social, political, and emotional subtext behind domestic turmoil. In one sense, Ryder was effectively performing a political role as he disciplined his householders, in the process encouraging them to be the very sort of self-governing people that Britain's ostensibly freer and freer society needed if it hoped to avoid social anarchy. Ryder's role in his family could in this sense be compared to that of the local reformers whom the sociologist Philip Gorski has identified as major players in the process of state formation in the early modern Netherlands. Much as the apparatus of the

Calvinist church in the Netherlands inculcated modes of self-restraint that gave the Dutch comparatively little need for external forms of regulation like the police force, Ryder participated in the "diffusion of disciplinary practices" that instructed people how to control themselves in a commercial society. In another sense, though, we can also glimpse that there were clear limits to the success of Ryder's efforts as a family prince and priest. As the historian Steve Hindle has shown, poor parents who had been compelled by parish officers and magistrates to apprentice their children in households like Ryder's might, for example, actually encourage their children to be disobedient to their new masters. What had these parents been told by officials, implicitly or explicitly, if not that they were incapable, as Hindle has written, of instilling the "diligence and deference upon which labour discipline and social order depended"? Ryder's words clearly echo in the language of the magistrates Hindle has followed. These officials who regularly enforced the practice of apprenticing poor and refractory children called such children "difficult," "troublesome and difficult," a "labour," "continual trouble," and so on. If their descriptions are as clipped as Ryder's, their subtext is no less clear: householders must have continually resisted forms of external control meant to make these children pliable, pious, and productive.[28]

We have to be careful, all the same, about the precise way that we characterize Ryder's particular ambitions. Compelling evidence that he was an iron-willed manager of the household who used religion as a mere instrument of discipline or oppression is not forthcoming. The goal he set for his family seems rather to have been the goal he set for himself: to avoid immersion and excess in the struggle to attain the material wealth that could be self-sustaining and manifest evidence of doing God's work on earth. As he once wrote after "trafficking in the affairs of this present Life & World . . ., I find my Thoughts & affections have been too much there, the Concerns of a numerous Family necessary calls for much care & concern Even for their temporall subsistence, & much more I think every Good Christian ought to have for their better part, Oh that God would help me sincerely to depend upon him in the use of the means of grace, & in the conscientious practice of doing justly."[29]

Where Ryder was noticeably more stern, his guilt, and occasionally his self-control, trailed closely behind. Family members who disturbed domestic order might be exiled from his home, but he might as easily welcome them back again. In the winter of 1737 what he called a "miscarriage" in his family nearly led him "to strike" before patience won out. Days later the same "two young persons" behaved badly, but rather than administering punishment he contemplated his own failings. Much more constant in the diary, however, are his worries about exactly how to operate as prince. "This Day or rather this Evening," he wrote in the late 1740s, "I find my Self much concerned in my mind about the right Government of those that are young Committed to my Care & Charge. I am afraid lest I should be too easy and so prove to encourage or however not Show that dislike to their Vices & follies of youth which is required, on the other hand I am timerous lest by any great Degree of resentment & anger prevailing I should lose the peace & comfort of my own mind. No one is able to help me, or to Give me council to saving purpose but God."[30]

But of course such comments tell us not that Ryder was uninterested in discipline; they tell us he was unsure about how to go about administering it. One of the subtler and far less problematic ways in which he could merge his interests in keeping family order was by routine prayer. He and his family engaged in prayer "Every morning & Every night both in secret, & if we [are] in a Sociall or Family Relation . . . Constantly," and such regularity could go hand in hand with the exertion of authority. In this same entry, for example, he also found himself having "rul'd with Somewhat of Rigor in my Family tho Lords Day." It was troubling to have to punish a family member on the Sabbath, but he reasoned that punishment "is better given on that day than Malice and Revenge & Rancour harboured to Another Day." He "would freely choose Clemency Love and Gentleness" over punishment "if [they] did not Encourage such as are under my care to persist in their folly."[31]

The material and spiritual also met in the process of family instruction. It may be an indicator of the cultural reach of Lockean psychology in eighteenth-century Britain that even Joseph Ryder could not help but to sound at times like an empiricist. In the verse titled "Family Instruction Necessary" Ryder writes that

> While in our Infant State we are
> To serve our Lord There's Little care
> Trifles Do mainly fill our mind
> To Good We little are Inclin'd.

"Parents Instructions" were therefore necessary to "keep us safe from Every Snare / Lest We Should Wander." But a blank slate, instruction, and experience were also good for only so much, and Ryder was careful to privilege the role of grace in shifting one in the right direction:

> . . . Grace is much more needfull still
> To change the mind, & bow the will
> Parents may teach, But God can bless
> And Lead in ways of Holyness
> If we a Gracious Ear do Lend
> To Kind Entreaties God Does Send . . .
> But if we will not Lend an ear
> To What God Does to us Declare
> But will go on, & still rebell
> Then may we Dread the Lowest hell[32]

The godliness here already overshadows the rational empiricism. Ryder could be even more puritanical when it came to pleasurable pastimes. He felt "some uneasiness" when one of his householders spent the day following "the pleasures and sports of the time & had neglected hearing a sermon which he had opportunity of attending with the experience of much less time." And yet these infractions might also be forgiven, even if more in the diary (we have to wonder) than in person: "my concern for him excited me to speak to him about it whether he hear, or whether he forbear. I can look back & remember when [sports] pleas'd me as well as him."[33]

There is, then, much reason to give Ryder the benefit of the doubt when it comes to the crude materialist reading of his family life even as we recognize that his family disciplining, like his provisioning, was about more than simply saving souls. Before he was married, he drew a clear separation between worldly and spiritual ends for the family he longed to start. More important than finding a "way whereby to grow great here below" was to be a "happy Instrument of doing good" for the "precious souls" of the children he might one day father. But years later, and with a large family of householders, his comprehensive hope for what was, after all, his labor force seems to have been to increase their piety without compromising the prosperity of his business, which alongside the spiritual guidance of family matters was a testament to his fulfillment of a higher calling: "This Day I Thought I was concerned at heart for the growth of Piety in my family, & Said to my wife, that as far as I knew my Heart I Thought I was more desirous after the Increase of Piety, than the Increase of Riches. Yet Am I just now a Little Concern'd what method of proceeding may be best for me in business."[34]

It is impossible to read through Ryder's countless references to his family and not wonder what these faceless people thought about their "father." But all of these children and young adults are even more obscure in the diary than Elisabeth. And when they appear in its pages, it is by virtue of what Ryder saw as their disruptive behavior. We therefore know them as "troubling," "argumentative," "careless," "disagreeable," "ungovernable," "insulting," "refractory"—all characterizations we can only imagine they would not have applied to themselves. Some, he tells us without giving names or context, had problems with lying and drunkenness. Others were more generally "contentious." Most remained distressingly unconverted or insufficiently pious. When he more kindly worried as they were stricken with illness or suffered injury after being thrown from a horse, he never tells us why they were worth worrying about.[35]

He nevertheless grew fond enough of three family members to break from form and actually mention their names: Hannah, Grace, and Linda Arey. The Arey sisters came into Ryder's life sometime after 1739—the precise day of their entrance is never recorded—when Hannah and Grace were infants or small children and Linda was an older child or early adolescent. From the beginning, and possibly because of her age when she came into the family, his relationship with Linda was turbulent. When Ryder had to make arrangements for her burial just before her seventeenth birthday (we're never told what led to her early demise), he described "a young woman for whom . . . I had a Great respect." The last word suggests an at least partly dynamic relationship. But he also wrote that he had been "often concerned" for her "eternall welfare." When grief demanded that he draw some kind of lesson from her death, he hoped God would "Sanctify the Stroke," allowing the death to serve as a divine admonition to help him, Linda's sisters, and "all concerned with and about her" to prepare for death. And he could not help but mention that "she left me in a Disagreeable manner." Grace and Hannah stayed in the family for much longer, and Ryder was "much affected" the day he saw them admitted into his church. Both occasionally appear as attendees of funerals alongside Ryder and Elisabeth, sometimes in their place. The paltry evidence suggests that each woman was becoming Joseph Ryder junior, at least as far as their spiritual lives were concerned, and possibly to reward them for their emulation, among other things, he designated them inheritors of some, if not all, of his diary. He may have shown them affection, in other words, and in return expected receipt and adoption of his spiritual values and the daily, diligent labor those values encouraged.[36]

Ryder had no doubt about the limitlessness of human fallibility: he considered himself flawed, saw himself in others, and believed, as the older generations sitting in Call Lane Chapel would have, that humans were fallen creatures. The reflection of himself he saw in others also made him empathetic as he sought to bring his family into line. But this put Ryder in a bind. On the one hand, he had an imperative to keep the sparks from straying—an imperative intensified by his inability to produce his own children. In the late 1740s, during their happier years of marriage, Joseph and Elisabeth sat together in the evening, lamenting the state of their church as they took "a survey through our congregation in our minds, & considering how few there were of professors children who had come up to a publick profession . . . yet what little mourning and crying after a departing God."[37] If they saw the increasing room on Call Lane's pews as a consequence, in part, of the older generation of parishioners dying unreplaced by the young, then the fact that the Ryders could not stem this demographic tide with their own children must have made Joseph's need to instill his spiritual values in others all the more pressing. But on the other hand, inheriting children who had lost or been taken away from their parents made the task of child rearing no less arduous. Some of Ryder's "troubles" must have come from social polarization. But some must have come from his urgent need to save the souls of the people who were closest to him emotionally.

Adoption, in particular, was also made complex by its symbolic weight. Becoming a father for the children who lived and worked in his house meant, in some sense, enacting the process of his own adoption. Ryder's regret over not having known his biological father was muted but not inaudible. This may have made thoughts of his spiritual adoption in Heaven all the more affecting. God was, after all, the "father of the fatherless" the London minister Samuel Wright preached in a sermon that urged his Dissenter parishioners to come to the relief of orphans and widows. Philip Doddridge, who had himself been adopted, sermonized to young readers that no piece of scripture was more comforting in his youth than Psalm 27:10:

"When my Father and my Mother forsake me, then the Lord will take me up."[38]

The spiritual resonance of adoption could also be heard closer to home. Back in Leeds, in the spring of 1748, Whitaker took to the pulpit with a fifty-three-year-old Ryder, now both motherless and fatherless, sitting in the pew. Men and women "should receive the adoption of sons," Ryder recorded. "Whence we were put upon the tryall whether we were adopted or no." To be adopted here ostensibly meant to be committed to Christianity, but the metaphor was extended enough to suggest the available choices in the Ryder household and the rewards they must have been seen to offer. "We must be Either the Children of God, or Children of Another Master," Whitaker explained. "If we love God with all our heart, if we are regenerated and born again, if we walk in the Spirit crucifying the flesh with its affections & lusts then are we the children of God." Ryder continued the thought that evening in a verse he titled "Of Adoption":

> Amazed with Gods love
> I would his wonders tell
> That I am rescued from the pit
> And from the Snares of hell
> But to be call'd a Son
> Still makes the wonder rise
> May every Gratefull thought hereof
> Fill me with sweet surprize.

"To be call'd a Son"—this is where the emotion rises in the verse, and we can hear in these words Ryder stressing the vehicle of the family metaphor that captured his relationship with God. God was to Ryder what Ryder hoped to be for his own family: a prince, a master, and a loving parent.[39]

In this nexus of emotion, economy, and piety the stakes for Ryder's affective and instrumental relationships with the children he brought into his home were as high, in other words, as those of his own spiritual adoption. Coming into the Ryders' family therefore would not simply have meant years of difficult, time-consuming labor and emotional turmoil. It could and often did mean those things, but it also meant entering a world governed by a father intent on guaranteeing that those around him adopted his piety along with his work ethic. This makes Ryder's family relationships sound top-down. They certainly were in more ways than they weren't. But there is one other thing we should not fail to notice. If Ryder's profound spiritual anxieties flowed to others by virtue of his paternalist influence, then his relationships with his householders also would have occasioned one of the great ironies of his life. Those anxieties and that sense of inborn trouble that likely passed from father to family came in part from the material surplus that the family, through the diligence and industriousness Ryder inculcated, was able to return to their father.

# 6. Mourning, Melancholy, and Money

> I oft walked but in a dejected and Disconsolate frame.
> —Joseph Ryder's diary, November 11, 1733

So many of Ryder's displayed emotions reside in the basic definition the West has long offered of depression and melancholy (the two words were often interchangeable in the eighteenth century and will be here).[1] To feel such emotions—dejection, sorrow, despair, sadness, unhappiness, despondency—at one time or another may simply derive from being human, and to articulate them in a religious culture that exalted self-abnegation is not necessarily the same as always feeling them. But there is an unmistakable specificity, consistency, and intensity in Ryder's expressions of, particularly, his remorse about his vain thoughts and worldliness, his expectations of eternal punishment, his mournfulness, and his criticism of his behavior and sinfulness in both his present and past.

Asking the question more directly—was Ryder depressed?—may nevertheless sound alarms. Precise psychological diagnosis requires a belief in the fixity of normative categories that many historians now approach skeptically. And even those who easily accept the existence of mental illness could at least admit that the cultural value of a condition like depression can vary. Certainly not everyone has thought, or currently thinks, of depression as a disease. Examples abound in the seventeenth and eighteenth centuries, especially in literary culture, of writers who wore a melancholic temperament as a "treasured identity badge" or found it in some other way artistically useful. To reach the conclusion that they needed an antidepressant would be to seriously misunderstand their motives. For these early modern literary types, whose numbers multiplied exponentially toward the end of the eighteenth century, melancholy could promise artistic breakthroughs.[2]

And yet if these qualifications should prevent automatic, value-laden diagnosis across the centuries, they are not particularly relevant in Ryder's case. Like so many of his coreligionists, Ryder saw melancholy as a serious problem. "The devill is a watchfull enemy & loves to fish in troubled waters," he noted after hearing "a very melancholy story of a neighbour who had been tempted and had attempted to put herself away by her own hands." There was nothing to be gained from experiencing or projecting sustained depression; by falling prey to dejected spirits, Ryder set himself up to lose, potentially, everything. Without slipping into anachronism or reifying medical categories, we can simply ask whether Ryder suffered from a state of mind that he himself thought was dangerous.[3]

There are deeper reasons to wonder this. Among the various authorities in the West to weigh in on what might lie behind depression, few have been more influential than Freud, who took on the subject in his essay "Mourning and Melancholia," written and published during the First World War. Freud's view is nuanced and complex, but at its heart lies the notion that the expressive characteristics of depression are the same as those of temporary mourning over a specific loss; melancholy, for all intents and purposes, *is* endless mourning. As it turns out, there was nothing particularly novel in the basic form of this view. In still the most comprehensive history of depression, Stanley Jackson showed that even if for some early modern physicians, Richard Napier for example, mourning over actual death could itself be so intense as to never abate and effectively make one melancholy, it was still the case that underneath the broader view of Napier and many of his contemporaries was a typically understood difference between mourning, which was supposed to be temporary, and melancholia, which was mourning that went on for so long as to eventually seem to be without cause.[4]

What is particularly striking about this view of depression that holds together so well over time is that despite what Ryder took to be the dangers of melancholy, and despite his tacit recognition that mourning and melancholy were not the same, he very particularly and consciously sought to experience a regular state of grief. "I comply with Solomon's assertion. It is better to go to the house of mourning than the house of mirth," he repeated almost like a mantra in the journal. This wasn't simply recitation. There was no more reliable way to enter a house of mourning than to experience death, and at least as early as his first volume Ryder had become a sort of junkie for funerals. "I desire I may not pass over one day without Serious Thoughts about my dying day," he wrote in his early sixties, supported by what by then was documentation that over the course of his examined life he had visited and recorded the details of hundreds of funerals of strangers, family, and friends.[5] Ryder's religiously sanctioned perpetual and deliberate mourning was already hardly distinguishable from melancholy.

Searching out mournful experiences was also only one part of the causal mix. As important as it has been for historians to recognize that the Puritan ethos didn't inevitably produce killjoys, no amount of revisionism in the historiography has overturned the notion that, as a recent study puts it, "Calvin's emphasis on human unworthiness and divine justice appears to have created or—in those with a disposition towards it—intensified tendencies towards an obsessive and psychologically damaging introspection, and to have produced the depressions and extremes of self-loathing which afflicted many individual English puritans."[6] If human depravity and divine wrath led to depressing conclusions, these were also major premises that Ryder accepted. And yet even this may only get us so far. "Many individual English puritans" still means: not all. Why some and not others?

Another and closely linked source of dejection was intense watchfulness itself, and, by extension, spiritual diary keeping, the medium through which this practice was made both material and more efficacious. R. H. Tawney reportedly once claimed that the "sufferings of the peasantry in the sixteenth century are due to the invention of printing." Tawney's student Christopher Hill took this to mean that "the prevalence of a literature of despair and conversion during the English Revolution may be the result of unprecedented freedom of publication." That may be true. How much do we fail to recognize that some men and women in early modern times were depressed simply because they were never able, or never bothered, to lastingly express their feelings? But the particular formal nature of what so many people were beginning to write in the later sixteenth century may have been more instrumental than the fact that they were writing and publishing at all. It is no accident that so much of our evidence of melancholy godly men and women comes from their diaries. At the beginning of this book we heard Ralph Josselin tell us from the pages of his journal that he desired to loathe himself; Nehemiah Wallington tried to kill himself nearly a dozen times; "Indispos'd in Body and greatly afflicted in Mind . . . I heartily mourn'd over, and lothed my self," was how the Puritan diarist Elizabeth Bury once glossed her state; even at the very end of the eighteenth century spiritual diarists like the Quaker Ann Dymond were similarly affected in part because diary keeping so readily told the diary keeper how much human behavior could fall out of line with the divine: "I am like one bereft of every enjoyment. I mourn; I abhor myself, and long to feel my mind brought into more subjection to the Divine Will." More examples are easy to find, and predictably so. Providentialism could breed "self-loathing, melancholy, and debilitating despair," one historian writes. And to the extent that watching was the praxis of providentialism, it made all the more methodical and regular the recognition of spiritual shortcomings.[7]

To discover through the process of relentless examination a feeling of piousness rather than moral corruption, however, could have occasioned delight rather than despair. Keeping a diary was also useful, after all, for expressing gratefulness for divine favors. But what brought on Ryder's dejection was the more regular outcome of his watchfulness, namely, his recognition of his capacity to sin. Much of this perceived sinfulness stemmed from what he had done during his youth. As he wrote in verse in later life,

> Such as in Early age of Life
> Seek God with their whole heart & Mind
> Have Gods Good word for their Support
> That the lov'd Object they Shall find—
> But ah! What time I Spent in Sin
> Which Justly may cause Grief & Shame.[8]

Even if we never know exactly what such vague references to early years entail, it is still worth noting that his recollection of a troubled past regularly attends his expressions of sadness. Two other major suggestions of his sinfulness nevertheless run more vividly throughout the diary.

The first was physical illness. As to be expected, Ryder's outlook was uneasy when his flesh was diseased. As a relatively young man he once wrote that he "was ready almost to Say No Sorrow like unto my Sorrow" until he realized that there were "many who had perhaps as Great Trouble of mind as I"—Ryder was already saying his mind was troubled—"or greater had the additionall Trouble of Tedious afflictions of Body."[9] To make matters more complicated, physical illness suggested his sinfulness in tandem with its obscurity, much as inevitable decay in later life confirmed that his sense of sorrow could be as complete as he imagined much earlier in life it might one day be. And yet to be too healthy, as we will see, could just as troublingly generate levity.

The second major sin was also rooted in his fear of extremes. In more than one sense, Ryder would have felt the force behind the modern economic meaning of "depression"; the earliest recorded use of the word in English print to signal an economic downtown appeared a few decades after his death, but he too grew depressed when thinking about poverty. Yet time and again in this book we have seen that just as worrisome was the prospect of abundance. As enlightened thinkers increasingly redefined acquisitiveness and the material rewards it could bring as instruments of happiness, what shaped Ryder's melancholy alongside his religiosity, perpetual mourning, physical maladies, and personal failings, was his immersion in activity designed to make him money.[10]

Death was not hard to find in the eighteenth century. Over the course of Ryder's seventy-two-year-long life, all but about a decade and a half witnessed Britain in military conflict with other European nations, with the dispossessed Stuarts, or somewhere in the empire. Epidemics that could affect both humans and livestock and "Cause thousands to fall on one side ... Ten Thousands on our Right" still lingered in and around Leeds (smallpox was rampant in 1741, for example, and distemper in 1749). For a century before Ryder's birth Britain may have had productive enough agriculture and a diverse enough economy to spare it widespread famine of the type that still struck Ireland during his diary-keeping years, but harvest crises and food shortages for the poor remained a common worry. "God could bless us, or he could blast us," Ryder noted during the uncertain harvest season of 1735. And few things could transfix the spiritually vigilant like natural disasters, the worst of which for Ryder, as for most of eighteenth-century Europe, was the 1755 earthquake that did in fact carry off tens of thousands of souls in Lisbon.[11]

Ryder kept a close watch on dismal events both at home and abroad, so many of which were worth noting in the diary as they bound together the meaning of mortality and morality. But he also sought out and brought into the diary a more direct experience of death. This was partly expressed in hundreds of morbid verses, which compose only a fraction of the number of prose entries that touch on the subject in one way or another. Death lingers even more conspicuously—and suitably, given the sequentiality of a book—in the final pages of nearly every volume. Here, where Ryder left a record of deceased family, friends, and neighbors, he reveals, for example, that over the course of one year he saw a body lowered into the ground once every seventeen days, and this was after having turned down a handful of funeral invitations because of business. So extensive is his record of demise that the diary is itself an archive of the Dissenter community: among hundreds of names of men, women, children, and infants he documented, the majority are unaccounted for in the town's official parish register (see Appendix 2).[12]

Death wasn't simply a late-life preoccupation, although the subject was unavoidably on his mind as an old man. In his mid-sixties he recognized that his life had been a mixed blessing. He had reached old age but as a lonely widower, wearied by a lifetime of witnessing his friends pass away and reasonably certain that his own time on earth was approaching an end: "This day I am in health. Blessed be God but would not boast of to morrow, because I know not what a day, or a night, nay what an hour may bring forth, therefore would I desire to enjoy life with patience and yet have death in daily expectation because I so frequently see, and hear of many call'd of[f] the stage of time upon very short." But Ryder sounds like the same person as a much younger man. In a poem unambiguously titled "On Sudden Death," he again invoked the metaphor of the stage, although here with an economic backdrop for the drama that had played out earlier in the week:

> This day a man in silent dust was laid
> who four days since was working on his trade
> such sudden changes knowledge should impart
> But little do we say such things to heart
> Some nipt are in the bud, others survive
> and are to flow'ring youth preserv'd alive
> now when their parents hopes begin to Rise
> God calls them hence and causes great surprise
> Others perhaps are spar'd to middle Age
> and then by sudden death call'd of[f] the stage
> Now seeing we such objects do behold
> The young are call'd away as well as old[13]

Immediate experience could confirm that last line with depressing ease. In April 1748 he "again had a call to a house of mourning" to attend the funeral

One of Ryder's death lists, here from the back of his tenth volume. Reproduced by courtesy of the University Librarian and Director, The John Rylands University Library, The University of Manchester.

of John Prince of Holbeck, "ye third son his aged Mother has now seen lain in the Dust—all grown to Manhood—in about two years." "I have been at the funerall of a Relations child, & there was three funeralls at one church besides," he recalled the next winter. In 1767, months away from his own death, he "was at the funerall of John Lodge who was as far as I can learn the oldest man in our Congregation. It is a common saying among us that the young may die, but the Old must dye. Experience prov'd it this day for there were four funeralls of different ages . . . we evidently see there is no discharge in that war."[14]

Funerals were simply one call to watch. Serious consideration of mortality had to attend countless other providential moments that brought to mind human fragility. Ryder once recalled in a daily entry from the 1750s the relative cheerfulness he felt on waking up to greet the day. "I eat my breakfast with Sweetness and was well refresh and I hope thankful," he wrote in unusual detail, as if specificity could make for a more dramatic letdown. "But presently came those thoughts that shortly it would be otherwise." Death could come in various forms, he reminded himself, and later that day a man was horrifically "Slain with a waggon running over him, as I was informed not far from where I dwell." The lesson was clear. "Death comes surely to all, & Suddenly to many, and to whom we cannot tell. It must certainly be our highest interest to Get our loyns Girt, our lamps Trimm'd, & our lights burning, & be in among those good Servants who are waiting for the Coming of their Lord."[15]

By itself, though, the regularity of death completely explains neither Ryder's intense preoccupation with his mortality nor his inability to "enjoy life with patience." He once reasoned that the mere frequency of death has no necessary moral meaning. If not properly interpreted—hence his uncharacteristic attention to its detail—death could actually inure one to its very spiritual consequences. When his neighbor Leonard Ryder was buried in 1741, Joseph considered that "ye Commonness of the Instances of mortality makes the Instance . . . but little notice taken of. Whereas, did we but seriously consider that now our Time for Improvement is over, and our Eternall State at Death Decided, it should have a Quite Different Effect."[16]

The deeper causes of the "different effect" death had on him lay in part in his religiosity. Like any pious Protestant, Ryder repudiated the doctrine of Purgatory. On hearing a minister identified only as a "stranger" preach in the late 1740s on the urgency to prepare for death because afterwards "ye State of the Soul is fixt & no redemption for it," Ryder observed "that the congregation appear'd well satisfy'd and commended his work." Assent was also given to Mill Hill's Thomas Walker, who sermonized on the rewards of the afterlife and "oppose[d] the notion of Insensibility and the Doctrine of Purgatory." In a larger cultural sense the Protestant response to Purgatory in the two centuries following the Reformation is uneven and complex; there was no single function of Purgatory that Protestant rituals and beliefs simply replaced after the pope lost his authority in England. But long after the dissolution of that doctrine, Ryder's ministers emphasized a simpler implication: the soul's immediate journey to either Heaven or Hell at the exact moment of one's passing made death a more urgent call to live a godly life. In the absence of intercessory prayer, Ryder may even have channeled into his funeral lists and the diary's other outward signs of bereavement the grief that came from bearing witness to so much loss of life. His behavior might in this sense fit with a broader change in the expressiveness of grief that one historian has noticed in public and private Protestant writings from the sixteenth century onwards.[17]

The religious imperative to watch for death in daily expectation did not, in any case, only follow from intense religiosity. Any avid reader of the Bible confronted the paradox that death should, in some sense, be eagerly anticipated. This was the more widely interpreted point of the koan-like maxims of Ecclesiastes that Ryder alluded to or reproduced throughout the diary. The High Church bishop Francis Atterbury preached in a funeral sermon in 1698 that the ecclesiast's paradoxes, "however they may startle and shock us . . . when closely examin'd, will appear to be clear unquestionable Truths, by which the whole Course of our Lives ought to be steer'd and govern'd." The notion that the day of one's death is better than the day of one's birth could be resolved by viewing death as an "Admittance into a State of perfect Rest and Tranquillity, of undisturb'd Joy and Happiness; whereas the Day of [man's] Birth was only an Inlet into a troublesome World, and the Beginning of Sorrows." Atterbury was far from alone in trying to unravel such mysteries. If "the heart of the wise is in the house of mourning," as pronounced in Ecclesiastes, actually to seek to reside in the house of mourning could only work "for a crack'd-brain order of Carthusian monks . . . not for men of the world," the novelist (and Anglican cleric) Laurence Stern sermonized with a sense of the tragicomic. "Are the sad accidents of life, and the uncheery hours which perpetually overtake us, are they not enough, but we must sally forth in quest of them?" With more of a utilitarian bent, Hugh Blair explained in much-reprinted sermons (published for the first time shortly after Ryder's death) that mourning was useful, but only as it "is calculated to give a proper check to our natural thoughtlessness and levity." One should "frequent the house of mourning, as well as those of the house of mirth," Blair advised. "Study the nature of that state in which thou art placed; and balance its joys with its sorrows."[18]

If softer ways to read this passage on which Ryder fixated in the diary were in the air, his tendency was nevertheless to interpret scripture literally and apparently feel its implications viscerally. He often cited the line about the house of mourning, for example, after he had stepped into the mourning households of dying and deceased friends and family on days that might have been more cheerfully spent. And he already struggled to keep up his spirits. The more upbeat Thomas Whitaker cited John 16:33—"be of Good Cheer; I have overcome the World"—to explain that he himself had conquered sorrow by faith, devout meditation, and fervent prayer. But Ryder could easily find evidence to dissent. The day after recording Whitaker's optimistic sermon he noted the trifles that diluted the solemnity and piety of his conversations with coreligionists and kept cheerfulness beyond reach. Or the next year he buoyantly began a mid-December day only to have his hopes shattered by the intrusion into his mind of "the worldly, the flesh & the devil." Or again, on a spring evening in 1741, he "found some difficulty upon the appearance of distress to gett into a chearfull frame notwithstanding the multiplyed favours which I enjoy . . . while many were ruin'd with the desolations of War. Oh that I had a more chearfull and thankfull and submissive fram of spirit to the will of God whatoever it may be concerning me." Or here was how he put it at the very beginning of the diary, hinting that watchfulness itself could make the balance between happiness and sadness that the sermonic literature recommended hard to attain: "This Morning upon Examination of my frame I was dejected Charging my Self with hypocrisy . . . what a mixture of Joy and Sorrow is this world at best."[19]

But Ryder was in more of a predicament than the hundreds of sullen comments like this in the diary suggest. His religious outlook may have encouraged him to seek out reminders of death and maintain a state of mourning, but even as the duration of mourning or the many occasions to bear witness to mortality may have made depression a likely possibility, the cheerfulness that the Bible and sermons also recommended—the very proof of one's triumph over the world—could just as worryingly pull him away from the sacred house of mourning. Here Ryder lay at a historical junction between the validation of pleasure that Roy Porter called "the Enlightenment's great historical watershed" and the tenacity of the Puritan condemnation of

levity. Equanimity was the obvious solution to the problem, but daily experience supplied abundant enough occurrences to throw Ryder off balance. "I
meditated in this or the Like manner," he wrote as a young man, "that saying
things that happened so much to heart might be prejudicial to my health." As
always, the Bible provided the basis for reasoning: "A Merry heart does good
like a medicine," he quoted from Proverbs, after which he made a resolution
in his entry "to carry more chearfully under whatever befell me." But his
recollection of the Bible superseded his ability to resolve its many contradictions. "Yet again," he countered himself while echoing the Gospel of John,
"[I] thought of perhaps giving way to chearfulness, Levity should come in
upon me and so I should fall short at last, may God in love show me the right
way and enable me to walk in it."[20]

Passages like this suggest another source of Ryder's anguish: his health.
To some degree, he clearly believed it was worth trying to overcome disease.
He went to see doctors when he was ill—at a depressing degree of personal
expense. In his early sixties, for example, he alluded to getting a doctor's
bill, "it being the Usuall time of payment." When he found it "a great
Sum, it rather sunk my spirits a little, thinking my self somewhat Imposed
upon." For whatever relief he could offer he also constantly visited
coreligionists sick "in both body and mind," "out of order," and so on, and
hoped and prayed for their improvement. Just as indicative of his fear of
disease is his record of the medical advice he got from others. At least something he possessed—possibly medicine—came from an apothecary in
London, according to a note in the back of one his volumes, while in the
front matter of another volume he jotted down two recipes for bringing
down a fever.[21]

Even when it came to his health, however, extreme states were spiritually dangerous. The fate of his soul was implicated in the simplest thoughts
of physical self-improvement by way of a change of heart: even, that is, as he
recognized that cheerfulness would ameliorate his physical health, and even
as he implied by that recognition that melancholy was affecting his flesh, he
worried that cheerfulness could also put him on a slippery slope toward
damnation, as was suggested above in his comment about the dangers, absent
adequate mourning, of "levity." And on one occasion when his health
improved, by his own estimation as a result of a happy encounter with
friends, he could then just as easily doubt the spiritual value of the merry
company he kept.

This Day hearing of Three Sudden Deaths and Considering upon them I was Desirous hereby to be Excited to be seeking after not only an habituall but an actuall readyness for this Solemn Change, not knowing but In a very Short Time It may be my own Case. In the Evening was Engaged in Company and by Some Chearfullness among them was ready to think I was Something better as to the health to my Body than I have been of severall days past. Thought upon these words, A merry heart does Good like a medicine, but a Broken Spirit Drieth the bones. But if Company keeping should prove any way detrimentall to the Soul what an unspeakable Disadvantage would this prove.[22]

The dilemma did not end here. Abstaining from a cheerful encounter that might bring health to the body could spare Ryder the spiritual consequences of being lighthearted, but remaining physically ill because of his depressed outlook could also be worrisome. In one of the sermons we came across at the beginning of this book, we heard Whitaker cite lines from the Gospel of Mark that read in Ryder's paraphrase, "they that are whole have no need of the Physician but they that are sick I came not to call the Righteous but Sinners to Repentance." "Physician" could certainly be taken allegorically; Ryder once titled a poem "Christ the only physician" and used the metaphor to stress Christ's psychotherapeutic powers:

> Sometimes a fear they find
> From Satan's cruell rage
> But Christ's Good Spirit heals the mind
> and does their fears assuage.

But we may recall that Ryder understood in literal terms the physician in the line from the gospel that Whitaker quoted. The need for a human doctor could therefore suggest sinfulness. This negative interpretation came to life in Ryder's early sixties, when after months of complaining of swelling in his chest, his doctor diagnosed him with an unnamed disease whose rarity enhanced its already ominous meaning. "When I heard from my physician the uncommonness of my case, I could scarce forbear being dejected under the apprehensions of being some uncommon sinner." And it was not just his diseases that registered this way. "Oh what a hospital of diseases has Sin made the world," he once exclaimed with more poetic punch than his verses usually deliver after visiting four sick friends in a single day, one of whom suffered a "disorder [that] appeard to me to be something of the melancholy."[23]

It is tempting to wonder whether at least some of Ryder's diseases actually had clear physical causes. We can of course never know this, but there is a psychosomatic logic in his attitudes about his health. He indicates, for example, that the very thought of using his mind or "heart" to cure his body was itself dangerous. Even as disease could signify sin, the cheerfulness that might help heal his flesh exposed him to the danger of lightheartedness. That might then imply a spiritual dependence on some measure of illness. And in any case, if he could selectively avoid therapeutically cheerful company, then at least some of his diseases may as well have been psychosomatic. Like his preoccupation with death, mind-forged maladies were a useful tactic to avoid too much of the mirth that by his own recognition made him feel better— before making him feel worse.

There was at least one other source of psychological disequilibrium: his awareness of his sinful acts. This awareness came in part thanks to his persistent memory of his corrupt youth, which could take on special meaning as the deaths of others made him realize that he was unprepared for the end of life. In old age he recorded the passing of "two ancient neighbours," Hannah and Mary Rider. He could only attend one funeral two days later and had to send his maid to attend the other. But as if to drive home the regularity of death, in the afternoon of October 28, and after hearing about the two Rider women, he also found himself at a funeral of "another old woman," which set him wondering "what more suitable Subject can I dwell upon than Death, In order to get into a prepared frame for it." The problem was immediately clear: at this point in his years (he was now sixty-three), he may not have been "much Intangled with the business of life," but he couldn't prevent the "youthfull sinns [that] come as fresh into my mind as if but lately committed, and I Scarce dare say as David did I hate vain thoughts, but I desire to be daily praying against them."[24]

In the absence of details we can only wonder what other sins Ryder committed during his youth before 1733. If his claim that his early years were worse than those squandered by Mr. Badman may have been an indirect way of calling attention to economic spiritual crimes, there is no mistaking the principal sin of Ryder's middle age as he perceived it from the 1750s and 1760s—a middle age that also could have qualified as the "youth" he recalled in 1758: in those earlier decades he had been consumed with business. "Take heed lest at any Time Your hearts be Overcharged with Surfeiting & Drunkenness or the Cares of this life," he wrote after calling to mind a warning given by Christ. It was "ye last of which I seem at present in danger to be overtaken." Four days earlier he gave a more precise definition to those "cares" when he explained that "having again much Business upon my hand I was necessarily put upon much Diligence. In some part of the Day at Least I thought upon the Words of the Psalmist, who said, In the Multitude of my Thoughts within me thy comforts Delight my Soul. But fear'd I could not Truly Say so, because my Thoughts were so Carri'd away with my Business." Much more explicitly could the Devil tempt with an excessively busy life. "This Evening I was purposing to set apart some Time for preparation for the approaching solemnity, & was by worldly business unavoidably (in a manner) hindered, which I was ready to take to be a Device of Satan." The parenthesis is telling: where exactly could he draw the line between economic choice and necessity? In what precise manner was business avoidable? In what manner was it not?[25]

Immersion in business, as we have seen over and over, was also not just an unsettling sin of the past on which Ryder reflected as an old man. His fluctuations between what counted as useful and excessive profits, or between diligence and misuse of his time, routinely threw him off balance while he was in his forties, fifties, and even his sixties. In this sense he makes us see the relatively simplistic nature of the modern link made between economic pursuits and mental disturbance. The modern link was of course taking shape in the eighteenth century as feelings of depression were developing strong associations with impoverishment, indebtedness, diminishing profits, and other forms of material loss. London alone saw six suicides in a single week in January 1721 after the bursting of the South Sea Bubble. "So closely associated were wealth and happiness in the minds of early modern Englishmen," Michael MacDonald and Terrence Murphy have written, "that they found it difficult to believe that anyone would kill himself while in possession of an adequate living, let alone a large fortune." But we should also add "some" to "early modern Englishmen." As these historians also note, reports of cases of wealthy suicides—nameless merchants with incomes anywhere from £1,500 to £60,000—were regularly scattered throughout the London papers. Suicide, then as now, has no shortage of causes. The intense unhappiness Ryder could feel when immersed in economic life raises the possibility that the most dangerous symptom of depression—a lost instinct to live—may have gotten a boost from excessive gain as well as from loss.[26]

So much of this book has up to this point been supported by information that Ryder gave away despite his diary's spiritual focus. But here we have admittedly been pursuing something trickier. How did he feel? Is it naive to assume that depression is something his language can reveal?

The question may at first seem unnecessary given the precise sorts of feelings Ryder expresses. George Orwell's (mostly) unassailable line about autobiography was that it "is only to be trusted when it reveals something disgraceful. A man who gives a good account of himself is probably lying, since any life when viewed from the inside is simply a series of defeats."[27] What *is* Ryder's self-account if not a record of perceived defeat and disgrace? But these are also relative terms, and for people who saw grace less as a learned social skill than as a gift from God, much as for those who understood that a measure of defeat in this world was irrelevant if victory could be attained in the next, bearing some marks of shame and defeat could demonstrate a spiritually appropriate awareness of human depravity and the inscrutable nature of God's ultimate plan. How do we know that Ryder was not simply using the pages of his diary to rehearse a suitably sullen godly role? In fact, two bigger questions are implicit here: how do we know we can recover Ryder's emotional life from the form in which it is supposedly expressed? And how do we know he was giving us the truth?

Literary critics have helped teach historians the important lesson that form matters, and rather than taking this simply to mean form *impedes,* we should think in specific ways about the implications of particular genres. More thoroughly and thoughtfully than anyone, Philippe Lejeune has done this with both "autobiography"—self-writing (of the sort Orwell had in mind) composed from a distant point of remembrance—and more diurnally observed and drafted journal or diary keeping. In one sense, Lejeune has argued, the classic characteristics of a daily or semidaily self-account can easily conceal a subject. Diaries are characteristically discontinuous, redundant, repetitive, nonnarrative, and allusive. As any reader who has made it this far is aware, Ryder was no exception: these are the very generic qualities that make knowing him and his immediate world so difficult. The gaps—the huge swathes of life missing from entries that he wrote, sometimes in a mere hundred words, to capture a full twenty-four hours of experience—further fragment a self that was already guaranteed by virtue of being a historical figure, if not simply a human being, to be lacking in continuity. Nonnarrative, or at least not typically narrative, characteristics—an abrupt beginning, a middle deprived of any but a diurnal sequence, an ending shaped by death and not by intent—have the effect of making him even more incoherent (if only he could have told us in a final entry what it all meant). Repetition and redundancy in the diary are so aesthetically off-putting that they function almost as a guarantee that no one would ever really want to get to know the diarist word for word and page by page. Most frustrating of all are his constant allusions, which hardly ever have recoverable referents. The present chapter in particular would have been easier to write had Ryder only been clearer in entries like this one: "By What has happened This Day I Scarce know upon reflection What Judgment to form of my [scratched-out word] Self. What from Dejection on the one hand and a readiness to Comply with Temptation upon the Least offer on the Other I am ready to wish my Self out of the World." We simply never know what happened on this day to give him what sound like suicidal thoughts. But the theoretical point is in any case that, on one level, the diarist behind the diary is elusive not because a diary is a text and all texts are opaque; diaries can be particularly opaque by their very particular formal nature.[28]

And yet to leave it at that, or even worse, to therefore call diaries "fictional" because they possess formal qualities that coalesce as a genre, is to miss the larger point. By virtue of their very opacity it is better to call diaries, in Lejeune's neologism, "antifiction." Their allusions, for example, are mostly communicative failures; their discontinuities and nonnarrative characteristics make the stories they tell disorganized, or at least hardly more structured than a normally messy life; repetition and superfluity further ensure artlessness. Ryder's diary, like most diaries, would be a terrible novel for the same basic reason Lejeune has argued that fictional diaries in novels make such recognizable fakes. Novelists know where their characters are headed (see Robinson Crusoe), as do many memoirists (see Benjamin Franklin); earnest diarists, in contrast, have no idea where they are going. These "antifictional" formal characteristics of diary writing, far from sealing off the author in the realm of untruth, are so artless, in other words, that they can actually corroborate some of a diary's apparent themes and suggest the diarist's preoccupations. Careless repetition of phrases may be stultifying, but it is precisely this characteristic that clues us in to what one historian calls "patterns of personal significance." That same repetition alongside Ryder's fragmented narrative may even be a formal signifier of depression. Julia Kristeva once observed that "the speech of the depressed [is] repetitive and monotonous. . . . A repetitive rhythm, a monotonous melody emerge and dominate the broken logical sequences, changing them into recurring, obsessive litanies."[29]

But if the diurnal form, especially when articulated over so many thousands of individual entries, would demand improbable artfulness in order to consistently conceal affect, the more damning question may in any case be one that Orwell leads us to: how do we know that an ostensibly unflattering self-account written by a self-denying Christian qualifies as honest? This may, however, be the easier question to let the content of the diary answer. For one thing, Ryder's language reflects ambivalence about an audience of outside readers; in one case, as we saw, he worried about anyone seeing his diary precisely because he suspected his doubt might be contagious.[30] He is categorically distinct, that is, from a famous, published memoirist like Salvador Dali, whom Orwell justifiably had a hard time trusting. For another, a quick tour through some of the hundreds of passages in which Ryder expresses depression makes clear that his state was far from spiritually commendable.

Here is how he once put it in his late thirties: "I have found my heart Strangely carried away with Vain Thoughts, So that upon Such prevalency I Scarce know what Judgment to form of my Self, under perplexity of heart with respect to what at Some times attends me I am at Times too much dejected notwithstanding the word of God Says Rejoyce in the Lord always, & again I say Rejoyce, Sometimes in the morning I am ready to say, would God it was Evening, thoughtfull how to get the day over free from guilt and sin and sorrow. Sometimes at Evening, would God it was morning, because of Trouble in the night."[31] Would any godly role worth performing in a spiritual diary demand such poor self-knowledge, or perplexity, or dejection out of sync with scripture? The Bible issues a command: rejoice. And yet Ryder tells us here that he can't comply, as his guilt, sin, and sorrow make the day as unbearable as his nights are sleepless.

Or here from his late forties: "Such Deadness Seizes me from time to time that I am very much Dejected & Cast Down, under the Dreadfull Apprehensions that the Spirit of God is Departing or Departed from me."[32] There was nothing pious about deadness (an admittedly vague word), especially as it led to a sort of depression occasioned by the thought that he had been abandoned by his spiritual father.

Or here at fifty: "I found Some Depressions of Spirit when I came to Consider how far I have yielded to the Temptation of Sin, Satan, & the world."[33] In few passages does Ryder so concisely make the point I have been trying to suggest here: submission to sin, to the world, and ultimately to Satan was causally linked to depression. And here something else is clear: the sort of depression he feels on this day far from suggests that he is bound for Heaven.

Or here in his mid-sixties: "This day I have Severall times found a great damp of my Spirit upon Severall accounts not-withstanding a Rule in Sacred Record, which is Rejoyce in the Lord always, & again I say rejoyce, But my evidences for rejoycing appear at present greatly clouded because of rising fears that I have not made God my chief good, a right hand or a right eye[.] Sin appears as I apprehend to gain ground upon me, what I am born down with at times the world are Strangers [to], my complaint I keep much to my Self, Because it is not in the power of man without God blessing to help me, And when I do pray against Sin, I am ready to dispute my Sincerity in asking."[34] Ryder sounds remarkably as he did twenty-seven years earlier: the Bible ("Sacred Record") says rejoice, but he still can't, at least not as much as he would like. And here he tells us something no less remarkable: he keeps his condition a secret between himself and his diary. No mortal can help. Even praying is fraught with ambivalence since in the second-order mode of reflection that apparently intruded into his prayers, he couldn't help but question the authenticity of his intentions.

The deep ambivalence that at one time or another marked virtually everything Ryder indicates he did, even praying, brings us back not just to the double-mindedness that has run through this book. It returns us to the essay in which Freud argued that in a state of melancholy, as opposed to one of temporary mourning, a person's relationship to any depression-inducing "internal object"—for example, disappointments suffered during childhood—is marked by love and hate. In a normal state of mourning, someone loses an external object, typically because of death, but eventually overcomes the loss. The melancholic instead imagines he or she has eradicated an internalized object but is incapable of life without it.[35]

We don't have to give Freud's idea ultimate medical authority to recognize that it is useful to think with. Ryder had good reason both to love and to hate his material acquisitiveness in particular: moderate rewards on earth implied his success in the hereafter; poverty represented failure, much as profits did when taken in excess. He made this connection perfectly clear while tying it to dejection when he wrote after a lifetime of reflection on the meaning of getting ahead in the world: "I well perceive the frailty of human nature in being apt to be dejected under temporall wants and too much lifted up Sometimes with a Supply of them." "Lifted up" tells us that he could occasionally feel some lightness when materially satisfied; "too much lifted up" tells us once again that levity made him worry. Attempting to curtail extreme acquisitiveness with daily watching may also have given him the occasional feeling of having eradicated the "internal object." But he was still dependent on his acquisitiveness for whatever measure of material success would bode well for his salvation: by the same drive to acquire that could lead him to sin, he could also transform indolence into diligence and set himself heavenward. "This morning . . . I was desirous that I might not hencefor-ward be slothfull in Business, But fervent in Spirit serving the Lord." But no less than business failure, too many profits, both the definition of business success and for many in the eighteenth century the ticket to happiness, could depressingly threaten his salvation. As he phrased it early on in a couplet that prefigured the rest of the diary, "If I'm concerned too much in things below / it makes my progress heavenwards but slow."[36]

So, then, was Ryder depressed? The evidence presented here as throughout much of this book suggests that, at least episodically, he was. A spiritually watchful awareness of his sins, especially his sinful immersion in commerce, was part of the equation. So was his wavering health. So was finding himself, almost from the moment we get to know him, living in a precarious world. "I attended the funerall of a poor neighbour. As I was walking over the graves in the churchyard, I thought it would not be long before I must make one of that number," he wrote just shy of his fortieth birthday—with what turned out to be nearly thirty-three years of his life left to live.[37] The admixture of causes encouraging depression also included daily doses of sermonic and scriptural prescriptions that, like the inversion of twenty-first-century pharmaceuticals, were spiritual depressants to be taken to maintain a solemn sense of watchfulness, which might in the end ensure the long-deferred happiness of a heavenly afterlife, as long as by overdose they didn't cause the dangerous sort of melancholy that Satan could exploit.

This is of course not to say that simply being religious or simply reading the Bible led inevitably to depression. The Bible's moral instruction, like the preachers and prescriptive literature through which it filtered, offered the hopeful message that in death there would be life. Ryder's beloved Bunyan, after all, hoped that *Pilgrim's Progress* would "divert thy self from melancholly," although it is worth noting Bunyan's implication that if diversion was necessary, melancholy was the presumed default setting of his imagined audience. What is important is Ryder's way of understanding the Bible, which to him stressed, potentially overwhelmingly, that every thought and action was loaded with salvational meaning. To live life with death constantly in mind may have been key to an eternal existence, which was far more valuable than the earthly lives of princes or wealthy merchants, but the comfort that this deliberate preoccupation brought depended on the degree to which one felt bound for the right destination. "If my interest in Christ was but secure and my title to heaven clear, then might I sweetly welcome the harbinger of death," Ryder wrote just after turning a mere thirty-nine. Weeks after his forty-eighth birthday, his preparation for the distribution of his material goods after his demise meant little without spiritual preparedness: "This day I have Executed my Last Will and Something of Satisfaction I find therein as being preparatory for Dying. But what will it avail to have done something for the Satisfaction of my Friends If I have not made Christ my Friend, what will it avail to have my house in order If My heart is unprepared[?]"[38]

We should also notice, finally, that Ryder's depression itself was not inevitable or perpetual. He could find relief if he could also find a way to keep one or more of the causes of despair at bay. A sense of mental well-being was often brought on by a positive change in his physical health, from which state it was easier to recognize melancholy in others. After weeks of good health, for example, he went to "visit an acquaintance, an Aged woman who has a long time been Sorely afflicted with clouds and Darkness upon her mind with respect to her State." Ryder articulated his mind-body diagnosis: "All us most around her think it to arise from Somewhat of a melancholy disorder of body, but let the foundation of the disorder be what it will, the fruits of it are very distressing to her Self and to Such as attend on her, and respect her." At first, the occasion called less for greater watchfulness than for gratitude that he was free from such melancholy (the fact that Ryder here expresses relief is also just one of the many subtle suggestions that he worryingly faced his own bouts with melancholy). "Oh what a call to Gratitude & thankfullness Have I and others to Almighty God who guards us from the power and policy of Satan, and from all Such tormenting fears, as Some Such are afflicted with." And yet, just as strikingly—and a further indication that his watchfulness could cut short any sense of relief—his recognition that he was better off than others, at least on this day, was a step toward sinful self-appreciation, which could undercut any health benefits he might have enjoyed. The next day he "call[ed] to mind the sad complaints of the afflicted person" he had visited the day before. "When I compare my own Inward conflicts with hers, I cannot think them far short, except in this, that she wants health which I enjoy. I often think surely not many can have more vain and vile thoughts than my self at times, notwithstanding all my care and watch-fullness."[39]

Being in good physical shape could also enable Ryder to play spiritual cheerleader for others and in the process delineate the social facet of his spiritual existence. In his mid-sixties he noticed that while he was "spared in health," at least for the moment, his friends were either "sick or weakley" or "falling asleep. One particularly I saw to day who is in a weak way. Her nurse told me she lik'd to see her Intimate acquaintance. I told her there was far superiour Company above, Upon the Mention whereof she, that is Mrs Moult, appeard to me to be in a kind of an Extasy, breathing out as well as her poor feeble strength would admitt the words of Dr [Isaac] Watts, There Shall I see and hear and know / all I desir'd or wish'd below. Oh it is delightfull, and what in life can be more desireable than to die rejoycing in the Dying love of Jesus, and well grounded hopes of Eternall life and happiness when we come to quit the stage."[40]

Where Ryder offers the impression that he had achieved some balance between success and excess in his economic life, he might also see himself on a course for the sort of suitable happiness he occasionally witnessed in others: "This day I was but in an Indifferent State of health yet went to my labour, & thought if I laboured as long as I was able, Nobody could accuse me of Idleness, neither Should I have cause to condemn my Self; do I but labour for a good end, namely to be usefull rather than richer. I esteem them very happy who have finished their course, & kept the faith."[41]

In fact when one traces the use of the word "happy" in the diary, it becomes clear how vital such balance was to cheerfulness, however imper-manent that cheer was in Ryder's outlook, which itself ebbed and flowed from the beginning to the end of the diary. In one sense, as evident in the above examples, "happy" characterizes Heaven and those who seem bound to make it there. Death, potentially, is a "happy state, where peace is enjoy'd without disturbance, and Quietness without end." "Happy they who enjoy perfect Love," he wrote as a young man. "Oh happy they who are prepared for that rest which remains for the people of God in another and a better world. Oh that I may have life in patience, & death in daily expectation that so when my Lord calls I may not be found sleeping," he wrote more sententiously thirty-two years later, a year from his death. "Oh that I may be found of that happy number that sleep in Jesus when I come to sleep the sleep of death," he prayed in writing only weeks before his time actually was up.[42]

Just as importantly, happiness could come on earth as he perceived social and economic balance. During the last months of his life, Ryder surveyed his world and "beheld a great variety in the dispensations of divine providence, some as it were swimming in prosperity and fullness, others in great distress . . . others in the middle station perhaps more happy than either of the others, for fullness is very apt to make us unmindfull of God and often excites such to sacrifice to their own net, and to burn incense to their own drag, as if by their own power and skill they had got all their abundance." This was the voice of a man who, in one way or another, had spent a lifetime considering the spiritual implications of social rank and could now give it a different sort of hierarchy. "Such as are very poor are too apt to envy those above them, and to quarrell with providence. But if any have fullness they have no cause to boast because we have nothing but what we have received, and he can take away at pleasure, and if the poor be enabled by grace to live resigned to Gods providence He can certainly make everything to work for their best good. Those in a middle state of life, and know neither want nor fullness, may by the blessing of God be both happy here and hereafter." Providence could bestow both poverty and prosperity. But it bestowed happiness—an earthly happiness—when it planted one in the middle station of life, a state of equilibrium that offered distance from the extremes of want and wealth. This was Ryder, at once, articulating the value of the middling sort and telling us that part of what made the middling sort so desirable was the moral and psychological balance it promised.[43]

And here, once again, he was far from alone. As a much younger man he had a friend who "oft compared his own heart to a glass full of muddy water, which if it stood still . . . grew fine and clear but when shak'd was all muddy again. Upon this I conceived the great benefitt of a still and resigned frame, and would desire to be found watchfull against contrary vice."[44] There was much in Ryder's life and the outside world that could shake up the muddy water: death, illness, the ominous signs of providence, family troubles, sins past, present, and future. But were he watchful like Ryder (as his comments suggest) and as involved in the cloth trade (as so many people Ryder knew were), how could this nameless friend not have shared at least some of Ryder's anxiety about the psychic pitfalls of poverty and excess? If Ryder's despair was in large measure shaped by all the spiritual dangers his watchfulness could expose, by his immersion in the booming cloth trade, and by his pursuit of death and mourning at a time when they were such depressingly regular facts of life to begin with, how unique could he have been? The externalities so likely to have given him a melancholic temperament made him indistinguishable from countless other men and women whose labors and broadening desires were making industrial Britain as they watched, prayed, and worried about the fate of their increasingly acquisitive souls.

# 7. The Changing Meaning of God and Man

At the beginning of Ryder's life, most Dissenters accepted the interlocked assumptions of the Reformed tradition: that God intervenes in the cosmos with a constancy and inscrutability that demand vigilance on the part of human beings who, by their nature, are morally depraved. At the end of Ryder's life, Mill Hill's young minister, the utopian polymath Joseph Priestley, was helping to invent a new denomination, Unitarianism, whose interlocked major premises were that Jesus was a mere human being, humans are perfectible, and the laws of the universe are Newtonian. This was no mere change that Ryder witnessed. A watchful God had become a watchmaker; once depraved humans were now dignified; once profoundly wrong ideas were now broadcast from the pulpit as truths, as beloved truths were recast as useful fictions. How did this happen?[1]

One answer has persisted in that single word "enlightenment," a word we still turn to Immanuel Kant to help us define. "*Sapere aude!*" Kant exclaimed in his essay-length definition: "'Have the courage to use your own reason!'—that is the motto of the enlightenment." This was also a motto Kant carefully qualified. Enlightened people should know how to tell moments when it was suitable to be so courageous apart from those when it was better to fulfill traditional duties. And no example in his short essay illustrated how change and continuity could coexist as fully as that of the Protestant minister, mulling over theology and pushing for cultural renewal among his intellectual peers while performing the basic pastoral functions that spiritually nourished his congregation.[2]

Ryder's most daring ministers operated with similar assumptions. Almost everywhere in the diary they can be found at the pulpit, trying to meet the needs of parishioners like Ryder with sermons and prayer, or convening privately with congregants, or leading funeral services, market lectures, days of public fasting—the list could go on. Never once does Ryder complain that his ministers were unwilling or unable to give their time or energy. When we take the long view and consider how many people on the eve of the Reformation craved more spiritual sustenance than the church had the willingness or the means to offer, Ryder's diary reads as proof that, at least in some corners, the Reformation had been a success: God seemed to be everywhere in the West Riding, in no small part thanks to the tireless work of his ministers on earth.

As many of Ryder's pastors nurtured their congregations, however, they were also increasingly—and daringly—wondering exactly who that God was. Was he three beings rolled into one? Was he still actively involved in his creation? Did he actually take the temporary form of a man, create a secondary divinity, or just invest one man with a special message? For that matter, and with no less iconoclasm, the same pastors were reconsidering the basic definition of humanity. Are we depraved by virtue of the sins of Adam? Or preselected to go to Heaven or Hell? Or deserving of the self-regard that Calvin had been so unwilling to admit? In theological terms, the more radical of Ryder's ministers embraced two related religious attitudes, a sort of heterodox package: anti-Trinitarianism and Arminianism. Anti-Trinitarianism, as it unfolded in mid-century English Dissent, tended to demote Jesus's divinity in stages: first by making him a deity subordinate to God, a view known as Arianism, and then by making him purely human, as in the religious outlook that coalesced in the 1770s as denominational Unitarianism. Arminianism promoted human dignity, also typically in two basic ways: by rejecting the doctrine of predestination, thus giving believers an active role in their salvation, and by rejecting the doctrine of original sin, thus freeing them from a criminal spiritual inheritance.[3]

From one angle, then, Kant's classic image rings true: religious life transformed in Dissenter Leeds, as it did elsewhere, thanks in part to the work of enlightened pastors who thought long and hard about the meanings and implications of doctrines and "-isms." But from many other angles, the idealistic sort of change that Kant expressed and made influential fails to capture the complexity of the pastoral experience that Ryder and others document. More daring ministers, for one thing, did not hesitate to cross-contaminate theological experimentation and traditional piety. Nor was change simply top-down. Especially in churches where the laity had the right to select their ministers, the congregations themselves could lead the way to heterodoxy, even as congregants like Ryder remained with the chapel but felt uneasy about its new direction. Not least, this new religious outlook was consonant with the level of prosperity that older Dissenters likely would have found morally suspect. If Puritanism could induce the diligence and industry that led to a measure of surplus, it also kept the watchful alert to the dangers of worldliness. The new religious mode that Ryder first saw take shape in Mill Hill Chapel and several years later at Call Lane, on the other hand, rejected Calvinist pessimism about human nature and laid out a different cultural vision in which people could more easily justify an expansive material life. In the run-up to industrialization, an elective affinity was developing between the more individualistic mode of selfhood that the free market was now understood to depend on and a more optimistic mode of spirituality that, in renouncing the theological basis of Puritan self-denial, was at the same time naturalizing self-interest. The religious change was about the needs of pastors and parishioners, to be sure, but those needs were simultaneously spiritual and material.

Anti-Trinitarianism had been the great heresy of early modern times, and it still remained criminal in the eighteenth century, thanks to the exclusion from the Toleration Act of 1689 of anyone who denied "in preaching or writing the doctrine of the blessed Trinity." By the time this position was lifted with the Unitarian Relief Bill in 1813, serious opposition to anti-Trinitarians had faded, but throughout the century after the Glorious Revolution deniers of the Trinity had been some of the unluckiest victims of religious intolerance. The last execution for blasphemy on the island of Britain—in Scotland in 1696—had been of an anti-Trinitarian; and by the terms of England's own Blasphemy Act passed two years later, downgrading Jesus's divinity could mean three years in prison and a loss of civil rights. It cost William Whiston his Lucasian chair at Cambridge in the 1710s, a scandal that made Samuel Clarke hedge trying to protect his career and reputation. Even by the more relaxed second half of the century, the threat of persecution could be renewed when the old law was invoked, as it was against John Wilkes, who suffered a longer sentence under the Blasphemy Act for the anti-Trinitarianism expressed in his 1763 *Essay on Women* than for his mockery of George III in *North Briton;* "ridicule of divine majesty," writes one historian, "remained a more serious crime in England than ridicule of human majesty." More famously, the prejudices reappeared in the paranoid 1790s—in the inimical association between anti-Trinitarianism and Islam; or when "Gunpowder Joe" Priestley (as he was then being called) was smeared as a Guy Fawkes–style terrorist and attacked by church and king mobs; or when, in 1792, Edmund Burke helped defeat an early attempt at the Unitarian Relief Bill in the Commons by comparing believers in this new denomination to "insect reptiles" that "fill us with disgust" and "if they go above their natural size . . . become objects of the greatest terror."[4]

The embrace of a heterodox package that included denying the Trinity was not simply about the adoption of a *different* religious outlook; it was about committing one of the graver spiritual crimes of the era. And not surprisingly, given the stakes, the motives of the heterodox were multifaceted. Attachment to the Bible mixed with rationalism and broad learning was routinely part of the equation. When the mid-seventeenth-century Oxford-educated John Biddle—the so-called father of English Unitarianism—found the "Holy Trinity ungrounded in Revelation, much less in reason," he still took the revelation seriously. According to the first English writer actually to use the word "Unitarian" in print, Stephen Nye, it was scripture that plainly said Christ was subservient to God—"My father is greater than I" (John 14:28), "The Head of Christ is God" (1 Corinthians 11:3), and so on. Newton and Locke, the latter of whom read Nye with interest, said much the same thing on the basis of textual criticism, and said it to each other. But the point to stress is that these authors were reading and quoting scripture using modified criteria. In a strain of biblical criticism developing around the turn of the eighteenth century, traditionalism was increasingly overshadowed by rationalism. And in a universe that Newton did so much to mathematize, there was something especially untenable about regarding three and one as the same number.[5]

Just as important was the fact that unorthodox implications could be drawn from staple reading in the Dissenter academies. Such places were not the inevitable incubators of radicalism that paranoid conservatives claimed, but their leading historian has written that students could nevertheless be encouraged to pick up heterodox ideas, or at least acquire an open-mindedness about doctrine, as tutors stressed free inquiry into differences of opinion. Ministers, for their part, could as easily arrive at heterodoxy as they continued to read about doctrinal controversies well into their ministries. Ryder made a detail-deprived reference to a preacher who in 1761, after eleven years of agreement with his church, was ejected "by a superior number of one vote" because he "had changed his method of preaching, and by reading other works had changed his sentiments on articles of faith to the great Dissatisfaction of many of the members of the Society." The comment speaks not only to the capacity of ministers to change their views, but to the fact that Independent and, by this era, Presbyterian churches had the right to select or dispose of their pastors as parishioners with political force saw fit.[6]

It is also the case that, like any big change, the shift to heterodoxy was informed by accident. This was especially true in the earlier years of the century. Before 1719, "Presbyterian" and "Independent" typically meant differences in church organization and administration. The contours of doctrinal division along denominational lines were in some evidence by the early 1690s, but a pattern appears much more clearly after 150 leading Dissenters met in 1719 in Salters' Hall Chapel in London in order to discuss whether or not to mandate professing belief in the Trinity. By a slight margin, the Presbyterians clustered among the "Nonsubscribers," namely those put off by a clause stating that denying the Trinity was a spiritual error, while Independents generally voted to uphold orthodoxy. It turns out that many who voted on opposite sides of the issue were Trinitarians—the real question in 1719 was about doctrinal freedom. But this did not change the fact that over the course of the next few decades the Presbyterians—whose founder had infamously burned Michael Servetus at the stake in sixteenth-century Geneva for anti-Trinitarian heresy—became something of a haven for the heterodox, while the Independents, whatever the connotations of their name, came to be known for their orthodoxy.[7]

Once radical ideas were in the air, however exactly they got there, a major determinant of whether or not they might settle into the lives of chapel-goers was the give and take between ministers and the laity. Ryder's diary offers us a rare chance to witness this dynamic relationship. So, just as remarkably, do a few other sources, which are worth considering before turning to mid-century Leeds.

By the late 1730s, a group of radical preachers was forming around one of the leaders of mid-century English Presbyterianism, George Benson.

Like so many Dissenters of his generation, Benson was a deep admirer of Locke, whose influence pervades the antiestablishment newspaper Benson helped write during the 1730s, *The Old Whig: Or, Consistent Protestant,* which was a sustained push for a third way in politics between Walpole and Bolingbroke that, among other things, brought together the republican tradition and a measure of commercialism. Benson had also been an Arian at least as early as the 1720s. But what else made him influential was his control between 1740 and 1762 of the Presbyterian Fund, a trust established in 1689 to support Dissenter clergy and the academies that was presided over by ministers, big donors, and elected leaders from the laity of contributing congregations. Running this fund made Benson a magnet for pastors looking for intellectual and financial support, and he in turn was a nodal point in a heterodox network made partly visible by his correspondence. It is not the case that Benson simply told his fellow ministers exactly what to believe, but he seems to have put his weight behind those who shared his more radical vision. Among other things, Benson's patronage meant that the connection between anti-Trinitarianism and Presbyterianism that was given an accidental boost in 1719 was becoming more deliberate.[8]

One minister who wrote to Benson (for friendly advice rather than financial support) was Samuel Bourn. Like Benson, Bourn had become an Arian at some early point in the wake of the Salters' Hall controversy, and his radical credentials were established by mid-century. (Priestley once called his own Birmingham New Meeting congregation "the most liberal, I believe of any in England," and then explained that "to this freedom the unwearied labours of Mr Bourn"—who had preached the opening sermon at New Meeting in 1732—"eminently contributed.") Bourn's radicalism also alienated him from orthodox Presbyterians, many of whom refused to attend his ordination. But Bourn had other friends. As he was abandoned by the mainstream, one contemporary source indicates that he found support thanks to an unnamed wealthy family. It may have been with such backing that he was empowered to publicly challenge Calvinism. As early as 1736 he attacked the standard Presbyterian catechism, the main problem of which was its Trinitarianism: "There are *not* three Persons, but one Person only in our Idea of God. For, what is a *Person,* but an individual, intelligent, free, active Being or Substance." He then went on to write a revised and expanded anti-Trinitarian catechism that pleased Benson and the *Old Whig* publisher Samuel Chandler, among others. This was the "first manifesto" of heterodox

Presbyterianism, in the words of a hostile late-nineteenth-century church history. It offered Jesus's life only as an "example" of how to be saved—a reading that hints at the sort of belief in the mere humanity of Christ that might have worried even Arians; and by the 1750s its multiple editions were themselves playing a role in the shift away from the Calvinist catechism in the Presbyterian schools and toward "the principles of common Christianity."[9]

Beyond what it exposes of a network linking radical ministers, whose lives appear only in fragments in the historical record, the Benson-Bourn correspondence reveals how much parishioners could play a role in transforming their religion. We can see this especially clearly in the early 1750s, when Bourn wrote to Benson looking for advice about whether or not to move to a different chapel. At the time Bourn was preaching in Coseley, a dozen miles northwest of Birmingham, while the offer to relocate had come from a Presbyterian chapel in Bolton, a dozen miles northwest of Manchester. These were both wealthy chapels in regions in the earliest stages of industrialization, and both wanted spiritual guidance by someone on the radical end of Dissent. Bourn would eventually decline the invitation from the Bolton congregation, where his father had once been minister, but not before sending two letters to Benson about the matter that explain why the offer was tempting. The Bolton congregation, Bourn wrote, consisted "very much of young thriving tradesmen, the old generation of my acquaintance being almost all gone." These were men of commerce on the eve of industrialization, promising Bourn a setup he found potentially "as agreeable as any I know in the kingdom." Not only would he have a house "over a river" in "a pleasant little town," but a lively spiritual life and "a weekly lecture, where several ministers usually attend" and where "worthy friendly brethren" would be "free from bigotry" (that is, open to heterodoxy). But more astonishingly, while the formal invitation was endorsed by "177 heads of families in Bolton," it had been *hand-delivered* by "100 Gentlemen," a virtual legislative assembly of self-governing and radical lay Presbyterians who journeyed a hundred miles to see whether they could persuade Bourn to shepherd their spiritual lives. As if the economic subtext of the sorts of people who made up the congregation was not already clear, Bourn was himself thinking like an entrepreneurial minister. And given that Dissenter pastors typically drew in the income of poorer Anglican clerics, while also having to pay for their living arrangements, these were not minor considerations. Bourn was careful to tell his friend Benson that while the Bolton party was now willing to raise his salary to keep him put, he took the congregation he would be leaving behind "to be three times as rich."[10]

That so many men made this far from trivial journey to deliver the invitation dramatically speaks to how much this new generation of tradesmen wanted ministers like Bourn to meet their spiritual needs. The scene also speaks to something central in the consideration of why particular Dissenter chapels welcomed heterodoxy: they did so when a portion of the laity that was significant in numbers or political power wanted to move the chapel in a different direction. Dissenter congregations in this era have rightly been characterized as "little democracies." If they disapproved of their ministers, they could simply eject them, as Ryder reminded us above. The logic of the structure of congregational self-governance already means, in other words, that some portion of laypeople were interested in new ideas at the moment that they pressed for a minister who held similar views. As much as it was undoubtedly about those standing behind the pulpit, religious change in chapels like Ryder's was about those sitting in the pews.[11]

The logic alone nevertheless tells an incomplete story. It was not simply the case that some congregants actively embraced a new outlook while others left the old denominations to go wherever else they could practice their traditions. There were also people like Ryder, uncomfortably watching the change while still listening to the sermons of ministers largely responsible for bringing it about.

Ryder complained about religious decay in general terms throughout his diary, but his worry took on specificity in 1748, a decisive year in large part because of Thomas Walker. The controversial Walker arrived in Leeds to replace Mill Hill's minister of eighteen years, Joseph Cappe, sometime— very possibly in May—between Cappe's death in February 1748 and Ryder's first reference to Walker five months later. Almost everything that is discoverable about this obscure minister is both intriguing and fragmented. A passing comment about him gets made, for example, in Priestley's memoirs, where Priestley recalled one of his homes from youth, his aunt Sarah Keighley's house, as a "resort of all the dissenting ministers in the neighborhood" and then singled out Walker as one of her two "most heretical" guests. Or there is a bundle of implications in the fact that Walker was the legal guardian of his much-better-known nephew, George Walker, whose republicanism, abolitionism, and broad learning suggest the outlook of the uncle whom the nephew cited as a major influence. Evidence of Walker's relaxed views on wealth, if not also of his social connections, is for that matter implicit in the success of his oldest son, who made enough money in the drysaltery trade to purchase a large country estate outside of Leeds.[12]

If Walker was the most important local source of religious division, however, he also may have simply given a green light to others who already held divergent opinions. The month Walker likely arrived in Leeds, Ryder was alluding to coreligionists becoming willfully indifferent to the specificities of religious tradition, the matters "for which our pious forefathers were ready to suffer the loss of all things." At least one other preacher, the obscure Mr. Owen, who appears earlier in the diary without any trace of heterodoxy that Ryder noted, was demonstrating the same sort of indifference by the next year. In late July 1749 Ryder put Owen down on paper as preaching that there are "many ways persons took up the opinion of themselves, that they walked worthy of the Lord. Many call'd it walking worthy whilst they indulg'd some singularity in fashion of dress, or meat." The rationalistic idea that religious particularities are irrelevant may not be entirely evident in the brief sermon summary. The next day, though, Ryder was troubled enough to say more. In the "evening I compared what I read in my bible with what I hear from some teachers who Exalt reason and plead very much for the Liberty of judging for themselves, but then is there not to be some rule to try by, and if in the Substantials of religion I Differ from my neighbour, Certainly in my Judgment One of us must think amiss." The question Owen was likely getting at was precisely the one that may have vexed Ryder on some deep level: what exactly constitutes the substantial part of religion? But Ryder didn't write in detail about any of the particularities Owen may have explicitly threatened. He irenically turned to the Bible to meditate on the meaning and dangers of religious debate itself: "I gett Strengthened in this way of thinking by reading the 10th verse of the 1st Chap: of the 1st Epis to the Corinthians, the words are these: Now I Beseech you Brethren by the name of the Lord Jesus Christ, that ye all speak the same things, and that there be no Divisions among you but that ye be perfectly joined together in the same mind." Ryder could accept some denominational pluralism, but not the sort of relativism that could cloud the path to salvation and endanger the church's vitality.[13]

Arguments like this must have been as emotionally distressful to Ryder as they seemed unsound. He had spent much of his life mastering the Bible and engaging in the very specific forms of practice that some ministers now trivialized, and he understandably did not want the sacrifices of his Puritan and Dissenter ancestors to be in vain. Mill Hill, where he had been baptized, had been born in struggle. The chapel was built between 1672 and 1674 in the wake of the Declaration of Indulgence, when "Indulgence" was more of an ideal than a reality, and the authorities harassed its worshippers until after the Toleration Act was passed in 1689, two years before the Independent chapel on Call Lane formally opened its doors. A decade and a half of persecution already may have been enough to reinforce a willingness on the part of later generations of congregants to stay true to Puritan culture, but such a message surely also came from Mill Hill's first minister, Richard Stretton, who preached in the age of Ryder's parents and grandparents. Stretton's radicalism is easier to trace after he moved from Leeds to London in 1678, a few years after which he was accused of having taken part in the Rye House Plot, was acquitted, and then still was thrown in jail for six months in late 1683 for refusing to take the "Oxford Oath." The Tory propagandist Roger L'Estrange called Stretton "one of the most peevish, subtle, active, leading men of their party." And if Stretton was in fact the author he claimed to be of the activist *The Case of the Protestant Dissenters Represented and Argued*, a text very possibly misattributed to the Whig Dissenter John Howe, there was something to L'Estrange's accusation. But it was likely not only the Tory offensive against Whigs and Dissenters in the early 1680s that radicalized Stretton. Before he came to Leeds, he was the chaplain of the civil war general Thomas Fairfax, a relationship it is easy to imagine tying him to the revolutionary face of Puritanism.[14]

Surely countless stories of discrimination and oppression like Stretton's lingered in Mill Hill's oral traditions, ready to be put to narrative use by self-persecutory parishioners like Ryder. But if we nevertheless have to guess about all the causes, we know the consequence: Ryder was undeniably committed to his religious culture. And this gave rise to yet another duality in his outlook. He tended, in one sense, to regard himself simply as a sincere Christian, yet he also valued the specificities of the older, more faithfully Calvinist form of Dissent. We have seen this reflected throughout this book in his devotion to practice and doctrine. But his sense of Dissenter identity can appear in other subtle ways. In a poem written in 1754, "Nonconformity to the world the Christian's Duty," "nonconformity" took on additional meaning as it metaphorically captured the necessary distance he kept from the world. "From every vicious custom keep me Lord," the poem began with the assumption that customs matter, "And Guide me by thy Spirit & thy word."[15]

It was for no shortage of reasons that Ryder felt as if his religion was particularly under stress beginning in the later 1740s. And as was true in Bolton and Coseley, ministers in Leeds were far from the only agents of change. Through a window Ryder cracks open onto one of his evening meetings with coreligionists in the fall of 1748, we can glimpse him sitting with several friends, "taken up with discoursing upon Religion and Severall Opinions Supported & held among Parties." His use of "parties" in the plural is already telling, and he walked away from the heated discussion lamenting that "the Practicall part" of religion was once again ignored. "I own it a valuable blessing to be well informed in matters of religion and to have some comfortable knowledge who we have believed in and rested our salvation on but after all what avails knowledge unless it lead to practice." The matter did not easily subside, although Ryder concluded that the best way to keep everyone together was to project the sort of irenicism he admired in his spiritual mentors. The next week he was again in the company of coreligionists, where he had "hoped to have spent a little time very comfortably, but debate arising about severall things in religion my peace was somewhat disturbed." Most of all he wanted "to speak evil of no man maliciously. Where any man differs from me I desire rather to pray for them than any way contentiously to dispute with them." The line of reasoning was straight from the pages of the conciliatory opinion makers of the "old Dissent." "If you are providentially led into Argument and Dispute whether on Themes of Belief or Practice," Isaac Watts advised in a text from the early 1730s, "be very watchful lest you run into fierce Contention, into angry and noisy Debate."[16]

No one, however, tested Ryder's willingness to accommodate divergent opinions like Thomas Walker, who would be little more than a composite of the fragments about him quoted above were it not for Ryder's record of sermons. Virtually as soon as he arrived in town, Walker went after Calvinist orthodoxy tenet by tenet, making a mess of the line Kant would in later years so famously draw between the public and private. Unfortunately, Ryder could be obscure about the sermonic details. The Mill Hill minister Charles Wicksteed, who read the diary in the 1840s to try to understand his own chapel's past, thought that Ryder would habitually bring attention to his faltering memory as "a quiet sign of disaffection" when trying to recollect an unsavory sermon. Maybe so, although Ryder also forgets things he very much seems to want to recall. What we are often left with, in any case, are allusions and suggestions whose meaning has to be read between the lines. In early 1749, for example, Ryder recorded a "sermon preacht by mr Walker about Christ mediation and of his undertaking." Christ's mediation could easily be spoken about in Trinitarian terms, and without context the reference would be innocuous. But Ryder further explained that after the sermon, "I was cast into company where we had a good many argument of a religious nature, which I desire may prove to me edification & growth in grace." In his eagerness to work out the doctrinal matters that were more and more dominating his religious meetings, he turned for clarification to Thomas Whitaker, who must have been encouraged by conversation with Ryder and other orthodox parishioners when he took to the pulpit at Call Lane weeks later to deliver an explicitly Trinitarian sermon, another sign that Walker was dabbling in the subject. Christ is "the Creator & former of all things," Whitaker preached, "being in the beginning with God and was God so that we must honour the son as we honour the Father."[17]

It seems clear enough that the Trinity was now up for debate, and despite Call Lane's orthodoxy, Walker was undeterred. Over at Mill Hill he would claim later that summer "that the things relating to our Salvation were very easy to a judicious considering, & diligent mind, & some things which were more dark in all probability were not materiall to our Salvation." One of those things immaterial to salvation, he was no doubt suggesting if not saying outright, was Jesus's divinity. By the next year, Ryder was still vague, but the suggestions were increasingly unmistakable. "Mr Walker preach'd from Luke 19:10," Ryder told his diary in early 1750: "For the Son of man is come to seek and to save that which was lost. In discoursing he show'd why Christ is called the son of man, and who they were that are here said to be lost. I endeavoured to give Diligent heed to what was Spoken and am very desirous to be profited by hearing, but must own at this time can remember but little methodicall." Maybe this time Ryder had an excuse for his memory failing. In the same entry he sadly noted the seventh anniversary of his mother's death. But it takes little effort to imagine that Walker's discourse on why Christ was called the son of man would have offered an occasion to explain that being the son of man did not necessarily amount to being one in the same with God.[18]

Throughout the 1750s, Walker persisted and Ryder seemed to get the message. In the fall of 1754, the minister offered a Thursday lecture that Ryder attended after a morning of labor. The sermon began with a list of the ways in which Christ is the "head over all things to the Church . . . in guiding them, & Giving the Holy Spirit, and being appointed to be the Judge having all power Given him." But then Ryder alarmingly heard Walker say that on the day of judgment, he "knoweth no man, nor the Son, but the Father." From this Walker "showd that Some would say that he knew it as God, but not as man, which way of arguing he showd to be trifling and Jesuiticall, which I must own gave me much Concern, while I took him in that Christ was not God." By tying the Trinity to popishness Walker was no doubt hoping typical anti-Catholic prejudices would help make his theological case. At the same time, there is a discernible sense here in which Walker was aware of the orthodoxy of some of his hearers. As much as he was again smearing the line between his intellectual pursuits and his pastoral duties, he must have been presenting his beliefs to satisfy some of the traditionalists. "And Yet afterward," Ryder continued his summary, "when [Walker] treated concerning [Christ] in heaven, he brought in that Scripture: Let all the Angells of God worship him, and also that command that we are to honour the Son as we honour the Father. In prayer he afterward pray'd that God would teach us to understand the Scriptures." The "and yet" in Ryder's prose is crucial. Walker surely asked his congregation "to understand the Scriptures" because he knew they were committed to that staple Reformation tenet, *sola scriptura*, which narrowed doctrinal certainties to what was contained in the Bible. The King James Version that Dissenters like Ryder read, after all, never mentions the Trinity. And Ryder, for one, seems to have been somewhat disarmed by this strategy of Walker's given the degree to which his concern over the Trinity diminishes in the diary after the late 1750s.[19]

The notion that Jesus did not share God's full divinity was not, however, the only heresy Ryder heard beginning in the late 1740s. More than one minister was also preaching that humans were not depraved. In many ways, this was a harder piece of theological revisionism for Ryder to stomach. He never indicated exactly what he thought about the Trinity before the controversies of the 1740s and 1750s, but he did reveal earlier in the diary that he was deeply attached to the doctrine of original sin. And precisely how he tells us this is intriguing on multiple levels. As we have seen elsewhere in this book, Ryder was not untouched by the rational morality of the Enlightenment. In one of the more surprising passages in the diary, well before heterodoxy noticeably made inroads into Leeds, he found Socrates's life to suggest that God's revealed word may not be the only route to correct moral behavior:

"In the Morning I was In some measure, overcome by hastiness of Temper, & was ashamed when I considered what I had heard the Day before of Socrates an Heathen Philosopher who being a Cholerick man in Temper So Overcame himself by reason without the help of Divine Revelation, that he became a very pattern of Patience." Ryder was ultimately making a case against himself: if a heathen could somehow do the right thing, what excuse was there for a Christian? Ryder would also nod in approval when Whitaker preached several months later that because the ancient Greeks had no access to the gospel they "fell prey to their own vain imaginations." But in thinking at all about Socrates in these terms Ryder was nevertheless flirting with the deistic argument that a moral life might not require exposure to Christian scripture. For that matter, if Ryder read Isaac Watts's work on logic alongside Watts's writings on practical divinity, he would have come into some kind of contact with Lockean empiricism. The diary tantalizingly offers up this passing comment from an entry in 1739, when Ryder found himself in some part of the day "Admiring the Goodness of God In making man a rationall Creature, with understanding memory & other faculties." It *sounds* Lockean. And yet the larger point lies in his Puritan qualification of his epistemological musings: "but saw on the other hand," he finished the entry, "the Great Reason to humiliation to Consider how mans nature was Depraved & Corrupted with the fall."[20]

Ryder had come to definite conclusions on the meaning of human nature that ultimately put him at odds with Enlightenment culture. There may have been a measure of open-mindedness inherent in his ambivalence, but he was predictably taken aback when he heard sermons characterize the concept of original sin—and predestination for that matter—as bankrupt. But what else is clear, and what makes Ryder's diary revealing about more than his own religious outlook, is that these issues were broadly under debate. Not only did Ryder explicitly address them early on in his diary, Walker was far from alone in tackling them from the pulpit.

Back in the summer of 1749, the other Thomas—the evenhanded Whitaker—was busy at Call Lane trying to mediate between heterodox and orthodox factions, preaching on several occasions against speaking evil words that could result from "an intemperate heat in Religious matters or a party zeal when others differ from them." Whitaker was no fan of religious enthusiasm, and more specifically he called on his congregation not to accuse "the ministers of Gods word or Elders but upon good evidence for they are

accountable to their great lord and master as to the fulfilling of their office."
It is a telling phrase—the source of the heresies was not simply ministers, but
the elders: the lay elites in the chapel who had brought in radical clergy to
preach. But Ryder's patience was nevertheless tested, and his pen activated,
when only a few weeks after Whitaker's conciliatory sermon a more obscure
minister questioned the legitimacy of staple Reformed beliefs. We noted this
sermon in a previous chapter, and it is worth returning to in this context. "To
preach that man was universally corrupted," a pastor identified only as
"Smith" claimed in Ryder's paraphrase, "and that God had chosen a certain
number to Salvation and left the rest in a state of reprobation was repugnant
to the Gospell." Ryder recoiled. This "gave some of us great sadness of heart
and it is to be feared helpt greatly to disrelish all the rest of his discourse . . .
oh that no minister may be carried away with the fear of man which brings a
snare from preaching the sound & plain doctrine of the Gospell in their
native simplicity."[21]

If it is clear that Ryder could be disturbed by heterodoxy, exactly what made
him return to Thomas Walker's Mill Hill, time and again, is something of a
mystery, especially when at Call Lane, his principal chapel, he could much
more reliably hear the gospel preached in its "native simplicity" in the
sermons of his beloved minister Thomas Whitaker. Did Ryder really need
the words of another pastor, especially one who was so dramatically swerving
from orthodoxy?[22]

One possibility we have to entertain is that Ryder simply did not catch
the full extent of Walker's radicalism. This is a tricky thing to consider given
that we can access only one voice in the pastor-parishioner relationship. All
of these Leeds ministers, aside from Priestley, were profoundly obscure.
They have a voice in the twenty-first century thanks to Ryder, and if Ryder
did not tune in to the full range of what they were saying, neither can we. But
there is one exceptional sermon that we possess in print form. It also happens
to have come from Walker, who in 1752 dedicated a new chapel at Wakefield,
one of the wealthiest congregations in Yorkshire, and published his sermon
the next year. Just as remarkably, given that this happened not in Leeds but
ten miles south, Ryder, as further testament to his diligence, happened to be
there that very day, sitting in the pews. With Ryder's diary and Walker's
printed sermon side by side, we have a singular chance to compare what the
minister preached with what the clothier wrote down.[23]

From Ryder's perspective, Walker stood at the front of the new Wakefield chapel and showed that "worship in spirit . . . differed from all bodily worship." The phrase already suggests Walker's rationalistic understanding of his religion. But it was more clearly annoying to Ryder that Walker did not "pretend to a Consecration" of the new building, instead using the occasion to argue that "ye Canopy over our heads, or the Starry Vault for our covering," was the house of God and gate of Heaven. If Ryder concluded with an endorsement of the minister, its tepidness can be felt in the double negative: Walker "did not discommend a Decent place for the worship of God, and Gave the Contributers a fine Encomium of praise for their Generosity in supporting the ministry, as well as building the place."[24]

These themes Ryder noted run through the published sermon, but assuming that little changed before Walker sent his text to the printer, it is striking to set these two voices alongside each other. Unlike his watchful parishioner, Walker sounds far less like a Puritan than a Newtonian aesthete. In an analogy he makes early in the lecture, he claims, for example, that "pure religion . . . is founded in the nature and truth of things, and when exhibited to the world in this light is an amiable and a grand thing; as far superior to what is commonly professed, as the original paintings of some of the greatest artists to the vulgar pieces of low performers. In the former, you see simplicity, proportion and truth; every thing calculated to instruct and please. In the other, so many unmeaning strokes, and unnatural attitudes, and such a vast quantity of whimsical and ill-judged drapery, as unavoidably occasion disgust or ridicule."[25] It is as if these two men believed in different Gods: the deistic God of "pure religion," as geometrically proportioned as the beautiful new Wakefield chapel, and the God "commonly professed" by the traditional and vulgar—a God that, like a bad painting, was worthy of ridicule.

Walker did not stop here. With possible intent in the order he gives the characteristics of worship, he explained that "no worship but what is intelligent and rational, spiritual or moral, can be acceptable or pleasing to him." (Nowhere do the words "intelligent" or "rational" appear in Ryder's summary.) Worshiping God in spirit varies by method across time and place, "and some [methods], it must be allowed, as absurd, ridiculous, and dishonourable to God, as could well have been devised. But still as in all ages and in all parts of the world something like the face of religion has been kept up." You can do as you wish with your body during worship, he continued (only here do we really start to hear the source of the echoes in Ryder's summary)—

you can kneel, look to heaven, fall on your face, just as Jesus did—"but the worship of the body *without the mind* is none." Walker then closed by finding in the new structure's completion the essence of a multivalent liberty—and note that all of these emphases in the text were Walker's cue to his reader to imagine the stress in his voice and feel the thrust of his argument: "In an age in which a taste for elegance in almost all things prevails I see not why a discreet and moderate degree of the *same taste* may not be allowed *in this.* . . . *This house,* not inelegantly finished, is an evidence and will be a monument of a pious munificence." It was "in the use of this liberty we both erect and support our places of worship." "You, my fellow Christians, are still steady. *This house* is proof of it. It shows you are yet the friends of liberty, piety and the rights of conscience."[26]

It was a stirring way to finish: liberty, piety, and the rights of conscience, a trinity for this anti-Trinitarian, were here built symbolically into the new church. And in the liberty, in particular, Walker located another sort of trinity—the confluence of political, economic, and religious interests. To put his argument baldly, one great virtue of the freedom to worship was that it allowed for prosperous members of society—including, if not especially, the newly prosperous—to support and practice a rationalized religion that doctrinally met their needs and, as the elegance of the new church attested, materially suited their tastes.

Did Ryder miss all of this? Maybe. But another possibility, which additional evidence supports, is that he to some degree tuned out what he did not want to hear in sermons. It is undoubtedly the case that Ryder continued to hear Walker preach even as it becomes crystal clear in the diary that he grasped the fuller extent of the minister's radicalism. In the fall of 1756, for example, Ryder heard a minister at Mill Hill (presumably Walker, though Ryder never discloses a name) say that many people profess many things. But true professors—truly pious believers, that is—become what they are solely "by a Good Education, or from Naturall conscience which may be awakened." Nowhere did the sermon point to the necessity of scripture. This is Lockean-inspired deism—the controlled experience of an education and "naturall conscience" offer the essential ingredients for leading a pious life. Despite the anguish Ryder had earlier felt over losing the texture of his religious culture, here in the diary there is silence—and a silence that did not result from aversion to admitting to controversy. Ryder still acknowledged that others were disturbed by what they were encountering at Mill Hill. Only three weeks later he heard "an ancient Christian complain with sorrow of heart, & I think either weeping or near it, of the Corruption of Doctrine delivered by the ministers he sits under, some in defence say, that every man has the Liberty to think for himself & ought to deliver his own Sentiments whether his hearers will believe them or [not]." Given that Ryder was himself now sixty-one and nonetheless noticing that this other Christian was "ancient," this was surely someone considerably older and even more tightly linked to traditional Dissent. We don't have to guess that this was someone emotionally distressed about religious change—Ryder tells us the man was virtually brought to tears. But still, however much more he had in common with the sad congregant than with Walker, Ryder upheld the principle of having the liberty to confront heterodoxy. According to Ryder, Walker preached in ways "quite contrary to the Direction given in Scripture"; even so, "we have the Scriptures to try false preachers by, and if they plainly differ from them, we have need to pray that we may disregard them." There is no mystery in what Ryder was saying: "disregard" involves not leaving the chapel, but rather learning how to deal with the minister. The mystery is why he was saying it.[27]

That mystery deepens as Walker's heterodoxy reached a tipping point for some of the congregants. After a minister Ryder only knew as "Mr. Pye" delivered a sermon in defense of original sin (from which chapel is never clear), Walker lashed out with so much "caviling" that "severall persons . . . resolve to leave him." If Walker was hoping that the personal make-up of Mill Hill's congregation would change—as he saw it for the better—Ryder, however much he favored Pye's message, stayed put. Hardly any time passed, in fact, before Ryder was once again quoting Walker with approval, finding it "pleasing," days later, when the otherwise heretical minister struck a familiar chord by exhorting his hearers against sloth and negligence. Few things appealed to Ryder as much as the extolment of industry and the execration of idleness. And still, Walker relentlessly deconstructed orthodoxy, asking his congregation in 1757 to "Grow in knowledge and holyness, as the most evident proofs of Christianity" rather than getting embroiled "in abstruse arguments, & knotty controversies and mysteries such as they could not defend, Such as Trinity in Unity, Election & reprobation, Grace and freewill and such like." Now Ryder hardly reacted, except to suggest that Walker was unfairly steamrolling some congregants who differed from him in matters of judgment. A year later, when a friend gave him reproof "for not speaking more freely in defence of a Gospell truth which he knew I heard

Struck at . . . Namely the Doctrine of the Trinity," Ryder responded that "if one is not duly furnished with convincing Arguments I yet rather choose to say little than to make ill worse, and the Point was Such as the greatest Divines cannot bring down to our reason." This should not be taken to mean that Ryder had simply abandoned his views. Five years later in 1762, after hearing Walker say something heretical—what, exactly, we are never told—we read this rejoinder, the voice of a late-stage Puritan, willingly held captive in a religion that was changing before his eyes: "I cannot deny but I am desirous of what I seldom meet with, even discourses of the depravity of our nature, and the healing remedies provided, the necessity of inward holiness and heart sanctification as well as outward reformation. But I desire patiently to wait at wisdom's gates, and wisely to improve the mercies I do enjoy." Sermon after sermon, Walker was, in essence, turning Calvin on his head. The religion was moving on. Ryder was ultimately unhappy about it, but by association, he was reluctantly moving along with it.[28]

Ryder's deeper motives and the larger meaning of this change might be found by asking a counterfactual question. Why didn't he show more interest in Methodism, whose adherents had been worshiping in Leeds at least since 1740? Probably no one we have on record looks more like Ryder than Joseph Williams, the Kidderminster Dissenter and clothier we met earlier. When Williams felt that the radical trajectory of Dissent was beyond his control, he joined the Methodists, whom he saw as more faithfully continuing the Puritan tradition.[29]

If by Methodism we mean the Arminian variety, the question isn't worth asking, given that Ryder was unmistakably unmoved by its doctrine. When he heard a description of the doctrine of "perfectionism" in 1745, he wrote that he did not "find any ground to take it in." Two years later, he waxed on the doctrine of justification and found that "if none are safe but those that can tell and explain the time of their justification, I must be reckoned among what number they please, for I cannot remember any such thing." As Herbert McLachlan aptly put it in his short article on Ryder from the 1920s, "doctrines of perfection and assurance were repugnant to a man constantly burdened with a sense of guilt, who in his old age expressed surprise 'to find himself this side of Hell.'" But the version of Methodism associated with the itinerant preacher George Whitefield was a different story. The Calvinist Whitefield actually upheld the doctrines that Walker and

others were rejecting, and he also regularly traveled to Leeds beginning in
1749. He was a ready and reasonable option for Ryder, and Ryder could not
help but be impressed by the large crowds Whitefield could draw to his open-
air sermons.[30]

What is so curious, though, is that Ryder also found something off-
putting even in this Calvinist variety of Methodism. In the fall of 1749, as
Thomas Walker was beginning his assault on orthodoxy at Mill Hill, a
neighbor invited Ryder to go hear Whitefield preach. Ryder praised any
revival of religion no matter who was leading the way but still turned the
invitation down, explaining a couple of weeks later that he "heard that Mr
Whitfield preacht near where I live, but did not hear him. I am afraid to be
deceived or turned aside. I have something of a jealousy I own relating to his
Intentions seeing he thus travells from place to place & abides not in one

The Rev.d M.r Whitfield Preaching at Leeds, 1749.

George Whitefield rendered Christlike in an engraving of an open-air sermon he delivered in
Leeds in 1749. Although we are given only the year the image was made, the haybail suggests the
recent harvest and that this could easily be the sermon from September 22 that Ryder turned
down an invitation to go hear. Reproduced by courtesy of the University Librarian and Director,
The John Rylands University Library, The University of Manchester.

particular place, but hearing that his doctrines as far as competent judges can find are agreeable to the word of God I would rejoyce to hear of a work of regeneration carrying on Whoever are the Instruments."[31]

It seems contradictory. Ryder could regularly sit, listen to, and then "disregard" Thomas Walker, a man who rejected Calvinism doctrine by doctrine. And yet Ryder ran the risk of being "turned aside" by Whitefield, who was actually reviving doctrinal Calvinism. It is strange, for that matter, that Ryder was suspicious of Whitefield's itinerancy, given how much Ryder himself rode back and forth into the countryside. And if Whitefield was also infamous for his alluring charisma, why exactly was that charisma threatening when Ryder could admit that the Methodist minister was reviving the very religious tradition that Ryder was so troubled to see fade in relevance?[32]

The contradictions are nevertheless more apparent than real. So many of Ryder's words in this book indicate that doctrine meant less to him than religious practice. As he put it in the description of an evening meeting with friends that we came across above: "Company was taken up with discoursing upon Religion & Severall Opinions Supported & held among Parties. But the Practicall part not so much taken notice of. I own it a Valuable Blessing to be well Informed in matters of Religion and to have some comfortable knowledge who we have believed in and rested our Salvation on but after all what avails knowledge unless it lead to practice."[33] This may be the closest thing we have to Ryder's theory of religion. In essence, "knowledge" and "practice" are the polarities, and the former without the latter is pointless. And rather than getting entangled in doctrinal controversy, Ryder suggests both in theory and in his actions that he felt it was better to practice his religion by simply continuing to be the creature of cultural habit we have witnessed him being—writing his diary entries and verses, meeting in the evening with friends, attending funerals or the sick at their bedsides.

And, of course, just as essential in his religious practice as any of these rituals was turning up, like clockwork, at Call Lane and Mill Hill. Ryder was as emotionally and spiritually attached to these places as anyone would be to a sacred space visited with such devotion. He may have never explicitly expressed his feelings on this point. Not surprisingly. He only really tells us how he felt about his wife and his mother after they die; had he seen either chapel's physical destruction, the emotion and description may have been similarly forthcoming. But we can still sense something in his silence. Like some of his coreligionists (obviously not those who abandoned Mill Hill altogether), he did not recognize a serious division between the two chapels. Parishioners, like him, could effortlessly attend both; ministers, like Walker and Whitaker, could as easily sermonize in both; the year after Joseph Priestley came to Mill Hill, he asked Whitaker to baptize his son at Call Lane. Nor does Ryder distinguish the two chapels in doctrinal or denominational terms, defining one as Presbyterian and the other as Independent. Both were for what by the mid-eighteenth century we can call traditional Dissenters. They were two expressions of the same culture, whoever the minister in charge.[34]

For that matter, the ministers of both chapels were also, ultimately, allies. Two Sundays after the thrashing Walker gave Pye over original sin in 1757, Whitaker rose to the pulpit at Call Lane to school his parishioners in global history: "there always had in every nation been some apprehensions of a Deity, and Some Religion in the world, never a Generation of Atheists." Don't fear Thomas Walker over at Mill Hill, Whitaker seems to have been saying: he is no atheist. A deist, maybe, but that is not the same thing. And, in fact, at this point Whitaker had himself begun to sound Arian to some of his parishioners, as this quotation dimly suggests. Ryder never gives us the evidence about Whitaker's heterodoxy that we possess about Walker's. The silence is again significant, if hard to read—after so many years, was Ryder too close to Whitaker to be critical, or was the conciliatory Whitaker simply more muted in his radical beliefs? But a Congregationalist history tells us that it was because of Whitaker's Arianism that a group of congregants left Call Lane in 1755 to start a new church, White Chapel, a haven of unchanging orthodoxy where Ryder would very occasionally go hear sermons, although never with any commentary that might indicate that he cared one way or the other about its atavistic mission. It is as if in Ryder's view White Chapel too—about which we unfortunately hear nothing of detail in the diary—had simply become part of the Dissenter fold. The terms of religious debate at the broadest cultural level may have shifted in a radical direction from their starting point earlier in the century. But the ever moderate, ever irenic Ryder still held to the via media, which by its nature shifted along with the extremes it lay between.[35]

From a more distant perspective, there is nevertheless something ominous in the way that Ryder found himself, as we find him in the diary, in a transitional world, trying to keep his religious practice on life support as so many of his beliefs were suffering a cultural brain death. It takes little imagination to find a correspondence for Ryder's distinction between knowledge and practice that we saw earlier in the way Clifford Geertz famously contrasted the worldview and ethos of a religion. In contrast to Ryder, however, Geertz argued that a worldview and ethos sustain each other—when one changes, the other necessarily changes with it.[36] As Walker and others were rethinking the meaning of the divine and the human, they were turning the Calvinist worldview upside down. But what Ryder seems to have expected by virtue of his willingness to hear Walker over Whitefield is that the character and the texture of his spiritual experience could somehow escape the process transforming the beliefs they depended on. Ryder considered the relationship between knowledge and practice, that is, in only one direction: it is knowledge that is aimless without practice, he regularly tells us. But how can a set of practices without the knowledge it was constructed with—how can an ethos without a worldview—not eventually find itself adrift?

The point is not that Ryder was naive. It is easier to know from our distance what was happening to the Puritan tradition. Living in the moment did not give Ryder a sense of the inevitable. However much the radical Walker challenged doctrine, he could still uphold for Ryder a satisfying degree of the practical part of religion as he indefatigably delivered sermon after sermon in the physical spaces where Ryder had worshiped throughout his life. Ryder could still *feel* connected to his religious culture even as he also felt it was in a woeful but not irreversible state of decay. George Whitefield, however much he might be seen from some angles as the logical continuation of Calvinism, was, to Ryder, simply too much of an outsider. And for that matter, when Ryder did eventually submit to going to see the Methodist dynamo speak in 1762, he said nothing about it in his diary. It is like his trip to London all over again. The silence is so incongruous given the significance of the witnessed event that it is impossible not to equate it with disapproval.[37]

The bigger question we have been concerned with here, however, is why the worldview itself changed. Why, in local terms, did heterodoxy take over Dissenter Leeds? We began by considering a litany of causes, all of which need to be taken seriously. But the one that Ryder's diary encourages considering at length—if only because this is the cause we know the least about—is the elective affinity that was developing between Unitarianism and material self-interest. Circumstantial evidence of this link has been interspersed throughout this chapter: in the exchange between Bourn and Benson; in the back and forth between Bourn and the two chapels near Manchester and Birmingham; in Bourn's wealthy benefactors; in the prosperity of the new Wakefield church; or for that matter in the prosperity of Mill Hill, far and away the Dissenter chapel of choice for the town's affluent cloth merchants and, by the nineteenth century, when it acquired the nickname "the Mayor's nest," the home of so many of its politicians. There is something suggestive too in the legacy of Ryder's younger cousin David, who in 1754 baptized his daughter and "denies the Trinity." Ryder found himself "much concerned that my kindred according to the flesh are not found walking in conformity to the life and power of godliness. I found much concern for the little infant." And yet the infant, Olive, must have had parents successful enough for her to marry into the Lupton family, one of the town's most successful and politically connected cloth merchant families from the time of Ryder's death.[38]

We can go further and cite the work of other historians who have shown that, after the denomination itself took shape in the 1770s, Unitarians became known for their wealth. In the late-eighteenth-century Midlands, and particularly in the diaries and personal papers of the steam engine magnate James Watt and his family, Margaret Jacob has found approval of Joseph Priestley's sermonic advice—Priestley had left Leeds in 1773—to mix with the world now that there was nothing wrong, as Priestley put it, with "riches, honors, and pleasures." From a different perspective, John Seed has shown that denominational Unitarians made inroads into the circles of Whig power because they possessed the necessary financial weight. E. P. Thompson and R. G. Wilson, for that matter, both briefly noted that Unitarians were unusually wealthy. Much more dramatic is Michael Watts's quantitative evidence of the connection. Watts figured out that if "Dissent as a whole produced fewer wealthy men than their strength in the total population would have predicted"—mainly because working-class Methodists bring the overall number down—it was also the case that for England and Wales by 1851 "there were nearly ten times the proportion of Unitarians among the millionaires and half-millionaires as in the general population."[39]

What do we do with this information? Does it entail a connection between the actual content of heterodoxy and a more unfettered capitalist spirit? Watts thought not, placing emphasis instead on Unitarians' greater receptivity to secular knowledge and engagement with polite society—forms of cultural and social capital that might lead to the accumulation of more tangible wealth. There is surely something to that explanation, but only insofar as we also connect it to shifts in belief. In renouncing the major tenets of Calvinism, the heterodox elevated the meaning of humanity in inverse proportion to the divinity of Jesus—a Jesus they also devoutly worshiped, even if in terms more befitting a human than divine being. This new system of belief aligned with major entrepreneurs precisely because it offered a basis for their increasing self-interest, without which accumulating cultural and social capital would be too sinfully tied to the vanity Ryder so hated. In effect, heterodoxy released the economic potential of Puritanism. Curiously, the same revision of the meaning of God and humanity happens in Quakerism—a religion beyond the scope of this book but one whose adherents we should note (as Watts also discovered) show up in the category of the nation's millionaires and half-millionaires at a proportion nearly *fifty* times higher than their proportion in the general population.[40]

The incentive behind greater capital accumulation, to put it another way, was not about a simple secularization of the Protestant ethic; it was about a shifting worldview that remained religious in character, notwithstanding the fact that its rationalism became its more celebrated feature. This is not to say that critics of Weber have been wrong to emphasize the limits Puritanism placed on capitalism. No one tells us about those limits more agonizingly than Ryder himself. But those limits were not antagonistic to *enterprise*, as Watts incorrectly writes; they were antagonistic to *excess*. Nor were ministers like Walker simply laboring at the pulpit to change the meaning of God and man because they operated in the service of protoindustrialists who were antsy to get rich. On the one hand, there is surely an element of truth to Watts's notion that "when, in the second half of the eighteenth century, a Presbyterian minister interpreted his commission 'to teach whatever Christ commanded' in the light of the theology of Arminius, Arius, or even Socinus, rather than of Athanasius or Calvin, he might suffer the departure of a large and orthodox section of his congregation, but he was likely to retain the confidence of the select group of laymen who held the deeds of his meeting-house and hence the key to his chief source of income." But on the other hand, ministers could (and can) accommodate careerism alongside conviction, much as parishioners like Ryder ran through calculations in their thinking about their religion that were far too complicated to be reduced to *either* spiritual *or* material.[41]

And yet, however complex the causes, one outcome of this change was relatively streamlined. The new worldview taking shape at the parish level encouraged the sort of economic life that an earlier generation would have found sinful. This is not to say that the younger generation of tradesmen that Ryder watched come into the world were simply greedy. The charitableness of Unitarians was as conspicuous as their wealth. A fuller discussion of this awaits us in the next and final chapter. But we might once more turn to a sermon of Walker's, in which much of what I have argued here coalesces. Ryder, a month away from his sixty-fifth birthday and obsessing about his inevitable departure from the earth, went to hear Walker speak at Mill Hill after a morning of labor. The springboard for the sermon was 3 John 2: "Beloved, I wish above all things that thou mayest prosper and be in health, even as thy soul prospereth," a line that Walker "Showd looks a little Strange in the reading that the Apostle Should desire health & prosperity above all things for his beloved Gains." The strangeness arose from the apparent notion that prospering in the world was all-important—a notion Ryder consumed a heroic amount of paper and ink in the effort to reject. Walker's interpretation solved the potential problem, however, by encouraging the interpreter (in Ryder's paraphrase) to "Imagine [the Apostle] very desirous of health and prosperity for him who was So Good a man, and who testifyd his Love to the Saints by relieving & Supporting them." It was acceptable for pious men—for the saints—to prosper on earth, in other words. Here Ryder could not help but borrow Walker's Enlightenment vocabulary. "And it is *naturall*," the clothier continued approvingly, "for us to desire the lives of Such Usefull and hospitable men and to desire prosperity for them who make such a good use of their wealth." We simply don't hear Ryder using the word "natural" elsewhere in the diary as a criterion for economic behavior. The message the heterodox minister was delivering, namely, that nature and the Bible converge in sanctioning a *desire* for prosperity, was settling in. But a key part of that message was that aspirations should also in some sense transcend the self. "For when [useful and hospitable] men decay or go back in the world," Walker concluded, "ye poor Suffer." Walker was not crudely saying that greed is good. He was investing admirable men with at least two virtuous qualities: their ability to acquire wealth, and their willingness to make good use of it.[42]

This may be the final reason why Ryder kept attending Mill Hill and Call Lane as they left orthodoxy behind. Having made the case that humans and their savior were of the same basic stuff, it was easier for the new generation of ministers to view the world itself less as a vale of tears than as a place that godly people might improve if given the moral go-ahead to accumulate in unprecedented ways. "Many things were delivered which I could have been glad to have retained but cannot," Ryder finished the entry. No doubt he would have been happier had he held on to the fuller message. Walker was saying, in effect: there is no longer reason to be so double-minded.

# 8. The Making of a Middle-Class Mind

Remove far from me vanity and lies; give me neither poverty nor riches; feed me with food convenient for me; Lest I be full, and deny thee, and say, Who is the LORD? or lest I be poor, and steal, and take the name of God in vain.
—Proverbs, 30:8–9

The man we have gotten to know in this book can admittedly look unusual. He was born posthumously, had no siblings, and lived in a childless marriage that did not begin until he was forty. He held to a fading religion while newer faiths were thriving and knew an urban life not in London but in Leeds, in the northern part of a country celebrated for the south. More anomalous is his self-account, a diary of exceptional length even in a religious culture obsessed with the word. Yet Ryder never encouraged these things that set him apart from others. He wished he had known his father, much as he wanted to be one himself. He longed for siblings and pined for a wife years before he found one. The contraction of his religious culture, however potent the metaphor of nonconformity, was depressing. If Leeds was provincial, he still lived like a traveling salesman. If his diary is immense, it may be a special case only because time is otherwise adept at destroying paper artifacts. What Ryder craved was distance from extremes. He didn't want to stand out. He wanted to fit in the middle.

Like many of his peers, he found his middle way in the various forms of the middling sort: a successful business, a sufficiently sized home, the occasional vacation taken to restore the health, an income allowing for a cushion of wealth. To experience such things did not exactly make him average. Even by the end of his life only a quarter of the country's population achieved the annual earnings—roughly £50 a year on the bottom end—that helped define what contemporaries variously called the middling sort, the middle station, and, increasingly, the middle class. But for various reasons, such an existence became a likelier possibility in the eighteenth century than it had ever been. Overall economic growth after the political and financial revolutions of the late seventeenth century offered more chances for building economic capital. Cultural capital came more easily in a society driven by a Lockean mandate for self-improvement through instruction and training. Relationships made in an expanding public sphere could pay dividends in social capital. And this buildup of capital was only part of the story. In the nation's cash-poor economy an array of credit networks financed everything from local shop keeping and cloth making to overseas ventures in the expanding empire. The family order, built on materialism and morality, gave a workable structure for making and passing down fortunes. For some, a spirit of consumerism rose with disposable income and drove the incentive to acquire—incentive made all the more appealing by the social prospect of entering the ranks of those more easily able to spend. Swelling Britain's "stout midriff" was as critically on the nationalist agenda in the drawn-out contest with the French, from Beachy Head to Waterloo.[1]

Ryder was nonetheless driven to the middle by something more. The relief it offered from the extremes of poverty and excess could benefit his spiritual life. As he put it one night in his forties, thinking about the transactions of yet another busy day, "I was somewhat afraid lest the world and the numerous Concerns of it Should Gain the Ascendant in my affections. On the One hand I am often afraid of Giving way to Such a measure of Ease as may prove my Snare, On the Other hand, I am afraid of too much Care & labour. The middle way which is well Consistent with True Christianity, & real practicall Holyness I would Long after."[2]

The core logic of sentiments like this had a natural ring to it in Ryder's Britain. David Hume, of all people, cited "Agur's Prayer," the proverb that opens this chapter, as he celebrated the middle station "as the most eligible of all others": "The Great are too much immers'd in Pleasure; and the Poor too much occupy'd in providing for the Necessities of Life, to hearken to the calm Voice of Reason. The Middle Station, as it is most happy in many Respects, so particularly in this, that a Man, plac'd in it, can, with the greatest Leisure, consider his own Happiness, and reap a new Enjoyment, from comparing his Situation with that of Persons above or below him."[3] Unlike Ryder, however, Hume cared nothing about a Heaven he didn't believe in. He valued distance from social extremes because it offered a relatively neutral space for making and keeping friends. It gave one a basis, that is, for sociability, which in one variation or another was becoming for more secular-minded British thinkers a means of both materializing and containing self-interest. As Albert Hirschman argued more than thirty years ago, reconceptualizing self-interest as a virtue rather than a vice was one of the major cultural projects and achievements of the eighteenth century, at least for thinkers coming to hold a labor theory of value. The traditional moralists had gotten it wrong, so Hume and others thought. Spiritually decriminalizing desire for gain wouldn't tear society apart but rather virtuously release the labor of individual men and women and empower the economy and nation. But as the various thinkers who inverted morality in their advocacy of the modern capitalist mindset well knew, the ego of *Homo economicus* had to be sublimated socially—to be redefined as a bridle for the passions—in order to avoid the risk of a greed-driven free-for-all. The variations in the answers that some of the major Enlightenment figures gave to the question of how to demoralize self-interest are far from trivial. But the intended effect of each answer was, in one way or another: moderation, the putatively normative goal of reasonable people.[4]

There is no evidence that Ryder was reading the more secular authors who shaped the debate about whether or not self-interest can help society. And could we somehow sit him in a room with Hume, the politeness would no doubt be strained. Sociability stripped of the spiritual was always vapid for Ryder. But even so, the industrious habits that more pious authors like Richard Baxter encouraged—that the Bible itself encouraged if a reader turned to the right pages—potentially led to conflict that was structurally similar to that latent in the demoralization of self-interest. What happened if industry, which moral traditionalists had themselves long praised as a virtue, turned to worldliness and excess?

The pious too had their solution. As we just heard Ryder put it as well as anyone, "the middle way" was "well consistent with . . . good practical holiness." But when the spiritual stakes were so high, when the cost of losing one's balance was so great, such a solution could be much easier to articulate than to perform. Ryder, for one, had no detailed, methodical blueprint for exactly how to pursue economic success. In one sense, this is where watching entered the picture as a habit cultivated to keep one aimed in the right direction. Isaac Ambrose made the obvious choice when he turned to a Latin word for "middle things" to title his diary-keeping guidebook, *Media*. The middle he invoked may have explicitly called to mind a temporal in-betweenness, framed by the cosmic beginning and end. But his metaphysical via media was not simply redolent of the middling sort; it was the very type of high concept that could underpin it, much as in an earlier era the cosmic order of the great chain of being underpinned traditional social hierarchy. Nor is it coincidence or a mere practical outcome of their relative wealth and literacy that spiritual diarists were disproportionately of the middling sort. There is a conscious concern with balance and the via media in the pages of godly self-writing. One study based on 135 early modern spiritual diarists and autobiographers found that "material prosperity was not greeted as the successful achievement of a personal goal." These authors pursued security rather than gain. "In the subjective perspective of reality framed by the middle sort," Michael Mascuch writes, "the openness of the abyss of poverty, into which providence might at any moment cast whole families, was more awesome than the openness of the elite in which individuals might at any moment cast whole families." If salvation was the goal of watching in an ultimate sense, attaining and then sustaining social and economic balance was the reason why one watched while in the middle of things on earth.[5]

But we have also seen that watching brought liability with security. It was an addictive technology of the self, I suggested earlier, because the more one watched—at least in writing, where there is solid evidence of this habit—the more noticeably there were things to watch against. And in the case of trying to lead a moderate life, exactly what counted as equilibrium could be elusive. Too little work led to poverty; too much to temptation. A life of careful moderation could stabilize the double-mindedness brought on by being both self-denying and in *the world*, but the process of discerning this moderation meant confrontation with the uncertainties of subjectivity. Middling folk were, after all, comparatively on their own. They were self-made, and they needed regular self-control, within parameters that were always to some degree self-defined, in order to hold themselves between idleness and worldliness. The image we get from the theorists and the moralists is that advice was given and then simply taken. It is admittedly an image lent support by the way in which the middling sort stood out to contemporary observers because of their voluntary restraint. But we also have to consider the image we get from Ryder, for whom moderation depended on an ability to discern the line between success and excess—an ability, and a line, that was always in some measure in question.[6]

The via media of Ryder's economic life by definition entailed two extremes that needed to be avoided. At one end were poverty and sloth; at the other, worldliness and abundance. The danger was that the industrious habits required to escape the former could easily lead to the latter. But besides watching there was another way to address this problem: charity.

The idea of giving to the poor was nothing new in Ryder's era. The Bible abounds with such advice, as did custom, the literature of practical divinity, sermons, and so on. We just heard Thomas Walker warn in the previous chapter that if prosperous men did not make good use of their wealth, the poor would suffer. What is interesting about Ryder's broader milieu is that some religious authorities could offer actual quantified advice about how to give. The philanthropically minded Restoration Dissenter Thomas Gouge argued in his widely read tract on charity that the more liberally a man gave away his money, "the more likely he is to thrive and prosper in the world." Gouge explained that his father gave one-seventh of his yearly income toward "maintaining poor scholars at the university . . . poor families, and distressed persons." Gouge himself gave away a third of his income. The London merchant William Pennoyer, Gouge approvingly wrote, donated £150 "to poor ministers, widows and others in distress," £20 to his poor tenants, £800 in woolen cloth and other commodities to his distressed kin in New England, and so on.[7]

It is hard to know if such advice was followed with numerical precision. The Essex minister and spiritual diarist Ralph Josselin, whose anxiety, like Ryder's, rose with his wealth, was willing to part with around 10 percent of his annual income, less than what Gouge suggested (though Josselin was also a man of relatively modest means). Ryder for that matter never disclosed a numerical measure of his altruism. But it is not only clear from a couple of unmistakable allusions in the diary that Ryder actually read Gouge; it is clear that as the diary begins he could be particularly anxious about how much was enough. On finding his worldly concerns "a great hinderance to Divine Meditation," he recalled Christ's advice to a young man to sell everything and give to the poor in order to find treasure in heaven. "Taxing myself with Such a Question, Corrupt nature was ready to say this is a hard Saying. Who can bear it?" And if the dilemma lessened as time went on, it was mostly the accidental result of childlessness, which worked to Ryder's advantage as it did to that of many others who freely gave away their surplus wealth. As Ryder once explained, he was "by Providence fixt in a capacity of Publick Usefulness by a Blessing upon my affairs and Concerns of Life" because he "had fewer family necessities than many others."[8]

The individual believer not only bore the ultimate responsibility of coming up with the calculus—Gouge himself ultimately not very helpfully wrote that "a charitable heart, with the help of prudence, is the best judge of the due proportion which we should give"; it was necessary to consistently assess true intentions in sometimes tricky situations. Gouge claimed, for example, that spending on luxuries could entail indirect benefits, as when a person might "entertain powerful men sumptuously in order to escape their displeasure and be able to do more good later." But when we find Ryder in exactly such a situation, the outcome was unsettling. A week after his first mention of charity in the diary—had he just read Gouge?—he found a moment to write while waiting for "Some few Guests of a Superiour Rank." Their arrival demanded that he "put upon Suitable preparations for their Entertainment," and he calmly admitted to being "led a little to meditate upon that preparation which was Daily made for the Rich and Great," which prompted the "Conclusion in my own mind, to Chose Rather, with Jacob to be a Plain man Dwelling in Fonts, with plain & Comfortable accomadations, rather than Enjoy all that Grandure which the World with all its fullness was Capable of Affording." Before the guests had arrived, in other words, it was easy enough for Ryder to mute social envy with a mantra on the virtues of moderation. But the next day, with the previous night's event in his memory instead of on the horizon, the tone of his voice had changed. His heart was now filled with "Great Stirrings of Corruption & Niblings at the Bait of Temptation, Insomuch that I am Sometimes ready to Question my State being Good and Thought what Sin and Guilt and Hypocrisy I was Guilty of for Begging God's Assistance against Sin & not using my best Endeavours against it, & Considered that tho' no human Eye Could see the Wandering of my heart after Sin and Vanity, Yet God Judgeth Thro the Thick Cloud, & knew my most Secret hypocrisy." Ryder seemed to accept the same logic Gouge used—mixing with social superiors might bring wealth that could later be used providentially. But in real time, in the midst of the sociable means that might serve a greater end, he was wracked by feelings of sin and vanity.[9]

The largest theme of the pious advice to be philanthropic was, however, that charity was not a mindless way of paying spiritual taxes. If Ryder did not get this from Gouge himself—although that's nearly unthinkable—he undoubtedly got it from Thomas Whitaker. Charity, the Call Lane minister preached, was a more important part of spiritual experience than faith and hope. Faith and hope were "instrumentall graces," or so Whitaker once reasoned from the book of Corinthians, since they could help one secure salvation, while charity was an "abiding grace . . . a lovely and benevolent frame, a love both to God and Man." Whitaker was consistent on this point, and Ryder's internalization of the message reappears in the diary. "This Day we had the excellency of charity set forth as being greater or exceeding Faith or hope," he wrote in the late 1740s as he approvingly summarized yet another Whitaker sermon. "For if we had faith . . . we could remove mountains & had not Charity it would profit us nothing, If we gave our bodies to be burned, or all our goods to feed the poor and had not charity, it would not profitt. Charity exceeds faith & hope in its duration for faith & hope tho necessary graces are but temporary one[s], for when this life ends faith is turned into vision and hope into fruition but charity and love is the employment of heaven. . . . Many excellent things were said of Charity, Oh that I may enjoy it." That charity is part of the "employment of heaven" is a particularly loaded phrase. Whitaker seems to be telling us (through his watchful amanuensis) that his congregation was so obsessed with work that they could never be at rest, even in the hereafter. They did not just conflate work and life. They conflated work and the afterlife, where charity would be the next stage of labor, the eternal promotion.[10]

Ryder nevertheless did not wait for Heaven to share his rewards with others. The diary is filled with bits of evidence of an earnest willingness to relieve the distressed. Earlier in this book we came across his reference in 1733 to a local woman giving birth to "three living children," a "wonderfull" event that also brought on a financial burden he hoped he was prepared to reduce. In 1740 he again came to the relief of a "tender mother weeping over the necessitys of her children, which at first," he frankly recorded, "did not much affect me." Or in 1749 he donated clothes to a shabbily dressed man whom he also welcomed into his house. In some sense even his family was a sort of charitable institution, if also one whose labor he had the option to exploit. When he adopted the Arey sisters after their parents died, he saved them from an undoubtedly worse fate, given that the alternative was the workhouse. Or when he took in people from the woeful workhouse, whose officials routinely tried to apprentice young boys and girls to the town's trades, it is hard to imagine those souls were not better off in Ryder's home. There is something to be said for a lesser form of exploitation.[11]

Ryder's heart could also occasionally turn cold. At the height of the winter in 1738 he had to undertake the "unpleasant work" of "selling up a poor mans Goods, which left the wife in a poor and low condition." However unpleasant the task, God and the law demanded punishment for certain debtors. "This was but for the payment of a Just Debt . . . the law was made for the Lawless and Disobedient." Reasoning so helped "much to reconcile me to the proceeding." Ryder could similarly be less than enthusiastic even as he felt the urge to be altruistic. In the fall of 1747, "with the Advice & Consent of my wife I made somewhat of a liberal contribution to the relief or comfortable supply of a Christian Friend, Yet had not that Inward Satisfaction which I have had at other times upon like Occasions, which rais'd my Syspicion that perhaps [charity] was not so properly bestow'd as it might perhaps have been done, Or that I had not done it with a proper disposition of spirit." Two years later, while Elisabeth was still alive and his business was flourishing, he admitted to having "some little struggle in my mind about the proportioning [of] my acts of benevolence to the poor . . . I look upon it as my bounden duty as a steward of the talents with which God entrusts me to help to bear others burthens in order to the fulfilling of the Law of Christ, and as God gives me ability [I long] to find my self more and more a chearfull giver, being sensible that without this it is no acceptable service in the sight of God. I took a small survey into my effects, & found all well blessed by God. Oh that my heart may be enlarged in praise as God enlarges his bounty towards me."[12]

By the time he wrote this last entry, Ryder already may have been tasked with distributing Call Lane's charities. We never know the date when he was given this role, nor does he ever tell us his official position, but even without such details it is safe to assume that he had become a deacon of the church, and by the 1750s it is clear that the church had entrusted him with its relief funds. Parting with money was no longer a dilemma. Now the problem was the parsimony of others. In the late 1750s, amid Ryder's allusions to declining trade, he and a neighbor went door to door to ask several people for aid for another neighbor "who had been exposing or designing to expose goods to sale contrary to some law now in force and was compell'd by some officer to pay the full sum of ten pounds, & is hereby impoverished." Two days later, Ryder and his friend resumed seeking relief but met with "indifferent success. . . . I saw it plainly appear that one who we esteem'd very able to give offer'd so small that it was refus'd by my partner, tho we commonly say beggars are not to be choosers." The comment sounds like the beginning of his resignation to failure. But he underlined his seriousness about giving by recalling how much charity had meant to Elisabeth during her life. The common saying that beggars can't be choosers, he explained in his capacity as a beggar for the charitable relief of others, "brings to my mind a Remark of my Dear deceased wife's who ranked covetousness among the greatest of crimes because it hardened the heart against relieving the most deplorably necessitous."[13]

In doling out Call Lane's funds Ryder still had to distinguish between the deserving and undeserving poor. His compassion ultimately triumphs in his outlook, but not without the occasional struggle. On a day mostly "taken up without business belonging to trade, As I am employ'd in distributing a part of the churches charity," he found himself at "Severall houses of the poor" where he "saw many objects which may well draw out pity and Compassion." The disappearance of the grammatical subject in that last clause seems deliberate, as if he is saying that such scenes of poverty could easily draw out pity and compassion in some people, but not necessarily in him. "How far charity or almsgiving is Consistent with Christian prudence is as I Judge hard to determine," he continued while wondering about the prudence—the moral economic validity—of persisting in giving money to people in such dire straits. "But when I saw severall persons who had liv'd till they Seemingly could take no pleasure in things here, In all probability weary of the world, especially such to whom they are or may become burthensome the world weary of them, Oh what a call is here for Christian patience."[14]

In one way or another, these comments cohere with the image we have seen develop throughout this book: Ryder approached even this greatest of Christian virtues with the sort of moderation characteristic of an emerging middle class that had made its place in the world through the hard work it sought to encourage in others. "We are far from the Example of the primitive Christians who for one anothers relief had all things common," he once reasoned after relieving a person in distress. The point was to "be enabled to use the World so as not to abuse it, & to be as charitable as opportunity & ability will allow." But what else is clear in these entries is that charity and the middle state where charity helped one to stay positioned offered a solution to

the tension between this and the other world. The younger Unitarian clothiers and merchants in Leeds may have embraced the sort of religion that
could justify more brazen self-interest—and they too could still see themselves as middling if the parameters defining the top and bottom had also
shifted. But even as Ryder continued to work in ways that demanded the
profit-seeking calculations of businessmen, he ultimately remained faithful
to a mode of spirituality premised on self-denial. "My reasons within my
Self, I think are Somewhat plausible, If the Great heart Searcher does but See
Sincerity in them," he wrote in his sixties, still delivering a message to himself
whose repetition imparts its ongoing necessity. "I am hoping hereby to
become more usefull and helpful to others in need by Self denyall and would
earnestly pray that God will fitt me and prepare for all events, mercifull or
afflictive, That I may never be lifted up by prosperity, nor too much dejected
in adversity, but be enabled in every Station of life to behave my Self."[15]

One of the few concrete facts known about Ryder's well-behaved life comes
from the ad for his property placed in the newspaper several months after his
death. This was his final address, at the head of Marsh Lane "where it joins
the turnpike to York," a spot now occupied by a boarded-up Catholic church
and overshadowed by a flyover on the A64. When Ryder lived here, this was
the northeast edge of Leeds. Fifty years later this general area east of Marsh
Lane and Beckett Street had been reduced to slums following the migration
of elites to the west side of town and the north of England's first planned
suburb, built to create distance from the very working poor who in Ryder's
era had often lived in cottages in the backyards of the homes of wealthy
merchants. After the potato famine, thousands of Irish Catholic immigrants
came to the neighborhood, mostly textiles workers, whose low-rent cramped
housing was soon surrounded by factories. Early in the next century,
major demolitions made room for the Quarry Hill Flats, once the largest
social housing project in the country, erected outside the ghost of Ryder's
southerly windows. In the 1970s, these homes too met the demolition crews,
and now Ryder's former vista looks out onto planned estate housing in a
setting that an early-twenty-first-century architectural guide to the city
describes as "open space, semi-derelict industrial land or . . . decimated by
road schemes."[16]

In the process of urban destruction and renewal, still unfolding in front
of an audience traveling on the highway at speeds unknown to the eighteenth

century, the home where Ryder and his family lived and labored is irrevo-
cably buried under an industrial layer, now itself yielding to a landscape
intended to be "postindustrial." But not quite a hundred feet beyond the A64,
alongside the northern perimeter of Ryder's former property, a road fewer
than five hundred feet long runs parallel to the highway, serendipitously
bearing the name "Rider Street." Since he had no namesake heirs and his
estate was up for sale in 1768, the reference seems unmistakable. The likeliest
explanation is that Ryder's collateral descendents who rose in political power
during the nineteenth century, the Lupton family, wanted to pay homage to
their pious cousin and used their influence to place him in public memory.[17] If
so, they were less than successful. Any evidence of this clothier who was
obscure to begin with was edged closer to the abyss after his death, as his
honorific street spelled with an "i" failed to capture the way he actually identified himself with a "y" on paper. And yet the fact that Ryder is still—but
only barely still—visible on the city map graphically captures the spirit in
which he lived. He was a self-effacing presence, limiting his economic
achievements while finding uncommon success, anticipating early death
while surpassing the average length of life, unsure of the value of his diary
while ensuring its survival, suppressing his ego while featuring himself in
poetry and prose. It takes an arsenal of qualifiers to tell a story of a life so
embodied by tension, contrast, and ambivalence.

Once again, this also makes Ryder sound like Weber's missing case
study: driven yet anxious, accumulating yet ascetic, self-interested yet self-
denying. But to quote Albert Hirschman, Weber was ultimately "interested
in the psychological processes through which some groups of men became
single-minded in the rational pursuit of capitalist accumulation."[18] This book
has meant to show what Ryder was, hand-wringing and all, at the expense of
where he leads. And even as his ambivalence may have found some stability
in the episodic triumphs in his quest for balance, it should be clear that was he
never single-minded.

I don't say this to deprive that ambivalence of the significance it holds
outside of his immediate time and place. It is rather that, finally, Marx may be
the more fitting founder of discursivity than Weber. Not because of Marx's
materialist explanation of change, but because, as the historian of economic
thought Robert Heilbroner once wrote, "the key to Marx's penetrative insight
lies elsewhere, in his perception that the concealed essence of capitalism is its
own forgotten past, its long-disappeared history."[19] Despite the structures

erected in Marx's name, the tireless recovery of economic life that he encouraged is, eventually, a call to search for ordinary people whose voices resonate with more fellow feeling than the undertones of tectonic shifts. The object of such recovery should hold most of the rewards, as is true of Ryder, who is worth hearing in all of his specificity, and who in any case could never tell us everything worth knowing about capitalism. Yet this obscure figure still points to something critical about its essence. Watchfulness, middling mindedness, selflessness in an acquisitive society—these religiously driven habits were expressions and instruments of self-control, which was itself the linchpin of early modern Britain's precocious, stable, imitable, and—for its eventual global supremacy—indispensable middle class. By endeavoring for so long to regulate himself, Ryder's double vision of this and the other world could occasionally come into focus as he held himself between extremes, in the space in the middle that offered compromise between his faith and fortunes. From there he could pursue sufficient prosperity, feel a measure of spiritual assurance, and augment the wealth of the nation. It sounds like a bourgeois success story, and by some standards it is. But the self-control that this pious middling type could project, like the balance he might achieve between ambition and sacrifice, was also made possible by decades of anguish and spiritual agony, hidden away in the pages of a nearly forgotten diary.

Ryder and his revelations were nevertheless about more than either passivity or struggle. When his recorded life is taken as a whole, he also offers something like analysis. He saw the economy as tied to the beginning of eternal life or the end of his soul, and it was up to human agency to ensure quiet success. Even as his needs were aimed heavenward, he expresses a social vision in his praise of the virtues of a middle class that offers both defense against greed and assistance for the poor. His self-reflection tuned him in, often painfully, to what he was doing with his commercial life and to the ways in which he might do better both materially and morally. And he regularly held up images in his diary pages of the watershed that saw the new economy abandon the old moral psychology as the limits that tradition placed on acquisitiveness became unworkable. He never used these words in apposition, but from his own angle of vision Ryder was as aware as anyone of the capacity of capitalism for creative destruction.

None of this makes him a perfect hero for the twenty-first century. Restoring his spiritual outlook would be as dissonant as resurrecting an eighteenth-century house in the shadow of a freeway. The Dissenters of

Joseph Priestley's generation were not clueless for unmooring their modernizing, self-expansive, and egalitarian hopes from a religion so easily defined by self-loathing and anxiety. But that doesn't mean that, in the end, Ryder's perspective offers us nothing. We still listen to eighteenth-century British voices telling us about the economic system that they did so much to invent, and we should add this clothier to the chorus, spirituality and all. It was because he was so pious and productive—so attuned to the danger of idols he ultimately helped to erect—that he knew what he was seeing as he watched the market becoming as totalizing and totemic as his religion.

# Acknowledgments

I wrote the first draft of this book at Brown University, where I also started amassing debts to the people who made the process easier. Tim Harris supervised my dissertation, taught me most of what I know about early modern England, and was still saving me from errors on the eve of sending off the final manuscript. Philip Benedict pressed me to look carefully into many things, but especially Calvinism and the Reformed tradition, and Joan Richards, my unofficial fourth reader, made me think more seriously about audience and the piety of Unitarians. I was also given generous financial aid by Brown's graduate school, history department, and program in early modern and Renaissance studies.

Correspondents and participants at conferences and lectures (at Brown University, Harvard University, Hobart and William Smith Colleges (HWS), Tufts University, UCLA, and Worcester Polytechnic Institute) have offered advice—big and small, and always in some sense influential—as they have read parts or all of the manuscript or heard me talk about bits and pieces of it. Whether or not they all agree with everything I've written, I thank, in particular, Joyce Appleby, Deborah Cohen, Carlo Ginzburg, Jeremy Gregory, Michael Grossberg, Pat Hudson, Lynn Hunt, Mary Lindemann, Deirdre McCloskey, Susan Pedersen, John Pocock, Guenther Roth, Catherine Secretan, Ethan Shagan, John Smail, Francesca Trivalleto, Deborah Valenze, Richard Wilson, Keith Wrightson, Mary Yeager, and several anonymous readers from *The American Historical Review,* my tenure committee, and Yale University Press.

I've been supported in various ways by every one of my departmental colleagues at HWS, but I've placed a special burden on Derek Linton, who read and made detailed notes on much of the manuscript, and Dan Singal, who also read several chapters and helped this book to see the light of day. My editors at Yale University Press—Laura Davulis, Chris Rogers, Jeffrey

Schier, and Christina Tucker—along with my friend Matt Gallaway, have to be thanked for simplifying the complex process of publication, much as Jessie Dolch must be thanked for her careful copyediting. Brett Harrison, formerly of the West Yorkshire Archives Service; Dorothy Clayton, Suzanne Fagan, John Hodgson, Peter Knockles, and John Woodhouse at the John Rylands Library in Manchester; and many other librarians at the British Library, Brown, Cornell University (where extended borrowing privileges were made possible by a series of fellowships through the Institute for European Studies), Harvard, HWS, the University of Leeds, the University of Rochester, the Thoresby Society, and Yale helped me during my research and book preparation. So did several undergraduate research assistants—Meghan Abbott, Nate Barickman, Moira O'Neill, and Ashley Yang—and the money to pay them, thanks to internal faculty research grants; Helle Folkersen, Alexander Lock, and Naomi Taback greatly helped with research overseas. Among my own teachers, I hope it is not invidious to single out Bill Beauchamp, John Lewis, and John-Paul Riquelme for their lessons in critical reading; Serge Kappler, who offered a model of clarity to me as an undergraduate and then took time twenty years later to read pieces of the book manuscript; William B. Taylor, who more than anyone helped me to believe I might become a historian; and the late Robert Heilbroner, who, along with my father George, never got to read a page of this book but was an ever-present face in its imagined audience.

I'm grateful to all of my students over the past decade—at Brown, Harvard, and HWS—for giving me a better sense of how to try to write for an audience made up, in part, of people like them. I'm no less grateful to my daughter Iris for coming into the world after I had written the final sentence. And in ways too varied to detail, I'm as indebted to a number of friends and colleagues for helping me to think through specific issues the book raises: Steve Albini, Matthew Barnhart, Chris Brokaw, Leslie Brokaw, Andy Cohen, Michael Dahlquist, Mike Donofrio, Laura Free, Melanie Gustin, Sara Hallisey, Irakli Kakabadze, Eric Klaus, Josh McKay, Mischo McKay, Tim Midyett, Colby Ristow, Nick Ruth, Peter Schmidt, James Woodard, Kim Woodard, Leigh Yetter, and not least, my brother, Bubba.

My wife, Claire, has helped me think through all kinds of things for more than a decade; she's also one of the most careful readers I've been lucky enough to have. The same goes for my mother, Lou, whose eyes miss nothing on the page and whose endurance as a listener is heroic. I hope these two women know that what I owe them can't be put into words. I hope the same is true for the person to whom I dedicate this book. Margaret Jacob turned me on to Ryder's diary after she rescued it, for all intents and purposes, from obscurity. She read the dissertation and manuscript and helped me to make sense of the diary in an article on Ryder and Weber that she and I coauthored in 2003. She gave me several chances to talk about my work publicly and generously shared her notes and resources. Without her unbounded support, this book would have never been written.

# Appendix 1. Ryder's Diary Volumes

Ryder wrote just over 12,350 pages and, based on the averages below, two and a half million words. I derived the data in the "words per volume" column by averaging the number of lines on four pages that are evenly spread out in each volume. I then selected a page in each volume that itself contained this average number of lines and chose from it four lines at random in order to draw an average word count per line. I multiplied this number by the average number of lines per page and the total inscribed pages per volume (a more exact number) to arrive at the approximate number of words per volume. To determine approximate words per page I multiplied average words per line with average lines per page.

These are obviously rough numbers, but it is still worth noting some of the impressions they suggest. One is that Ryder grew more affectionate for writing as he aged. His first twenty volumes, which contain 5,578 pages, cover nineteen and a half years while the second twenty volumes, 6,777 pages, cover fifteen years. Since he produced a manuscript, it is necessary to account for possible changes in his handwriting and line spacing. In what may be additional testament to his constancy and diligence, the number of words he wrote per page did not discernibly change as a consequence of age or diminishing eyesight. His handwriting was actually more consistently small in later years (had he gotten eyeglasses?). Note too that Ryder wrote more largely and using fewer words per entry in volumes 11 through 22. These volumes cover years—1742–1754—when his business was booming, his marriage was happy, and his experience was slightly less marked by death, at least as indicated by his funeral lists.

| Volume no. | Dates covered | Size (in.) | Pages | Words | Words per page |
|---|---|---|---|---|---|
| 1 | May 25, 1733–Apr. 13, 1734 | 6.5 × 8 | 278 | 51,152 | 184 |
| 2 | Apr. 14, 1734–Feb. 23, 1734/35 | 6.5 × 8 | 273 | 48,048 | 176 |
| 3 | Feb. 24, 1734/35–Nov. 2, 1735 | 7.5 × 9.5 | 162 | 42,120 | 260 |
| 4 | Nov. 3, 1735–Dec. 31, 1736 | 6.5 × 8 | 274 | 59,184 | 216 |
| 5 | Jan. 1, 1736/37–May 23, 1738 | 6.5 × 8 | 276 | 66,240 | 240 |
| 6 | May 24, 1738–Apr. 15, 1739 | 7.5 × 9.5 | 180 | 34,560 | 192 |
| 7 | Apr. 16, 1739–Feb. 1, 1739/40 | 7.5 × 9.5 | 174 | 37,584 | 216 |
| 8 | Feb. 2, 1739/40–Nov. 23, 1740 | 7.5 × 9.5 | 180 | 48,600 | 270 |
| 9 | Nov. 24, 1740–Feb. 5, 1741/42 | 6.5 × 8 | 266 | 57,456 | 216 |
| 10 | Feb. 6, 1741/42–Nov. 28, 1742 | 7.5 × 9.5 | 176 | 39,424 | 224 |
| 11 | Nov. 29, 1742–Feb. 26, 1743/44 | 7.5 × 9.5 | 186 | 35,712 | 192 |
| 12 | Feb. 27, 1743/44–June 28, 1745 | 6.5 × 8 | 276 | 52,164 | 189 |
| 13 | June 29, 1745–Nov. 1, 1746 | 6.5 × 8 | 370 | 62,160 | 168 |
| 14 | Nov. 2, 1746–Oct. 25, 1747 | 6.5 × 8 | 353 | 59,304 | 168 |
| 15 | Oct. 26, 1747–Aug. 12, 1748 | 6.5 × 8 | 278 | 38,920 | 140 |
| 16 | Aug. 13, 1748–June 10, 1749 | 6.5 × 8 | 382 | 58,828 | 154 |
| 17 | June 11, 1749–Apr. 4, 1750 | 6.5 × 8 | 375 | 63,000 | 168 |
| 18 | Apr. 5, 1750–Feb. 5, 1750/51 | 6.5 × 8 | 378 | 52,920 | 140 |
| 19 | Feb. 6, 1750/51–Dec. 1, 1751 | 6.5 × 8 | 356 | 54,824 | 154 |
| 20 | Dec. 2, 1751–Nov. 7, 1752 | 6.5 × 8 | 385 | 64,680 | 168 |
| 21 | Nov. 8, 1752–Sept. 19, 1753 | 6.5 × 8 | 373 | 77,211 | 207 |
| 22 | Sept. 20, 1753–July 27, 1754 | 6.5 × 8 | 374 | 77,418 | 207 |
| 23 | July 28, 1754–May 21, 1755 | 6.5 × 8 | 377 | 94,250 | 250 |
| 24 | May 22, 1755–Dec. 31, 1755 | 6.5 × 8 | 283 | 58,581 | 207 |
| 25 | Jan. 1, 1756–Nov. 3, 1756 | 6.5 × 8 | 377 | 74,646 | 198 |
| 26 | Nov. 4, 1756–Sept. 4, 1757 | 6.5 × 8 | 378 | 78,246 | 207 |
| 27 | Sept. 5, 1757–Apr. 5, 1758 | 6.5 × 8 | 270 | 53,460 | 198 |
| 28 | Apr. 6, 1758–Sept. 4, 1758 | 7.5 × 9.5 | 184 | 36,432 | 198 |
| 29 | Sept. 5, 1758–July 8, 1759 | 6.5 × 8 | 376 | 77,832 | 207 |
| 30 | July 9, 1759–Dec. 2, 1759 | 7.5 × 9.5 | 183 | 35,136 | 192 |
| 31 | Dec. 3, 1759–Oct. 12, 1760 | 6.5 × 8 | 374 | 87,516 | 234 |

| | | | | | |
|---|---|---|---|---|---|
| 32 | Oct. 13, 1760–Aug. 12, 1761 | 6.5 × 8 | 377 | 94,250 | 250 |
| 33 | Aug. 13, 1761–Jan. 11, 1762 | 7.5 × 9.5 | 185 | 44,400 | 240 |
| 34 | Jan. 12, 1762–Nov. 12, 1762 | 6.5 × 8 | 369 | 84,870 | 230 |
| 35 | Nov. 13, 1762–Sept. 25, 1763 | 6.5 × 8 | 378 | 85,050 | 225 |
| 36 | Sept. 26, 1763–Aug. 3, 1764 | 6.5 × 8 | 378 | 49,500 | 250 |
| 37 | Aug. 4, 1764–May 28, 1765 | 6.5 × 8 | 410 | 94,300 | 230 |
| 38 | May 29, 1765–Apr. 4, 1766 | 6.5 × 8 | 371 | 90,480 | 240 |
| 39 | Apr. 5, 1766–Feb. 1, 1767 | 6.5 × 8 | 373 | 85,790 | 230 |
| 40 | Feb. 2, 1767–Dec. 17, 1767 | 6.5 × 8 | 372 | 89,280 | 240 |
| 41 | Dec. 18, 1767–Jan. 3, 1768 | 6.5 × 8 | 15 | 3,450 | 230 |

# Appendix 2. Deaths and Burials

Ryder's avidly kept record of deaths and burials of the congregants of Call
Lane and Mill Hill makes the diary a valuable source of information on
Leeds's Dissenter population because many names recorded here are absent
from the parish register or other official documents. The "Register of the
Day & Year of the Baptism of the Churche's Children" (The National
Archives, Public Record Office, RG4/3674), which the churches produced,
does not include deaths. For those people whose names also appear in the
parish register, Ryder on occasion offers a few other pieces of information:
age at death and time of burial, both of which are consistently missing from
the parish records; and cause of death, which the parish records only record
from 1764 on, and then typically in cases involving physical disorders.
However much his labors were partly driven by his own fear of death, Ryder
took on an important community responsibility by recording all these names.

Ryder's funeral lists at the back of many of his volumes are incomplete
when compared with the diary as a whole. The following list of roughly
three hundred names has therefore been compiled from both the diary's back
material and main entries. Information in brackets represents what can be
gleaned from the parish register and typically concerns the neighborhood
where the person in question lived. Also in brackets are spelling variations or
other discrepancies between the parish and Ryder's records, neither of which
should automatically be assumed to be correct, though Ryder's attendance at
many funerals about which discrepancies exist suggests his familiarity with
the person in question. I have excluded from this list a handful of deaths that
Ryder noted (the death of George II, for example) that have no direct
relationship to the population in and around Leeds.

## *Abbreviations and Symbol Key*

| | |
|---|---|
| f.d. | Funeral discourse |
| * | Name also mentioned in Leeds Parish Register |
| † | Joseph Ryder in attendance |
| †† | Joseph and Elisabeth Ryder in attendance |
| (†)† | Elisabeth attended without Joseph |
| ††† | Joseph, Elisabeth, and Joseph's mother, Mary, in attendance |
| (†)(†)† | Mary but neither Joseph nor Elisabeth in attendance |
| ‡ | Joseph invited but did not attend |

| Name of deceased | Residence | Age | Cause of death | Attendees | Date of death (d.)/burial (b.) |
|---|---|---|---|---|---|
| Mrs Airey | | | | | d. Mar. 30; b. Apr. 2, 1739 |
| Jane Altha | | | "sudden death" | | d. Aug. 24, 1748 |
| Mrs Ambler | | 86 | | | b. Jan. 17, 1761 |
| anon. child | | | | † | b. Feb. 25, 1752 |
| anon. child | | | | | d. Jan. 18, 1761 |
| anon. "young boy" | | | "short illness" | | d. Feb. 25, 1742 |
| anon. "young man" | | | "sudden death" | | d. Feb. 14, 1742 |
| Mrs Anslessey | | | | | d. June 20, 1760 |
| Linda Arey | | "under 17" | | † | d. Mar. 9, 1742 |
| Joseph Armitage | | | | | d. Jan. 19, 1750 |
| Child of Stephen Ashburn | Holbeck | | | † | b. Sept. 25, 1740 |
| William Askwith | | | | | d. Feb. 27, 1761 |

| Name of deceased | Residence | Age | Cause of death | Attendees | Date of death (d.)/burial (b.) |
|---|---|---|---|---|---|
| Daughter of Nathan Atkinson | | | | ‡ | b. Oct. 31, 1744 |
| Mary Atkinson | | | | | b. Mar. 2, 1739 |
| *Nathan Atkinson | [Headrow] | | | † | b. May 22, 1738 [d. May 20, 1738] |
| Son of Nathan Atkinson | | | | † | b. Nov. 3, 1744 |
| James Bailey | | | | † | b. Mar. 11, 1740/41 |
| *Mary Balmer [Bowmer] | [Northall Bridge] | 81 | | † | b. Aug. 5, 1762 |
| *William Barley [Batley] | [Kirkgate] | | | † | b. Jan. 1, 1743 |
| Alice Batley | | | | † | b. Apr. 6, 1739 |
| John Batley | | | | | d. Dec. 13, 1760 |
| *Joseph Batley | | 43 | illness | † | d. Mar. 27, 1760 [b. Mar. 29] |
| *Sarah Battey | | | | | d. Apr. 21, 1735 [b. Apr. 22, 1735] |
| Jane Baynes | | 44 | | † | July 14, 1767 |
| Eldest son of Joseph Baynes | | 9 | | † | b. Sept. 25, 1752 |
| *Joseph Beamont | [Bank] | | | ‡ | b. Sept. 4, 1743 |
| *Child of Joseph Beaumont [daughter of J. Beaumont] | | | | † | b. Dec. 24, 1760 |
| *Sarah Beckwith | [Workhouse] | | | | b. Jan. 30, 1739 |
| George Bell | | | | | d. Mar. 10, 1760 |
| "beloved child of a neighbours" | | | | † | b. Feb. 26, 1750 |

| | | | | |
|---|---|---|---|---|
| Ruth Bentley | | | | d. June 22, 1749 |
| Samuel Bentley | | | † | b. Apr. 30, 1755 |
| Benjamin Bibby | | | | b. Apr. 30, 1755 |
| Daughter of Benjamin Bibby | "a child" | | † | b. May 28, 1741 |
| William Blith | | | | b. Feb. 3, 1742 |
| *Phe[o]be Bridgewater | | | † | b. Sept. 14, 1741 |
| *James Brown | [Quarryhill] | | †† | b. Dec. 18, 1743 |
| *Joseph Brown | | | † | b. Apr. 8, 1743 |
| Daughter of William Burn | | | | b. Aug. 20, 1760 |
| Daughter of William Burn | | | | b. May 2, 1761 |
| *Benjamin Burnley [Burley] | [Bank] | | | d. Dec. 23, 1748 |
| *James Burnley | [Workhouse] | | | b. Mar. 31, 1739 |
| Joseph Burnley | | | | d. Dec. 23, 1748 |
| Son of Mrs Bush | | | | d. Oct. 4, 1760 |
| Son of Mr Cadman | | | | b. Aug. 21, 1760 |
| *Martha Capitt [Cupid] | | childbirth | † | d. (morning) and b. (evening) Aug. 3, 1735 |
| *Wife of Joshua Chapman [Anne] | | | †† | b. Mar. 2, 1742 |
| Joseph Chapman | | | †† | b. Oct. 15, 1743 |
| A "Christian Friend" | | | | d. Mar. 5, 1742 |
| Mr Cowell, "a man in ye neighbourhood" | | | | d. Sept. 10; b. Sept. 11, 1755 |
| Mrs Cowell | | | † | b. June 12, 1745 |
| *Margaret Craven | [Marsh Lane] | [old age] | † | b. Feb. 5, 1765 |

| Name of deceased | Residence | Age | Cause of death | Attendees | Date of death (d.)/burial (b.) |
|---|---|---|---|---|---|
| *W. Craven [William] | | 77 | | † | b. Mar. 12, 1762 |
| Christopher Darnton | | | | | b. Feb. 2, 1739 |
| John Darnton | | 49 | | † | b. May 3, 1759 |
| Mrs Darnton | | | | † | b. Dec. 16, 1761 |
| Susannah Darnton | | | | ††† | b. Mar. 5, 1742 |
| Joseph Davison | | 8 | short illness | † | b. Feb. 23, 1742 |
| Grace Denison | | | | ††, Olive Arey | b. Jan. 7, 1743 |
| Joseph, son of Jonathan Denison | | | | †, Joseph Ryder (Ryder's cousin) and William Moult | b. Feb. 23, 1742 |
| *Joseph Denison | [Marsh Lane] | | | † | b. Dec. 11, 1743 |
| Joseph Denison | | | | † | b. Aug. 29, 1760 |
| Robert Dixon, son of Joseph | | | | Henry Ibitson | b. Nov. 7, 1742 |
| *Sarah Dodgsham [Dodgson] | [Weetwood] | | | † | b. Dec. 16, 1741 |
| Samuell Dodgson | | | | † | b. May 23, 1745 |
| Thomas Dodgson | | | | † | b. May 26, 1756 |
| *John Dove [Joseph Dove] | [Mill Hill] | | | † | b. Nov. 14, 1756 |
| Mrs Dunswell | | | | | d. Apr. 23, 1761 |
| *Child of Mr Ellis [daughter of Robert Ellis] | [Upper head Row] | | | | b. Oct. 2, 1758 |
| Thomas Elsworth | | | "after a long illness" | | b. July 21, 1767 |

| | | | | |
|---|---|---|---|---|
| Grandchild of Matthew Erinshaw | | 3 | † | b. June 13, 1763 |
| Lydia Falkiner [Falkner] | [Mabgate] | | † | b. Jan. 24, 1744 |
| *Son of John Fearnside[s] | [Bank] | | † | b. Dec. 22, 1760 |
| Mary Frankland | | "short sickness" | † | b. Feb. 13, 1734 |
| Wife of John Gales | | | | b. Feb. 10, 1740 |
| James Garnett | | "ancient" | † | d. Jan. 19; b. Jan 20, 1748 |
| John Gergson | | 86 | † | b. Sept. 11, 1756 |
| George Gillam | Leeds | suicide by hanging | | d. Aug. 6, 1754 |
| *Lydia Gilpin | [Bank] | | † | b. May 21, 1742 |
| *Jonathan Gray | [Bank] | | | d. May 10, 1761 [b. May 12] |
| Son of Joseph Gregson | | | † | b. Oct. 31, 1760 |
| *Grace Gutherick [Goodrick] | [Mabgate] | | † | b. Feb. 1, 1737 |
| *Lydia Gutherick [Goodrick] | [Mabgate] | | † | b. Oct. 21, 1744 |
| *Hannah Hague [Haigh] | [Kirkgate] | | ‡ | b. Jan. 25, 1744 |
| Widdow Hall | | | † | b. Mar. 14, 1756 |
| *Elizabeth Hallyday | [Marsh Lane] | "an aged woman" | † | b. Dec. 2, 1759 |
| *Son of John Hardcastle | [Boar Lane] | "8 or 9" | † | b. Jan. 7, 1759 |
| "Mr Hardcastle" | | 36        "sudden" | † | b. Sept. 3, 1754 |
| Widdow Hardcastle | | 69 | † | b. May 16, 1765 |
| *Susannah Harper | [Quarry Hill] | 84 | † | b. Dec. 27, 1758 |

| Name of deceased | Residence | Age | Cause of death | Attendees | Date of death (d.)/burial (b.) |
|---|---|---|---|---|---|
| Thomas Harper | | | | † | b. Sept. 17, 1761 |
| *Son of Benjamin Harrison | | | | † | b. Mar. 16, 1756 |
| Hannah Harrison | | | | | d. Apr. 21, 1735 |
| Rebecca Hick | | 11 | | | d. 1762 |
| *Matthew Higgins [Higgons] | [Briggate] | | | † | b. Dec. 18, 1740 |
| *Benjamin Holdsworth | [Bank] | 58 | | † | b. July 7, 1759 |
| *Mr [John] Holdsworth | [Bank] | | | † | b. Apr. 10 [Apr. 2], 1748 |
| *Rebecca Holdsworth [wife of Richard Holdsworth] | | | | † | b. Sept. 14, 1742 |
| *Richard Holdsworth | [Bank] | | | † | b. Oct. 19, 1750 |
| Joseph Holmes | | | "suddenly" | | b. June 10, 1739 |
| Josiah Horsman | | | | † | b. Feb. 19, 1742 |
| Brother of Josiah Horsman | | | | William Moult | b. Mar. 19, 1742 |
| *Ann Houghton | [Marsh Lane] | 45 | | † | b. Sept. 6, 1758 |
| *Hannah Huggon [Higgon] | [Workhouse] | | | † | b. Apr. 14, 1745 |
| Mary Huggon | | | | † | b. Nov. 6, 1742 |
| Thomas Ibbitson | | 75 | | † | b. Feb. 1, 1764 |
| Sarah Ibetson [Ibbetson] | Buzlinthorp | 80 | old age | † | b. June 22, 1766 |
| *Mr [Hephziba Ibbetson] Ibitson | [Kirkgate] | "old" | | † | b. June 22 [June 15], 1740 |
| Hannah Iles | | | | | d. c. Apr. 1741 |
| *John Iles | [Bank] | | | † | b. Jan. 12, 1745 |

| | | | | | |
|---|---|---|---|---|---|
| *Hannah Ingham [Ann, wife of John Ingham] | [Holbeck] | | | | b. Jan. 24, 1742 |
| John Ingham | | | | † | b. Mar. 19, 1745 |
| *John [Joshua] Inskip | [Marsh Lane] | | | | b. Mar. 17 [16], 1755 |
| *John [Margaret] Inskip | [Woodhouse] | | | † | b. Feb. 22, 1737/38 |
| Benjamin Jackson | | | | † | b. Aug. 8, 1741 |
| Mary Jackson | | | 74 | † | b. Apr. 12, 1766 |
| Alice Jebbs | | | | | b. Dec. 9, 1760 |
| *John Jefferson | | | | | |
| | [Mabgate] | | | † | b. Nov. 5, 1745 |
| *Mrs Jefferson [wife of Richard Jefferson] | | 26 | | † | b. Nov. 16, 1758 |
| *Edward Kilner | [Marsh Lane] | 84 | | | b. Mar. 23, 1757 |
| *Robert Kirkman | [near Timble Bridge] | 72 | [old age] | † | b. May 13, 1767 |
| *John Knot [Knott] | [Bank, Taylor] | | | | b. Apr. 26, 1739 |
| Ellimer Knowles | | | | ‡ | b. Jan. 3, 1741 |
| Joseph Knowles | | 70 | | † | b. Dec. 2, 1764 |
| Widdow Knowles | | 82 | | † | b. Oct. 20, 1756 |
| Robert Knutton | | | | † | b. May 25, 1760 |
| Matthew Lader | | | | ‡ | b. Apr. 12, 1743 |
| Widdow Laun | | | | | b. May 14, 1760 |
| *Martha Leadbeater [wife of David Leadbetter] | | | | (†)† | b. Mar. 1, 1742 |
| Sarah Leadbeater | | 80 | | † | b. Feb. 19, 1757 |
| Wife of John Linsley | | 36 | | † | b. Feb. 13, 1763 |
| *Lydia Lister | | | | † | b. Nov. 17, 1740 |

| Name of deceased | Residence | Age | Cause of death | Attendees | Date of death (d.)/burial (b.) |
|---|---|---|---|---|---|
| *Richard Lister | [Bank] | | | Hannah and Grace Arey | b. May 15 [14], 1745 |
| Sarah Lister | | | | | b. July 30, 1739 |
| Widdow Lister | | | | † | b. Oct. 12, 1756 |
| *John Lodge | [Quarryhill] | 82 | [old age] | † | b. Aug. 25, 1767 |
| Martha Lucas | | 62 | | | b. Oct. 27, 1762 |
| Jack Mackdonald | | | | † | b. July 12, 1764 |
| *John Mand | [Quarryhill] | | | † | b. May 20, 1756 |
| Mary Marshall | | | | † | b. Nov. 16, 1742 |
| *William Marshall | [Quarryhill] | | | † | b. Mar. 6, 1756 |
| Caleb Metcalf | | | | † | b. Jan. 14, 1760 |
| David Metcalf | | | | | b. Aug. 3 or 4, 1762 |
| Rebeckah Motley | | | | | f.d. Apr. 12, 1747 |
| John Moult | | | | | d. May 18, 1736 |
| Mrs Moult | | | | | b. Dec. 12, 1760 |
| *Hannah Musgrave [wife of William Musgrave] | [Bank] | | | † | b. Mar. 29, 1767 |
| Mary Musgrave | | 37 | | † | b. July 22, 1757 |
| *Rachell Musgrave | [Bank] | 79 | | † | b. Jan. 6, 1758 |
| Son of Joshua Musgrave | | | | † | b. Nov. 4, 1740 |
| Richard Naylor | | 88 | | † | b. Mar. 18, 1761 |
| "neighbour" (female) | | | | † | b. June 11, 1752 |
| *Sarah Nelthorp [daughter of Joseph Nelthorp] | [near the Church] | 2 | [smallpox] | † | b. Sept. 13, 1767 |

| | | | |
|---|---|---|---|
| *Joseph Netherwood | [Mabgate] | | b. Apr. 23, 1740 |
| Wife of William Nettleton, | | † | b. June 1, 1756 |
| Mr Newport | | | d. Dec. 14, 1760 |
| *Ann Nicholson [wife of John Nicolson] | | † | b. Mar. 20 [21], 1744/45 |
| Son of John Parker | | ‡Mercy Ross | b. June 3, 1764 |
| Mary Parker [wife of Samuell Parker] | [Workhouse] | † | b. Jan. 25, 1763 |
| Samuell Parker | [Workhouse] | | b. Feb. 15, 1763 |
| Samuell Powell | 85 | † | b. May 2, 1766 |
| Jonathan Priestley | | † | b. at Halifax, July 12, 1743 |
| John Prince | Holbeck | † | b. Apr. 6, 1748 |
| Thomas Prince | | † | b. Nov. 2, 1745 |
| *John Rammoll [Ramhill] | [Workhouse] | | b. Oct. 17, 1739 |
| Mr Read | 84 | † | b. Mar. 27, 1764 |
| *Henry Reynolds | [Briggate] | † | b. July 16, 1745 |
| *Abraham Rider | 72 | † | b. Nov. 10, 1760 |
| *Jonathan Rider | 74 | † | b. Mar. 29, 1758 |
| Joseph Rider | 5 | † | b. Jan. 11, 1764 |
| Joshua Rider, son of cousin John | Hunslett | | d. Dec. 5; b. Dec. 7, 1754 |
| *George Robinson | | † | b. Dec. 31, 1741 |
| Mrs Robinson | | † | b. Oct. 3, 1757 |
| Child of Ralph Robinson, | | † | b. Mar. 31, 1742 |
| Ralph Robinson | | † | b. June 29, 1742 |

| Name of deceased | Residence | Age | Cause of death | Attendees | Date of death (d.)/burial (b.) |
|---|---|---|---|---|---|
| *Sarah Robinson | [Mabgate] | "a young woman" | | † | b. Mar. 22, 1756 |
| *Benjamin Ross [son of Joseph Rosee] | [Marsh Lane] | 2 | [consumption] | † | b. June 27, 1766 |
| Joshua Ross | | 3 | | † | b. Feb. 19, 1764 |
| Wife of Joseph Rothery | Hunslett | | | † | b. Sept. 28, 1740 |
| Joseph Rothery | | 71 | | † | b. July 9, 1761 |
| *Elizabeth Ryder [wife of Abr. Rither] | | | | †† | b. Dec. 3, 1743 |
| Elisabeth Ryder (wife of Joseph Ryder) | | 49 | illness | † | d. Apr. 25; b. Apr. 27, 1754 |
| *Esther Ryder, youngest daughter of John Ryder | [Marsh Lane] | | | † | b. Aug. 26, 1757 |
| Hannah Ryder | | 75 | | † | b. Oct. 30, 1758 |
| *Jonathan Ryder [son of Nath. Rither] | | | | †† | b. Apr. 28, 1744 |
| *Jonathan, son of John Ryder | | | | † | d. May 20; b. May 22, 1749 |
| Joseph Ryder, son of Nathan | | 4 | "a long and tedious flight of afflictions" | † | d. Jan. 13; b. Jan. 14, 1751 |
| Leonard Ryder | | | | † | b. June 25, 1741 |
| "My Dear Mother" Mary Ryder | | 77 | | † | b. Mar. 2, 1742/43 |
| *Mary Ryder, cousin | [Mabgate] | 70 | | † | b. Oct. 18, 1758 |
| Mary Ryder | | 76 | | Ryder's maid | b. Oct. 30, 1758 |

| | | | | |
|---|---|---|---|---|
| Mary Ryder [daughter of John Rider] | [Marsh Lane head] | 11 | [swellings] | † | b. Apr. 29, 1766 |
| *Rebechah Ryder [daughter of John Rider] | [Marsh Lane] | "about 20 days" | | † | b. Aug. 27, 1758 |
| Robert Ryder | | 75 | "Palsy fitt" | † | d. Jan. 14; b. Jan. 17, 1757 |
| Daughter of Mr Scot | | | | | d. Jan. 29, 1752 |
| John Scot | | | | | b. at Mill Hill Dec. 27, 1754 |
| *Son [Thomas] of John Servant | | | "drowned at Burnitops in Samll Walkers well" | † | b. Aug. 13, 1743 |
| David Servant | | | "sudden" | † | b. Feb. 23, 1757 |
| Elizabeth Servant | [Marsh Lane] | 79 | | † | b. Nov. 13, 1757 |
| Joseph Servant | | | | † | b. Nov. 23, 1740 |
| Joseph Servant | | | | † | b. Jan. 1, 1765 |
| *Marmaduke Servant | [Quarryhill] | "about 76 or 77" | | † | b. Dec. 2, 1759 |
| Child of Banjamin Shadwick | | | | | d. c. Sept. 1760 |
| Thomas Share | | "20s" | | † | b. July 10, 1766 |
| John Sharper | | | | † | b. Apr. 28, 1745 |
| Son of William Shaw | | | | Olive Ryder | b. June 11, 1745 |
| *Sarah Shibden | [Kirkgate] | | | | b. Oct. 12, 1739 |
| Mrs Shipley | | | "sudden death" | | b. Aug. 24, 1748 |
| John Sigston | | | | † | b. Aug. 24, 1754 |
| *Joseph Sigston | [Marsh Lane] | 80 | [old age] | † | b. Nov. 18, 1766 |

| Name of deceased | Residence | Age | Cause of death | Attendees | Date of death (d.)/burial (b.) |
|---|---|---|---|---|---|
| *[Eliz] Sigston [wife of Joseph] | | | | † | b. Nov. 17, 1744 |
| *Margrette [Margaret] Simm | [Quarryhill] | 78 | | † | b. Mar. 17, 1758 |
| *Hannah Skelton | [Quarryhill] | | | † | b. Oct. 28, 1758 |
| *Benjamin Smallpage | [Quarryhill] | | | | b. Feb. 13, 1760 |
| Leonard Smallpage | | 36 | | † | b. Dec. 15, 1757 |
| Daughter of Alderman Smith | | | | | b. Jan. 29, 1752 |
| Benjamin Smith | | | "sudden" | † | b. May 26, 1747 |
| *Dinah Smith [wife of James Smith] | | | | † | b. Sept. 4, 1743 |
| *"A Scotchman call'd" John Smith | [Bank] | | | † | b. Oct. 8, 1743 |
| Leonard Smith | | | | † | b. Mar. 18, 1757 |
| Jonathan Smithy | | | | † | b. Sept. 1, 1761 |
| Abraham Snell | | | | † | b. Dec. 7, 1761 |
| *May Snipe [wife of George Snipe] | | | | † | b. Sept. 13, 1741 |
| *Hannah Sparrow | [Quarryhill] | 65 | | † | b. Aug. 24, 1758 |
| *Jonathan Sparrow | [Quarryhill] | | | † | b. Feb. 2, 1744 |
| *Wife of John Spawton [Spalton] | [Cross Green] | | | † | b. Mar. 27, 1756 |
| Jonathan Squire | | 63 | | † | b. Jan. 15, 1764 |
| *Grace Stead, daughter of Jane Brown [wife of Thomas Stead] | [Northall Bridge] | | [childbirth] | † | b. Aug. 23, 1765 |
| Mary Stead | | | | † | b. Apr. 7, 1738 |

| | | | | |
|---|---|---|---|---|
| Ann Stephenson | | 74 | † | b. June 5, 1766 |
| John Stephenson | | | † | b. Mar. 11, 1756 |
| *William Stephenson | [Kirkgate] | | | b. Apr. 4, 1740 |
| Widow Stirk | | 72 | † | b. May 26, 1766 |
| Joseph Story | | | † | b. Dec. 9, 1741 |
| Richard Syker | | 24 | † | b. June 1, 1754 |
| Dr Sykes | | | † | b. Marsh 20, 1757 |
| George Sykes | | 71 | † | b. July 27, 1761 |
| Mary Sykes | | | (†)† | b. Nov. 7, 1742 |
| Hannah Taylor | | 84 | † | b. Sept. 29, 1759 |
| Jeremiah Taylor | | | † | b. June 4, 1742 |
| Martha Taylor | | 70 | † | b. June 6, 1766 |
| Thomas Taylor | ?ulton | 64 | † | b. June 28, 1762 |
| John Tebbs | | | † | b. Nov. 25, 1761 |
| Benjamin Theakston | | 18 | † | b. July 1, 1767 |
| Child of Christopher Theakston | | | †† | b. Mar. 9, 1745 |
| Son of Christopher Theakston | | 15 | † | b. Dec. 12, 1763 |
| Hannah Theakston | | 81 | † | b. Apr. 4, 1763 |
| Joseph [Christopher] Theakston | [Workhouse] | | † | b. Feb. 27, 1767 |
| Josh Theakston | | 76 | † | b. Nov. 5, 1758 |
| Hannah Thompson | "Hinslett" | illness | † | b. Feb. 14, 1734 |
| Son of Matthew Totty | | | † | b. Oct. 5, 1756 |

| Name of deceased | Residence | Age | Cause of death | Attendees | Date of death (d.)/burial (b.) |
|---|---|---|---|---|---|
| *Child [daughter] of Eliz. Tyros [Levi Tyas] | [Marsh Lane] | | | † | b. Apr. 16, 1758 |
| *Son of L. Tyras [Tyas] | [Marsh Lane] | 15 | [consumption] | † | b. Nov. 6, 1765 |
| Wife of Mr Wainman | Pudsey | | "died suddenly" | | d. Mar. 21, 1755 |
| Sarah Wainman | | 33 | | † | b. Jan. 25, 1758 |
| *William Wait | [Mabgate] | | | † | b. Oct. 8, 1742 |
| Son of Benjamin Walker | | 12 | | † | b. Nov. 26, 1764 |
| Elizabeth Walker | | | | † | b. Dec. 2 or 3, 1761 |
| Hannah Walker, wife of Samuell | | "a mother to many children taken away as it were in the midst of usefulness" | "affliction" | † | d. Nov. 8, 1750 |
| John Walker | | | | | b. June 6, 1761 |
| Daughter of John Walker | | | | | b. Jan. 29, 1752 |
| *Jonathan Walker [son of Richard] | [Shipscar] | "15 or 16" | | † | b. June 17, 1762 |
| *Richard Walker | [Shipscar] | | | † | b. Aug. 30, 1757 |
| Son of Samuell Walker | | | | † | b. July 25, 1742 |
| *Sarah Walker | [North Part] | | | (†)(†)† | b. May 6, 1741 |
| Thomas Walker (minister Mill Hill) | | | "a brief illness" | † | d. Nov. 10; b. Nov. 11, 1763 |
| *James Walton | [Marsh Lane] | 22 | | † | b. Dec. 31, 1757 |
| *Martha Walton | [Near Church] | | | † | b. Aug. 10, 1760 |

| | | | | | |
|---|---|---|---|---|---|
| Wife of Edward Ward | | | | | d. c. Sept. 1760 |
| James Ward | | 42 | | † | b. Aug. 28, 1758 |
| *Mary Ward [daughter of Edward Ward] | [Bank] | 22 | | † | b. July 7, 1766 |
| "Aunt" Sarah Ward | | | | †† | b. June 1, 1743 |
| John Warham | | 55 | | † | b. Nov 25, 1766 |
| *Catherine Watson [wife of John Watson] | [Marsh Lane] | 55 | | † | b. Nov. 1, 1758 |
| *Hannah Watson, daughter of Samuell Ryder [wife of Joseph Watson] | [Mabgate] | 28 | childbirth | † | b. Apr. 14, 1762 |
| *Rachell Wauborn [Walburn] | [Caw-Lane] | 63 | | † | b. May 23, 1762 |
| John Webster | | 48 | | † | b. Jan. 29, 1765 |
| *John Westerman | [Quarryhill] | | "Gored with a bull when baiting" | | b. Sept. 7, 1755 |
| Samuall Wharum, son of John | | "around 10" | | † | b. Oct. 6, 1750 |
| *"My Uncle" Moses Wheelhouse | | | | † | b. Aug. 11, 1739 |
| Thomas Wheelhouse | [Woodhouse] | | | ††† | b. May 19, 1742 |
| *Mr [Mrs] Whitaker | [Lydgate] | | | † | d. Nov. 19. 1736 |
| | | | | | b. Nov. 22, 1736 |
| *"younger son of Mr Whitaker" | | | | | b. Feb. 8, 1738/39 |
| Deborah Wilkinson | | 63 | | † | b. Nov. 27, 1760 |
| *Joseph Wilkinson | [Bank] | 76 | | † | b. June 11, 1758 |

| Name of deceased | Residence | Age | Cause of death | Attendees | Date of death (d.)/burial (b.) |
|---|---|---|---|---|---|
| Matthew Williams | | 23 | | † | b. Mar. 7, 1764 |
| Widow Williams | | | | † | b. May 30, 1766 |
| Milliah Winter | | | | † | b. Mar. 29, 1743 |
| Edward Wokfolk | | 31 | | † | b. July 16, 1763 |
| *William Wolfolk [son of Ja. Woolfoot] | | | | † | b. Apr. 30, 1745 |
| David Wood | | 70 | | † | b. June 14, 1759 |
| Joseph Wood | | 53 | | † | b. Jan. 27, 1764 |
| Son of Joseph Wood | | | | † | b. Oct. 1744 |
| William Woolgar | London | | | | d. May 6, 1761 |
| John Wright [a child of Sam. Wright] | | | | † | b. May 12 [13], 1741 |
| Samuell Wright | | 59 | | † | b. May 14, 1761 |
| Alice Yates | | | | †† | b. May 16, 1742 |

# Notes

ABBREVIATIONS

JRD      Joseph Ryder's Diary
ODNB  *Oxford Dictionary of National Biography*, ed. H. C. G. Matthew and
       Brian Harrison (Oxford: Oxford University Press, 2004)
PTS     *Publications of the Thoresby Society*
WYAS  West Yorkshire Archives Service, Leeds

## I. DOUBLE-MINDED MEN

1. On the historiography of the Weber debate, see Chapter 4, note 1. On
   ordinary entrepreneurs and protoindustrialists of Ryder's milieu who said
   little about religion in their personal writing, see John Smail, *Merchants,
   Markets and Manufacture: The English Wool Textile Industry in the
   Eighteenth Century* (New York: Palgrave Macmillan, 1999), and Smail, ed.,
   *Woollen Manufacturing in Yorkshire: The Memorandum Books of John
   Brearley, Cloth Frizzer at Wakefield, 1758–1762* (Woodbridge: Boydell,
   2001); S. D. Smith, *'An Exact and Industrious Tradesman': The Letter Book
   of Joseph Symson of Kendal, 1711–1720* (Oxford: Oxford University Press,
   2002); K. H. Burley, "An Essex Clothier of the Eighteenth Century,"
   *Economic History Review* 11 (1958): 289–301; Julia de Lacy Mann, "A
   Wiltshire Family of Clothiers: George and Hester Wansey, 1683–1714,"
   *Economic History Review* 9 (1956): 252. For a recent overview of some of
   the titans of the new economy, see Joel Mokyr, *The Enlightened Economy*
   (New Haven, CT: Yale University Press, 2010); for some of its victims, see
   Jane Humphries, *Child Labour in the British Industrial Revolution* (Oxford:
   Oxford University Press, 2010). A mostly optimistic account of the
   eighteenth-century consumer is found in Maxine Berg, *Luxury and Pleasure
   in Eighteenth-Century Britain* (Oxford: Oxford University Press, 2005);
   more negative is in Margot C. Finn, *The Character of Credit: Personal Debt
   in English Culture, 1740–1914* (Cambridge: Cambridge University Press,

2003), and Martin Daunton and Matthew Hilton, eds., *The Politics of Consumption* (Oxford: Oxford University Press, 2001). The closest (accessible) person to Ryder in outlook, occupation, and time may well be Joseph Williams, on whom see more below. For an analysis of Williams's diary, see Isabel Rivers, "Joseph Williams of Kidderminster (1692–1755) and His Journal," *Journal of the United Reformed Church History Society* 7 (2005): 359–80. Two accounts that consider the ambivalence of middling folk inter alia are Margaret Hunt, *The Middling Sort: Commerce, Gender, and the Family, 1680–1780* (Berkeley: University of California Press, 1996), and Deborah Valenze, *The Social Life of Money in the English Past* (Cambridge: Cambridge University Press, 2006).

2. I owe some of these observations about the diary's neglect to conversation with Brett Harrison, formerly of the West Yorkshire Archives Service, and correspondence with Pat Hudson and Richard G. Wilson. Ryder first appears as a historical source on a few pages of Charles Wicksteed, *Lectures on the memory of the just: being a series of discourses on the lives and times of the ministers of Mill-Hill Chapel, Leeds . . .; with a farewell sermon delivered on the 14TH OF MARCH, 1847* (London: Chapman, 1849). Wicksteed married the daughter of Arthur Lupton, Ryder's nephew by marriage to his niece Olive; Olive and Arthur Lupton also possessed their uncle's massive diary, and Wicksteed presumably turned to it as it was part of the private family archive; on Wicksteed's marriage into the Lupton family, see R. K. Webb, "Wicksteed, Charles (1810–1885)," in *ODNB*. Wicksteed, who was also minister of the Unitarian Mill Hill Chapel from 1835 to 1854, in turn was apparently the only source on Ryder in another study of Mill Hill by another of its ministers: William Lawrence Schroeder, *Mill Hill Chapel Leeds, 1674–1924, Sketch of its History; with some account of the development of the congregational life and of the men who have served as Ministers* (Hull: Elsom, 1924). Schroeder very briefly mentions Ryder, as does Bryan Dale in "Early Congregationalism in Leeds," *Transactions of the Congregationalist Historical Society*, May 1906. Herbert McLachlan's more substantial essay on Ryder first appeared as "Diary of a Leeds Layman, 1733–1768," *Transactions of the Unitarian Historical Society* 4, 3 (1929–1930): 248–67. A very slightly altered version later appeared in his *Essays and Addresses* (Manchester: Manchester University Press, 1950). McLachlan, one of the great historians of Unitarianism and the Dissenting Academies, clearly read the diary thoroughly, and despite his tempered estimation of its overall value, he pulled from it some of the most

important passages related to the details of Ryder's life. I nevertheless don't always agree with his interpretations of the text, and his citations of the diary are often inaccurately dated; the places where I think these things matter are indicated in my footnotes. It is also McLachlan who explains that the diary was given by Edgar Lupton, a descendent of the same Arthur Lupton mentioned above, to the Unitarian College Library, which eventually merged with the John Rylands Library in 1925. For this and the comment about "small beer," see his *Essays and Addresses,* 22, 28.

3. See "The Registers of the Parish Church of Leeds, from 1722–1757," *PTS* 20 (1911, 1914), and "The Register of the Parish Church of Leeds," *PTS* 25 (1917, 1918, 1920, 1922).

4. On the peculiarity of Calvinism in England, see Patrick Collinson, *Godly People: Essays in English Protestantism and Puritanism* (London: Hambledon, 1983), and for the fleshed-out comparative perspective, Philip Benedict, *Christ's Churches Purely Reformed: A Social History of Calvinism* (New Haven, CT: Yale University Press, 2002), 317–29. Although what constitutes a spiritual diary can be hard to determine, William Matthews uses the word "spiritual" or some comparable qualifier to identify at least 50 of the 375 diaries written between 1570 and 1700; of the 629 written between 1701 and 1760, he found at least 75, roughly the same percentage, to be spiritual in nature. This is an imprecise way to categorize texts, but a more detailed breakdown of diaries awaits fuller study. Matthews, *British Diaries: An Annotated Bibliography of British Diaries Written between 1442* AND *1942* (Berkeley: University of California Press, 1950).

5. On the broader social relevance of individual cases, see Carlo Ginzburg's thought-provoking "Latitude, Slaves, and the Bible: An Experiment in Microhistory," *Critical Inquiry* 31 (2005): 665–83. E. P. Thompson, "Anthropology and the Discipline of Historical Context," *Midlands History* 1, 3 (1972): 42; this was Thompson's lengthy review of Alan Macfarlane's *The Family Life of Ralph Josselin.*

6. The importance of the financial revolution of the 1690s is classically covered in John Brewer, *The Sinews of Power: War, Money, and the English State, 1688–1783* (Cambridge, MA: Harvard University Press, 1990); Steven C. A. Pincus adds nuance to this picture in *1688: The First Modern Revolution* (New Haven, CT: Yale University Press, 2009), ch. 12. The Licensing Act (1662) did not die quickly, although it took its final breath on May 3, 1695. Nor did it lapse because of high-minded ideas about freedom of the press. But however economic the causes of its lapse, the

constitutional and cultural consequences were major. On the causes, see N. M. Dawson, "The Death Throes of the Licensing Act and the 'Funeral Pomp' of Queen Mary II, 1695," *Journal of Legal History* 26, 2 (2005): 119–42. The assumption of the cultural importance of the consequences underpins Roy Porter, *The Creation of the Modern World: The Untold Story of the British Enlightenment* (New York: W. W. Norton, 2001).

7. On the library, see Dennis Cox, "The Leeds Library," *Library Review* 44, 3 (1995): 12–16. On Leeds, see Steven Burt and Kevin Grady, *The Merchants' Golden Age: Leeds 1700–1790* (Leeds: Grady and Burt, 1987). On music and plays, see Emily Hargrave, "Musical Leeds in the 18th Century," *PTS* 28, 3 (1926): 320–44. Announcements of horse races and cockfights regularly appear in the *Leeds Mercury* and *Leeds Intelligencer*. Football was being played as early as 1715 and on the frozen River Aire—so noted the diarist and schoolteacher John Lucas. For Lucas's diary and a concise introduction to eighteenth-century life in Leeds, see Jonathan Oates, *The Memoranda Book of John Lucas, 1712–1750* (Leeds: Thoresby Society, 2006). The two most important works on the city during this period are R. G. Wilson, *Gentlemen Merchants: The Merchant Community in Leeds, 1700–1830* (Manchester: Manchester University Press, 1971), and Maurice Beresford, *East End, West End: The Face of Leeds during Urbanisation, 1684–1842* (Leeds: Thoresby Society, 1988). For the religious geography of the city, see Terry Friedman, *Church Architecture in Leeds, 1700–1790* (Leeds: Thoresby Society, 1997).

8. Maxine Berg, *The Age of Manufacture, 1700–1820: History, Innovation and Work in Britain* (London: Routledge, 1994), 208.

9. On theories of protoindustrialization, see the editors' introduction in Sheilagh C. Ogilvie and Markus Cerman, eds., *European Proto-industrialization* (Cambridge: Cambridge University Press, 1996); for England and Leeds, see Pat Hudson's contribution to the same volume as well as her *The Genesis of Industrial Capital: A Study of the West Riding Wool Textile Industry, c. 1750–1850* (Cambridge: Cambridge University Press, 1986). Fiennes quoted in John Wilhelm Rowntree, *Essays and Addresses* (London: Headley Brothers, 1905), 41. Defoe first published his tour of Britain from 1724 to 1726 but is quoted here from the fourth edition of the book: *A Tour Thro' the Whole Island of Great Britain . . .* (London, 1748), 119. We never know exactly when Ryder established himself as a clothier, but the earliest dates where he records buying cloth in his trade notebook are from the mid-1720s; see WYAS MS GA/B27. Ryder also never describes the scene from his window, but the view can be inferred

from the short description of his estate given a few months after his death in the *Leeds Intelligencer*, No. 780 (May 31, 1768).

10. Linda Colley, *The Ordeal of Elizabeth Marsh: A Woman in World History* (New York: Random House, 2007), xix.

11. For the authoritative account of providentialism, to which watching was so closely related, see Alexandra Walsham, *Providence in Early Modern England* (Oxford: Oxford University Press, 1999).

12. On this paradox of spiritual self-writing, see Michael Mascuch, *Origins of the Individualist Self: Autobiography and Self-Identity in England, 1591–1791* (Stanford, CA: Stanford University Press, 1996); Tom Webster, "Writing to Redundancy: Approaches to Spiritual Journals and Early Modern Spirituality," *Historical Journal* 39, 1 (1996): 33–56; Paul Seaver, *Wallington's World: A Puritan Artisan in Seventeenth-Century London* (Stanford, CA: Stanford University Press, 1985), 42–43; and Jürgen Schlaeger, "Self-Exploration in Early Modern English Diaries," in *Marginal Voices, Marginal Forms: Diaries in European Literature and History*, ed. Rachel Langford and Russell West (Amsterdam: Rodopi, 1999). Barker's diary can be found at the John Rylands Library, Burgess MSS xvii, D18, "Portion of the Diary of Pentecost Barker (fl. 1690–1731)." I deal with the messiness of early "diaries" in Chapter 3. Josselin is quoted in Christopher Durston and Jacqueline Eales, "Introduction: The Puritan Ethos, 1560–1700," in *The Culture of English Puritanism, 1560–1700*, ed. Durston and Eales (London: Macmillan, 1996), 13. On Wallington's fears of losing the right balance, and for details of his diary, see Seaver, *Wallington's World*, 2. On Katherine Gell, see William Lamont, "Gell, Katherine (bap. 1624, d. 1671)," in *ODNB*. On Baxter's (and Cotton Mather's) worries about excessive diary writing, see Webster, "Writing to Redundancy," 39.

13. "Le diable, autant que le bon Dieu, peut inspirer le diariste"; Philippe Lejeune and Catherine Bogard, *Le Journal Intime: Histoire et anthologie* (Paris: Textuel, 2006), 88. The authoritative survey of the demoralizing efforts of Smith and others is still Albert O. Hirschman, *The Passions and the Interests: Political Arguments for Capitalism before Its Triumph* (Princeton, NJ: Princeton University Press, 1977), a short and thought-provoking book that nevertheless says nothing about how this cultural debate affected the sorts of people, like Ryder, whom the debate was ultimately about. Note too that this wasn't simply an eighteenth-century debate. Also see Joyce Appleby's no less thought-provoking *Economic*

*Thought and Ideology in Seventeenth-Century England* (Princeton, NJ: Princeton University Press, 1978).

14. The St. Peter's of Ryder's day was not the one standing today. The current church was built in the 1840s and is one of the largest Anglican churches erected in Britain since industrialization. But even the earlier medieval church dwarfed Call Lane, which did not outlast the 1880s. JRD, April 22, 1741.

15. The marriage registry notes "Joseph Ryder m. Elisabeth Wheelhouse, Leedes," on the same day Ryder makes a more general note of the event in his journal. See "The Registers of the Parish Church of Leeds, from 1722–1757," *PTS* 20 (1911, 1914): 330. The same register lists her name as "Ann, wife of Joseph Rider" on the day of her burial, April 27, 1754, which occurred two days after Ryder recorded her death in the diary. The spelling of Ryder with an "i" is common throughout the register, so it seems highly unlikely that this would not be the same man and woman. (Ryder did have a cousin named Ann, but he does not mention her death on or around April 27, 1754.) His wife's name may have been Elisabeth Ann or Ann Elisabeth. Wheelhouse seems in any case to be the right maiden name, but that doesn't resolve the question of what Ryder would have called her. For the sake of consistency, I have made the decision—with the admittedly arbitrary rationale that a happier wedding day (notwithstanding Ryder's misgivings) should trump a funeral—to call her Elisabeth throughout this book. Details on Whitaker are scarce outside the diary. Also see Ralph Thoresby, *Ducatus Leodensis: or, The topography of the ancient and populous towns and parish of Leedes . . .*, 2nd ed. (Leeds, 1816), 44 (with notes and additions by a direct descendent of Whitaker's, Thomas Dunham Whitaker). JRD, April 26, 1741.

16. JRD, April 19, 1741.

17. Ryder's poems can certainly be called his own creations, but one can often locate possible sources of inspiration for his imagery. For example, John Flavel, an author Ryder read, uses the phrase "swarms of vanity." See *The Whole Works of the Revered Mr. John Flavel In Two Volumes, Volume II* (Glasgow, 1754), 466. But in many ways this is the point: the godly often spoke with something like one voice. On the meaning of "vain" and the godly, see Patrick Collinson, *Birthpangs of Protestant England: Religious and Cultural Change in the 16th and 17th Centuries* (New York: Palgrave Macmillan, 1988), 97. On Aristotle's axiom, see Keith Thomas, *Man and the Natural World: Changing Attitudes in England, 1500–1800* (Oxford:

Oxford University Press, 1983), 17. On Bunyan's "Vanity Fair," see John Bunyan, *The Pilgrim's Progress,* 2nd ed., ed. James Blanton Wharey, rev. Roger Sharrock (Oxford: Oxford University Press, 1960). JRD, August 22, 1758.

18. Joseph Addison, *The Spectator,* 69, May 19, 1711. Bernard Mandeville, *The Fable of the Bees; or Private Vices, Public Benefits* (London, 1714). Adam Smith, *The Theory of Moral Sentiments,* vol. 1 of the *Glasgow Edition of the Works and Correspondence of Adam Smith,* ed. D. D. Raphael and A. L. Macfie (Oxford: Oxford University Press, 1976), 50–51, 257, 259. All quotations from Smith are taken from his heavily revised sixth edition of *The Theory of Moral Sentiments,* which appeared in 1790 and which is the version used for the *Glasgow Edition of the Works and Correspondence of Adam Smith* cited here. The cultural effort to decriminalize words such as "vanity" apparently affected Smith himself: cf. the less lexically iconoclastic first edition, published in 1759. On changes Smith made to various editions of this work, see D. D. Raphael, *The Impartial Spectator: Adam Smith's Moral Philosophy* (Oxford: Oxford University Press, 2007), ch. 1. The point here is not, I should stress, that Smith, Mandeville, and Addison were one in the same. Smith may have admired Addison, but he was at great pains, like his teacher Francis Hutcheson, to distance himself from the cynicism of Mandeville, who was far more flippant in reversing the meaning of moral terms. See Nicholas Phillipson, *Adam Smith: An Enlightened Life* (New Haven, CT: Yale University Press, 2010), 21–23, 47–50.

19. JRD, January 28, 1738/9; August 26, 1733.

20. See the entry for "vain" in the *Oxford English Dictionary.* JRD, April 19, 1741.

21. Ignacio Carbajosa, *The Character of the Syriac Version of Psalms: A Study of Psalms 90–150 in the Peshitta* (Leiden: Brill, 2008), 214. John Calvin, *Commentary on the Book of Psalms,* Vol. 4, trans. James Anderson (Edinburgh: Calvin Translation Society, 1843), 448.

## 2. "MY CHARACTER & CONDUCT"

1. Laurel Thatcher Ulrich, *A Midwife's Tale: The Life of Martha Ballard, Based on Her Diary, 1785–1812* (New York: Alfred A. Knopf, 1990), 35.

2. JRD, June 29, 1733.

3. For Ryder's trade notebook, see WYAS, MS GA/B27. For his will, see Borthwick Institute, York, Leeds Wills, 1700–1830, "Will of Joseph Ryder of Leeds (1695–1768)." The ad for Ryder's property appears in *Leeds*

*Intelligencer,* No. 780 (May 31, 1768). For his baptism, see The National Archives, Public Record Office, RG 4/3724. For his marriage, see "The Registers of the Parish Church of Leeds, from 1722–1757," *PTS* 20 (1911, 1914): 330, and for his death, "The Register of the Parish Church of Leeds," *PTS* 25 (1917, 1918, 1920, 1922), 289.

4. Louis Menand, "A Critic at Large," *New Yorker,* December 10, 2007, 107. On Pepys, see Claire Tomalin, *Samuel Pepys: The Unequalled Self* (New York: Knopf, 2002).

5. Ryder is here also echoing Lam. 3:22–23. Paul Seaver, *Wallington's World: A Puritan Artisan in Seventeenth-Century London* (Stanford, CA: Stanford University Press, 1985), 9; the phrase Seaver quotes is Spinoza's. Ryder's comments are from July 4, 1734. Wallington quoted in Seaver, *Wallington's World,* 7. *Diary of Cotton Mather, 1681–1708* (Boston: Massachusetts Historical Society, 1911), 356–58; the entry is from June 1700, and we know that Mather meant to convey a sense of humor because he tells us that such reflections can not only be "delightful Entertainment" in his solitary thoughts, but they can be "made savoury with some little sort of Witt" when they are made public and instructive for others.

6. JRD, February 24, 1756. Ryder's passing comment about reading might mean that he read quickly, although "considerable part of a book" would be less impressive if there were relatively few words per page and/or relatively few pages in the book as a whole. Ryder does also suggest he read quickly in at least one other equally cryptic entry: "I have had a book put into my hand to read, which I have read the most of this evening, containing disputes about articles of faith" (JRD, April 11, 1761). But the same qualifications apply here too as the same question goes unanswered: what book was it? In the same way, on one occasion, and in a particularly distressed state after the death of his wife, Ryder hints at his diet, at least at this time in his life—"as for the benefit of eating & Drinking I think very little of in any thing of a superfluous kind[,] good wholesome plain food I hope is very satisfactory"—but he never explains what counted as wholesome and what as superfluous (JRD, May 20, 1754).

7. The phrase "autobiographical abstract" is from Andrew Cambers, "Reading, the Godly, and Self-Writing in England, circa 1580–1720," *Journal of British Studies* 46, 4 (2007): 803–4. Ryder himself tells us that he was born three months after his father's death (JRD, May 20, 1756). In fact, it is not absolutely clear that Ryder was born March 25. The birth register from Mill Hill lists his birthday as March 26 and his baptism on

April 4. It also records his father's name as Joseph. Since Ryder himself
celebrates his birthday on the 25th, this is the date I accept throughout this
book. See "Birth Register from Mill Hill," Reel 26, No. 3724, Leeds
Central Library. There is no hard evidence that Ryder went to a Dissenting
Academy—in any case, there was not one in Leeds. On Dissenting
education, see Herbert McLachlan, *English Education under the Test Acts*
(Manchester: Manchester University Press, 1931). On apprenticeships, see
Steve Hindle, *On the Parish? The Micro-Politics of Poor Relief in Rural
England c.1550–1750* (Cambridge: Cambridge University Press, 2004),
191–226; Keith Wrightson, *Earthly Necessities: Economic Lives in Early
Modern Britain* (New Haven, CT: Yale University Press, 2000), passim;
and although it mostly covers the period just beyond Ryder's death, Jane
Humphries, *Childhood and Child Labour in the British Industrial Revolution*
(Oxford: Oxford University Press, 2010), ch. 9. The fullest list of authors
Ryder read that I have been able to compile on the basis of his allusions,
citations, or loose quotations is Joseph Alleine, Isaac Ambrose, Richard
Baxter, John Bunyan, William Burkitt, Philip Doddridge, Benjamin
Fawcett, John Flavel, Thomas Gouge, Matthew Henry, Philip Henry,
George Herbert, John Mason, Christopher Nesse, Elizabeth Rowe,
possibly Ralph Thoresby (see Chapter 5, note 20), Isaac Watts, and
Thomas Whitaker the elder. On the place that some of these authors held
in the eighteenth century, see Isabel Rivers, "Dissenting and Methodist
Books of Practical Divinity," in *Books and Their Readers in Eighteenth-
Century England*, ed. Rivers (Leicester: Leicester University Press, 1982),
127–64.

8. Ryder claims to surpass Badman in sinfulness, for example, on June 5, 1756;
for another allusion, see JRD, July 11, 1760. John Bunyan, *The Life and
Death of Mr Badman* (1680). On Bunyan's capacity to exaggerate in his
recollection of his own sinful youth, see R. L. Greaves, *Glimpses of Glory:
John Bunyan and English Dissent* (Stanford, CA: Stanford University Press,
2002), 5. If godly descriptions of youthful sinfulness could be hyperbolic
and prescribed, they could also occasionally delve into particularity. John
Winthrop, for example, made the qualification that he was drawn to "all
kind of wickedness, except swearing and scorning of religion"; quoted in
Seaver, *Wallington's World*, 16. In his first volume Ryder says several times
that he hadn't been guilty of obvious and scandalous sins, though he says
this to point out that he has sinned nevertheless, even if furtively; see JRD,
July 7, October 28, November 27, and December 17, 1733. Bunyan's title is

itself an allusion to Rom. 5:20 ("where sin abounded, grace did much more abound," in the King James version). Ryder's affection for Bunyan is implied by many references, but rarely does he so specifically praise an author as he does when he writes, "I read a piece of Mr Bunyan's work, and I thought he made such remarks upon what I find in my heart as if he had been alive and heard my complaints" (JRD, October 7, 1748).

9. Sharrock quoted in Stuart Sim, "Bunyan and the Early Novel: *The Life and Death of Mr Badman,*" in *The Cambridge Companion to Bunyan,* ed. Anne Dunan-Page (Cambridge: Cambridge University Press, 2010), 96. Bunyan, *Mr Badman,* 156, 181. Ryder once wrote (JRD, December 6, 1735) of being overjoyed on hearing the news of the reformation of a man who was "wild and Extravagant" in his youth and implies that he was the same way in his own past. The same year (August 10) he also agreed with Thomas Whitaker that particular sins are particular to life's stages: vanity to youth and covetousness to old age.

10. Wool trade statistics are from R. G. Wilson, *Gentlemen Merchants: The Merchant Community in Leeds: 1700–1830* (Manchester: Manchester University Press, 1971), 2–6. On credit and capital accumulation, see Pat Hudson, *The Genesis of Industrial Capital: A Study of the West Riding Wool Textile Industry, c. 1750–1850* (Cambridge: Cambridge University Press, 1986), passim; and John Smail, "The Culture of Credit in Eighteenth-Century Commerce: The English Textile Industry," *Enterprise and Society* 4 (2003), 317. On average wealth, see Hudson, *Genesis of Industrial Capital,* 30–31.

11. Hudson, *Genesis of Industrial Capital,* 32–33. "Will of Joseph Ryder of Leeds (1695–1768)." *Leeds Intelligencer,* No. 780 (May 31, 1768). WYAS, MS GA/B27. On dyers in this area of England, see Herbert Heaton, *The Yorkshire Woollen and Worsted Industries, from the Earliest Times up to the Industrial Revolution,* 2nd ed. (Oxford: Clarendon, 1965), 286–87, and John Smail, *Merchants, Markets and Manufacture: The English Wool Textile Industry in the Eighteenth Century* (New York: Palgrave Macmillan, 1999), 23.

12. "Almost certainly" because the only sort of travel Ryder detailed in the diary was religious or social; by implication, when he gives no details about travel, it was likely an indication of a business trip simply because those would have been the only other sorts of trips he would have been required to take so regularly. John Locke, *Two Treatises on Government,* 2, ch. 5, sec. 34. David Hume, "Of Interest" (1742), in *Essays, Moral, Political, and*

*Literary,* ed. T. H. Green and T. H. Grose (London, 1898), paragraphs 6, 9, and 14. Baxter quoted in William Lamont, *Puritanism and Historical Controversy* (Montreal: McGill–Queen's University Press, 1996), 107. Hogarth wasn't the only artist to offer visual illustrations of the dangers of idleness and the virtues of industry; see George Morland, *The Comforts of Industry and The Miseries of Idleness* (1790), reprinted in John Styles, *The Dress of the People: Everyday Fashion in Eighteenth-Century England* (New Haven, CT: Yale University Press, 2007), 190–91. On broader disputes surrounding the labor theory of value, see Steve Pincus, *1688: The First Modern Revolution* (New Haven, CT: Yale University Press, 2009), ch. 12. JRD, June 17, 1733. The minister Ryder heard was not Thomas Whitaker but "Mr Lacks," an obscure figure who rarely appears in the diary. We should note too that the emphasis in the Puritan tradition on maximizing time and resisting idleness had Calvinist and not simply English roots; for a thorough account of this, see Max Engammare, *On Time, Punctuality, and Discipline in Early Modern Calvinism,* trans. Karin Maag (Cambridge: Cambridge University Press, 2010), passim, but esp. ch. 3 and the conclusion.

13. The *Leeds Intelligencer* put Denison's worth at his death at £500,000; the *Leeds Mercury* put it at £700,000. R. G. Wilson, "Denison, William (1713/14–1782)," in *ODNB.* Wedgwood was worth approximately £500,000, although inflation would have made the real value of his wealth considerably less than the worth of that nominal amount in the early 1780s. Robin Reilly, "Wedgwood, Josiah (1730–1795)," in *ODNB.* JRD, July 26, 1733. Ryder made strikingly similar comments on noting (but not attending) a funeral of another Denison nearly twenty-five years later. On the one hand, Ryder clearly admired Thomas Denison; on the other, he (and others) couldn't help but notice that riches mean nothing at the end of the day: "This day as I was going to visit a Friend I saw many Grand People attending the funeral of Mr Thomas Denison, merchant who I may reasonably think will be much lamented, because so able and honourable a dealer in the world. He was buried in great splendor, but dust to dust would be read I doubt not at the Grave Side, and I heard one Observe That this fine appearance was all the difference at last between poor & rich" (JRD, February 27, 1756). "Descend with Pomp into the pit" is a remarkable image, but it is not Ryder's; it appears verbatim in ch. 24 of Thomas Gouge, *The Young Man's Guide* (1672): "Of Moderation in Seeking after Riches." This is also just one of many indications that

Ryder read Gouge; at the very least he must have heard someone else use this line.

14. JRD, June 18, 1733.

15. JRD, July 1, 1733.

16. Local officials actively sought to apprentice boys and girls to the town's trades, and Ryder must have assembled some of his "family" from the workhouses. See the reference in his cryptic notebook of cloth transactions during 1733 and 1741 to a man who later died while living at the workhouse, Joseph Theakston(e), whose death on February 27, 1767, Ryder records at the back of volume 40 (see Appendix 2). Note too Ryder's entry from February 15, 1763, yet another instance of the class consciousness that deaths and funerals aroused: "I was at the funerall of a poor man from the workhouse I saw his coffin was very plain, and his covering in the Inside was Sheets of paper, while I was in the church, another man was brought into the Church in a Coffin much ornamented and as the outside was so grand I make no dispute but his grave cloths were proportionable but from short observation, they were both laid in the Earth, and consequently all the extraordinarys in the whole are but show."

17. On the advice to marry, see David Cressy, *Birth, Marriage, and Death: Ritual, Religion, and the Life-Cycle in Tudor and Stuart England* (Oxford: Oxford University Press, 1997), 296–97. On the general economic meaning of gender roles, see Wrightson, *Earthly Necessities*, 42–48. Ryder reveals the size of his family in an entry from May 29, 1761. This is consistent with the image of the family size of a protoindustrial clothier in Leeds that Hudson offers in *Genesis of Industrial Capital*, 30.

18. The varieties of eighteenth-century shops are detailed in Claire Walsh, "Shops, Shopping, and the Art of Decision Making in Eighteenth-Century England," in *Gender, Taste, and Material Culture in Britain and North America, 1700–1830*, ed. John Styles and Amanda Vickery (New Haven, CT: Yale University Press, 2006), 152–53. JRD, October 20, 1735. Wallington also spiritually glossed his house getting robbed, which signaled God telling him that "the world is ready to steal away my heart," and therefore he needed "to set my heart on that which no thief can steal away"; Seaver, *Wallington's World*, 9. On later evangelicals and home décor, see Deborah A. Cohen, *Household Gods: The British and Their Possessions, 1830–1945* (New Haven, CT: Yale University Press, 2006). The first mention of Ryder's move is made on February 7, 1736/37; he revealed more details on February 15. The guilt reappears with other

similarly vague details later that summer as he fears "rising of pride" when a friend, revealingly, views "the conveniences of my habitation and [finds] them very commodious" (JRD, July 4, 1737). This fear of his own materialism while surveying his home furnishings needs to be set alongside the spiritually trouble-free picture of home decorating presented in Amanda Vickery, *Behind Closed Doors: At Home in Georgian England* (New Haven, CT: Yale University Press, 2009). On the garden, see JRD, May 20, 1737. We also learn about the garden when Ryder later notices its providential meaning (see Chapter 3).

19. On the "great uncertainty," see JRD, April 7, 1741. The reference to the will is made on July 1, 1740. JRD, March 25, 1741. On the quantitative meaning of the middling sort, see Margaret Hunt, *The Middling Sort: Commerce, Gender, and the Family in England, 1680–1780* (Berkeley: University of California Press, 1996), 15. Ryder does actually reference a barn and cow for the first time in the back of volume 8; the word "cattle" reappears in his will. For Arey's house, see the probate inventory that attends his will, Borthwick Institute, York, Leeds Wills, 1700–1830, "Will of William Arey of Leeds."

20. See JRD, August 16, 1744, for Ryder's entry written while in London (the lacuna in the diary lasts from August 9 to September 6). On Alice Wheelhouse, Elisabeth's sister in London, see Chapter 5 (Ryder records the death in London of his brother-in-law, William Woolgar, on May 6, 1761). There is also a list of names and addresses for people in London at the back of volume 13: "Directions for Brother Sparrow For Joseph Sparrows att Mrs Stewards att the three Golden Sugar Loaves att the corner of Mary Lebon near Golden Square London / Directions to Mr Wm Smith For Mr Smith Att the Company's Wharf near the King's Printing Office Black Fryers London / Directions to Mr John Pearson For Mr John Person att the two Green Canisters near St Anne Soho Richmond Street London / For William Woolgar in Pennington Street nigh old Gravell lane in Wapping / For Mr Joseph Sparrow Now at Mr Grantd Over against Gebsons Court in Marrow bone Street London." William Smith is hard to identify, but Joseph Sparrows was almost surely Ryder's brother-in-law, given the similarity in name to a woman he identifies in his will as his sister-in-law, Sarah Johanna Sparrow (Lupton MSS item 126); John Pearson also appears in his will as the beneficiary of £10. But note too that this list appears in volume 13, rather than volume 12, which covers the actual trip to London. This may have been one of the occasions when

Ryder already had his next diary volume lying around in the form of a blank book and used it to record some practical information. For a descriptive account of the luxuries some middling men and women sought to acquire and experience, see Maxine Berg, *Luxury and Pleasure in Eighteenth-Century Britain* (Oxford: Oxford University Press, 2005), ch. 6. Ryder went to Harrogate from August 10 to 19, 1757, and recorded only a single entry while there (in which he lamented the worldliness of the place and chided himself for not having been more willing to reprove others). The dancing and feasting were on September 18, 1747.

21. The vivid entry comes from JRD, March 31, 1766. Numerous other references to letter writing pervade the diary; for just the later years, see May 6, 1761, and September 1, 1763. William Woolgar, also spelled Woolagar, was Ryder's brother-in-law (see Lupton MSS item 126 and the will there that Ryder wrote dated June 8, 1757) by marriage to Elisabeth's sister Alice, but that doesn't entirely explain why Woolgar's address occasionally appears in diary volumes preceded by the word "for." Did this mean that Ryder wanted Woolgar—either "senior" or "junior," both of whom he mentions—to one day have the volume in which the name appears? Woolgar junior, who Ryder tells us was living at Wappin Wall, Shadwell, was almost surely the author of *Youth's Faithful Monitor, or, The Young Man's Best Companion* (London, 1761), a composite work that was one part English grammar and one part accounting guidebook. It also went through several editions, but see the title page of the 1761 edition for the confirmation of Woolgar's address. As for what was in Ryder's letters, we can only guess. "Suffering circumstances" indicates letters that were in part emotionally expressive, which lends general support to the argument in Sarah Pearsall, *Atlantic Families: Lives and Letters in the Later Eighteenth Century* (Oxford: Oxford University Press, 2008), ch. 3. But it is also worth noting that among the godly this cultural expression in letters well predated the eighteenth century. For a more descriptive account of eighteenth-century letter writing, see Susan Whyman, *The Pen and the People: English Letter Writers, 1660–1800* (Oxford: Oxford University Press, 2009).

22. Although Ryder likely read the *Leeds Mercury* and the *Leeds Intelligencer*, he doesn't tell us so directly, and he certainly doesn't evidence that he was copying information from these papers into his diary, as did the diarist John Lucas; see Jonathan Oates, *The Memoranda Book of John Lucas, 1712–1750* (Leeds: Thoresby Society, 2006). But Ryder effortlessly, if not occasionally unconsciously, quoted from the Bible—"rejoyce with

trembling," to take only the nearest example, is from Ps. 2:11. On Leeds and elections, see Wilson, *Gentlemen Merchants,* 166. The elections were in 1734, 1741, 1747, 1754, and 1761, with by-elections in 1742, 1751, and 1759. Ryder does not comment on the elections in 1747, which had no contest in York; he was also too consumed in early 1754 by the death of his wife to think about politics. More curiously, he says nothing about the election in early 1761, but he does complain in the spring about feeling ill; he simply may have been too sick to care. JRD, October 27, 1734 ("Hearing much of the talk"); January 13, 1741/42 (on divine agency in voting). Turner (1685–1757) represented Yorkshire from 1727 until 1747; see Romney Sedgwick, *The History of Parliament: The House of Commons, 1715–1754,* Vol. 2 (Oxford: Oxford University Press, 1970), 487. JRD, January 22, 1741/42. For the disturbances, see JRD, January 23, 1741/42. Walpole's government fell after this election on February 2, but Ryder alludes to "rumors about change of government" only on February 9.

23. On Ryder's brief but loaded reference to Israel and Ai (from Josh. 7:1–26), see JRD, August 3, 1756. Ryder notes Byng's execution on March 19, 1757, though Byng had been executed on March 14. News didn't always travel so slowly. Ryder expressed gratitude on November 26, 1748, that George II had returned safely from a journey. In fact, George had returned from Hanover only three days earlier on November 23. See E. B. Fryde, D. E. Greenway, S. Porter, and I. Roy, eds., *Handbook of British Chronology,* 3rd ed. (Cambridge: Cambridge University Press, 1986), 46. It took only two days for Ryder to find out about George II's death; see Chapter 3.

24. See Barker's diary at the John Rylands Library, Burgess MSS xvii, D18, "Portion of the Diary of Pentecost Barker (fl. 1690–1731)." As regards the earthquake in Lisbon, Ryder initially thought that two-thirds of the town and one hundred thousand people had perished; see JRD, November 28, 1755. (The actual number of dead has been hard for historians to derive, but it was likely around twenty-five thousand. See Nicholas Shrady, *The Last Day: Wrath, Ruin, and Reason in the Great Lisbon Earthquake of 1755* [New York: Viking, 2008], 49.) Ryder later revised his estimate in the back matter of volume 24. Alongside his wild speculation that fourteen thousand priests were killed, he wrote that a king's chapel that cost £100,000 to maintain had also been destroyed. See JRD, December 2, 1755.

25. On grinning and bearing it, see JRD, January 6, 1766. The woman accused of a scandalous sin is from JRD, December 21, 1748. The late-night visit happened on December 28, 1756.

26. The plundering Ryder mentioned on April 28 was probably driven at least partly by need. A week earlier he mentioned that the price of grain was high and the poor legitimately pitiable (JRD, April 22, 1740). On the Turnpike riots, see JRD, June 23, 30, 1753.

27. Ryder's last housekeeper, Mercy Ross, also happens to be one of the only domestics in his life whose name we can recover. See his will from 1757 (Lupton MSS item 126), where she was a recipient of just over £3; also see Appendix 2, where she is noted as having attended a funeral on Ryder's behalf.

28. On retirement, see Susannah R. Ottaway, *The Decline of Life: Old Age in Eighteenth-Century England* (Cambridge: Cambridge University Press, 2004), 81–89. Ryder's comment on May Day is in some ways one of the most revealing comments he ever made about his business life, probably because the occasion was extraordinary, but the fact that he was so loyal raises another question he never permits us to answer: was he loyal by choice or because there were limits to the independence of the town's ostensibly independent clothiers, given their inevitable relationships with the merchants? "Not slothfull in business" is from JRD, April, 18, 1760; notice that Ryder is also here combining biblical passages: Rom. 12:11 and Eph. 4:28. Note too that Ryder was already contemplating retirement as early as August 1754 (JRD, August 12, 1754), in part because of exhaustion from travel in the absence of his wife's help (JRD, September 7, 1754).

29. JRD, April 26, 1760; September 9, 1744. This is a recurring theme in the diary. For another example, from September 10, 1747: "This Day I heard several things in my own praise, viz.: Peoples having a good opinion of me & the like, but considering upon them I found very abasing thoughts of my self."

30. Regret about Ryder's prolonged bachelorhood appears early in the diary. The first allusion is made on July 13, 1733; a more specific mention appears on September 11 the same year; the quoted words are from JRD, October, 15, 1733. On Ryder being called on to resolve legal disputes, see JRD, September 9, 1748; on the divorce, see JRD, July 22, 24, 1749. The entry from July 31 gives evidence that the divorce happened anyway.

31. JRD, February 23, 1756 ("Gospell duties preacht up"). For more on these controversies, see Chapter 7. Ryder describes a Methodist as a "friend" on February 13, 1747. Seaver, *Wallington's World*, 109.

32. JRD, February 11, 1747 (on the saints); October 31, 1749 (for the book auction). On book auctions more generally, see James Raven, *The Business*

*of Books: Booksellers and the English Book Trade 1450–1850* (New Haven, CT: Yale University Press, 2007), 106–10.

33. Decades before Leeds established its circulating library, Ryder once recorded loaning to three friends Isaac Watts's *Horae Lyricae,* Elizabeth Rowe's *Meditations,* and the first volume of Matthew Henry's *Expositions*—all works of practical piety and all suggestive of the sort of pious books that scattered references in the diary tell us could be found in his library. Ryder dated the loan October 17, 1745, and recorded it not in the entry for that day, but, consistent with his use of the back pages for practical matters, at the end of volume 13.

34. JRD, January 12, 1749.

35. JRD, January 1, 1734.

36. Evidence of Ryder's handwriting shrinking at the end of a volume can be found in volumes 4, 9, 30, 31, and 33. It is also worth noting the absence of such examples from Ryder's most prosperous years.

37. The bookplates mentioned and quoted are in volumes 10 and 13, from 1742 and 1745–46, respectively. On the experience and the inventories of bookstores, see Raven, *The Business of Books,* passim, and Richard B. Sher, *The Enlightenment and the Book: Scottish Authors and Their Publishers in Eighteenth-Century Britain, Ireland, and America* (Chicago: University of Chicago Press, 2006), 110–14, 439–40.

38. Ryder also admits to reading a history of the assassination attempt on William III: "[I read] a piece of hystory I had in the house relating a conspiracy for assasinating King William of Glorious Memory, and of the Wonderfull appearance of providence in his deliverance and also in delivering our Nation from an Intended Invasion by the French, in order to reenstalling King James which affected me much" (JRD, January 28, 1757). Richard Baxter, *A Christian Directory: or, A summ of practical theologie . . . Directing Christians, how to use their knowledge and faith . . .* (London, 1673), 921. On Baxter's eclectic library, see my "Les bibliothèques de deux théologiens réformés du 17e siècle, L'un puritain anglais, l'autre pasteur huguenot," *Bulletin de la Sociètè de l'Histoire du Protestantisme Français* 147 (2001): 67–100.

## 3. "THAT SINGLE WORD WATCH"

1. On watching with the dead, see David Cressy, *Birth, Marriage, and Death: Ritual, Religion, and the Life-Cycle in Tudor and Stuart England* (Oxford: Oxford University Press, 1997); on sleep cycles, see A. Roger Ekirch, "Sleep We Have Lost: Pre-industrial Slumber in the British Isles,"

*American Historical Review* 106, 2 (2001), 364–65. *Hamlet,* Act III, sc. ii. On the use of "watch" as a timepiece, see the entry for the noun form of the word in the *Oxford English Dictionary.* On the social and economic meaning of timepieces, see E. P. Thompson, "Time, Work-Discipline and Industrial Capitalism," *Past and Present* 38, 1 (1967): 56–97; on wearing them, John Styles, *The Dress of the People: Everyday Fashion in Eighteenth-Century England* (New Haven, CT: Yale University Press, 2007), ch. 7; on the technology, David Landes, *Revolution in Time: Clocks and the Making of the Modern World* (Cambridge, MA: Harvard University Press, 1983).

2. Rogers quoted in Tom Webster, "Writing to Redundancy: Approaches to Spiritual Journals and Early Modern Spirituality," *Historical Journal* 39, 1 (1996): 37. The *Seven Treatises* was published in 1603 but emerged from a set of devotional exercises developed in the 1580s. Francis J. Bremer, "Rogers, Richard (1551–1618)," in *ODNB.* Excerpts of Ward's (and Rogers's) diary can be found in M. M. Knappen, ed., *Two Elizabethan Puritan Diaries by Richard Rogers and Samuel Ward* (Gloucester, MA: Peter Smith, 1966), 118. For important ways in which Knappen's edition can be misleading, see Margo Todd, "Puritan Self-Fashioning: The Diary of Samuel Ward," *Journal of British Studies* 31, 3 (1992): 236–64. John Oxenbridge, *A Double Watch-word, or the Duty of Watching . . . by one that hath desired to be found faithful in the work of a watchman* (London, 1661), 11, 13–17. Ryder, too, often refers to the devil as a "watchfull enemy"; for one example, see JRD, May 23, 1749. John Owen, *Of Temptation, the Nature and Power of it. The Danger of Entering into it. And the Means of Preventing that Danger. With a Resolution of Sundry Cases thereunto Belonging* (London, 1721), 24. On Owen and his "high Calvinism," see Richard L. Greaves, "Owen, John (1616–1683)," in *ODNB.*

3. Thomas Wilson, *The Principles and Duties of Christianity . . . .* (London, 1738 [1707]), 69–70. The Cambridge-educated Wilson later became the bishop of Sodor and Man. Wilson was nevertheless of no cool religious temperature. According to his biographer, he placed a great deal of attention on "private devotional initiatives" and was read by Whitefield. Carole Watterson Troxler, "Wilson, Thomas (1663–1755)," in *ODNB.* I make my comment about few Anglicans using the word with specificity on the basis of keyword searches using the electronic database *Eighteenth Century Collections Online.* For one other example, however, see the Royal Chaplain Edward Littleton's *Sermons upon Several Practical Subjects. Vol. 1* (London, 1735), 185–86. "Watching" is no less a loaded word in dozens of

Methodist hymns. See John Wesley, *A Collection of Hymns, for the Use of the People Called Methodists* (London, 1780).

4. "Hotter sort" was a phrase contemporaries used; for the metaphor of temperature to describe the most strenuous Protestants in the historiography, see Patrick Collinson, *The Elizabethan Puritan Movement* (Berkeley: University of California Press, 1967), and Peter Lake, *Moderate Puritans and the Elizabethan Church* (Cambridge: Cambridge University Press, 1982).

5. On the origins of some of the long-term patterns within English Calvinism, see Patrick Collinson, *Godly People: Essays in English Protestantism and Puritanism* (London: Hambledon, 1983), and for the comparative perspective, Philip Benedict, *Christ's Churches Purely Reformed: A Social History of Calvinism* (New Haven, CT: Yale University Press, 2002), 317–19. Owen quoted in Michael Walzer, *Revolution of the Saints: A Study in the Origins of Radical Politics* (Cambridge, MA: Harvard University Press, 1965), 170.

6. Alexandra Walsham, *Providence in Early Modern England* (Oxford: Oxford University Press, 1999), 9, 10, 15. On providential symmetries in the calendar, see David Cressy, *Bonfires and Bells: National Memory and the Protestant Calendar in Elizabethan and Stuart England* (1989), and James Joseph Caudle, "Measures of Allegiance: Sermon Culture and the Creation of a Public Discourse of Obedience and Resistance in Georgian Britain, 1714–1760" (PhD diss., Yale University, 1996), ch. 4. Thomas Sherlock, *A Letter from the Lord Bishop of London to the People of London and Westminster; on Occasion of the Late Earthquakes* (London, 1750), 10.

7. Richard Baxter, *A Christian Directory . . . Part III* (London, 1673), 679. Philip Doddridge, *The Rise and progress of religion in the soul . . .*, 4th ed. (London, 1748), 66. Isaac Ambrose, *Media: The Middle Things, In reference to The First and Last Things: Or, The Means, Duties, Ordinances, Both Secret, Private, and Publike, for continuance and increase of a Godly life . . .* (London, 1649), 41, 47. Every work that I have seen mention the *Media* cites 1650 (or later) as the publication date of the first edition, but the annotation on the Thomason copy at the British Library crosses out the "50" and offers as the correction November 17, 1649.

8. For Ambrose's diary entries, see Ambrose, *Media*, 71–85. Michael Mascuch writes that Ambrose's was the "first manual of piety to advocate diary-keeping explicitly"; Mascuch, *Origins of the Individualist Self: Autobiography and Self-Identity in England, 1591–1791* (Stanford, CA: Stanford University Press, 1996), 75. Spiritual diaries were nevertheless

being written at least as early as the moment when Calvinism was failing to fully transform the English church. Philip Benedict has, for example, found evidence of spiritual diary keeping in England as far back as a 1574 account of the life of the Marian martyr John Bradford (d. 1555); Benedict, "Some Uses of Autobiographical Documents in the Reformed Tradition," in *Von der dargestellten Person zum erinnerten Ich, Europäische Selbstzeugnisse als historische Quellen (1500–1850)*, ed. Kaspar von Greyerz, Hans Medick, and Patrice Veit (Köln: Böhlau Verlag, 2001), 357–58. The account of Bradford's life is in John Bradford, *The Writings*, Vol. I (Cambridge, 1848–1853), 35, where the journal is called "a book of daily practices."

9. For a rich discussion of Agur's Prayer, see Ethan H. Shagan, *The Rule of Moderation: Violence, Religion and the Politics of Restraint in Early Modern England* (Cambridge: Cambridge University Press, 2011), 229–36. Shagan's point is that the recommendation to be moderate during the Tudor-Stuart era was as much about the cultivation of civic as economic habits, but the two habits easily overlap even if Ryder, in a more commercial age, was more tuned in to the economic. For the number of editions of the *Media*, see the frontispiece of Isaac Ambrose, *Prima, Media, et Ultima: or, The First, Middle and Last Things* (Glasgow, 1765). Ambrose himself makes the reference to preaching in Leeds in the 1649 edition of the *Media*, 75. Ryder's mention of Ambrose occurs on March 9, 1745/46. The "Ambrose" is almost certainly Isaac; an author search of *Early English Books Online* and *Eighteenth Century Collections Online* reveals no other remotely likely candidates.

10. Spiritual diary writing awaits a book-length study—ideally something like James Amelang, *The Flight of Icarus: Artisan Autobiography in Early Modern Europe* (Stanford, CA: Stanford University Press, 1998), or D. Bruce Hindmarsh, *The Evangelical Conversion Narrative: Spiritual Autobiography in Early Modern England* (Oxford: Oxford University Press, 2005). But a handful of recent articles nevertheless importantly take on the subject. See Webster, "Writing to Redundancy"; Todd, "Puritan Self-Fashioning"; and Andrew Cambers, "Reading, the Godly, and Self-Writing in England, circa 1580–1720," *Journal of British Studies* 46, 4 (2007): 796–825. Two recent book-length studies consider the matter of godly self-writing more broadly: Mascuch, *Origins of the Individualist Self*, and John Stachniewski, *The Persecutory Imagination: English Puritanism and the Literature of Religious Despair* (Oxford: Oxford University Press, 1991). Also filled with insights about spiritual diary writing are Paul

Seaver, *Wallington's World: A Puritan Artisan in Seventeenth-Century London* (Stanford, CA: Stanford University Press, 1985), and Alan Macfarlane, *The Family Life of Ralph Josselin: A Seventeenth Century Clergyman* (Cambridge: Cambridge University Press, 1977). Some of this important work hints at the significance of watching—"Rather than mystical contemplation, a militant watchfulness seems to characterize the lay saint" (Seaver, *Wallington's World*, 20); "A recurring theme [in Richard Rogers's diary] is 'watchfulness'" (Webster, "Writing to Redundancy," 49). But these authors go no further into its precise meaning.

11. For a curious exception to the rule about blank pages, consider Ryder's entry from June 10, 1747, which is written on the left page. The facing page on the right is blank. When you turn that blank page, his next entry (written on a new page) is from June 13. Does this mean he had stopped writing the diary for two days and then, on resuming on the 13th, felt a need to leave a page blank for entries he might later write to deal with the missing days? In any case, the page remained blank, and June 11 and 12 remained unaccounted for. For an example of two pages having been stuck together when Ryder originally wrote the journal, see the pages that divide the entry for April 27, 1749. I have not come across a lay spiritual diary from the eighteenth century longer than Ryder's. For a more massive clerical diary, however, see that of the Calvinistic Welsh Methodist Howell Harris, collected in some three hundred manuscript volumes at the National Library of Wales, Aberystwyth.

12. The point that later editions of diaries can misleadingly present the original manuscripts as polished has become an accepted premise of the scholarship since Todd's "Puritan Self-Fashioning."

13. I am not suggesting that Ryder never read his own diary but rather that the material evidence that he strenuously read his diary as part of his devotional practice isn't there. For that matter, there is also often evidence that Ryder never bothered to read through certain entries at all. In some cases, for example, he failed to draw a line through obviously repeated words—words that on other occasions he would cross out. See, for example, the opening sentence of the entry from May 20, 1754.

14. For an elaborate version of the argument that increasing neatness of diaries formally reflects individualism, see Mascuch, *Origins of the Individualist Self*.

15. *A Critical Edition of John Beadle's "A Journall or Diary of a Thankfull Christian,"* ed. Germaine Fry Murray (New York: Garland, 1996), 28.

JRD, October 18, 1747. "Mine and *others* practice" reminds us not only that Ryder was far from alone in keeping a diary, but that he was also well aware of this fact.

16. For the resolutions, see the back material of Ryder's second volume. On the role of covenants in diary keeping, see Cambers, "Reading, the Godly, and Self-Writing," 805–6. For nearly identical resolutions, see the advice given in the mid-eighteenth-century edition of *A Call to the Unconverted,* a work that Ryder read (see note 44 below). The book drew on the works of Baxter and Philip Doddridge and could almost be superimposed over the image the diary offers of how Ryder spent his days. The table of contents provides the most concise summary: "Secret and family devotions in the morning . . . Seriousness in devotion . . . Diligence in business . . . watchfulness against temptations . . . Government of the thoughts when in solitude . . . Management of the discourse when in company . . . The value of time . . . Temperance in eating and drinking . . . Observations of Providence . . . Dependance on divine influences . . . The conclusion of the day . . . Family and secret devotions of the evening . . . Lying down with a pious temper . . . A serious view of death, proper to be taken at the close of the day . . . Meditations when we awake in the night." *A Call to the Unconverted. By the late Reverend and pious Mr. Richard Baxter. To which are added, directions how to spend every ordinary day, and every Lord's day. Collected from the works of Mr. Baxter and Dr. Doddridge. With a collection of psalms, hymns, and prayers, for Morning and Evening, in the Closet, and in the Family* (London, 1746).

17. *The Diary of James Clegg of Chapel en le Frith, 1708–1755,* 3 vols., ed. Vanessa S. Doe, (Derbyshire: Derbyshire Record Society, 1978), xlvii. Seaver, *Wallington's World,* 6–12. Todd, "Puritan Self-Fashioning," 249, 259. Ambrose, *Media,* 71 (although note that there is no way of knowing whether Ambrose's first entry in the excerpts of his journal that he includes in the *Media* was in fact the first entry in the diary itself, which apparently has not survived). *Extracts from the Spiritual Diary of John Rutty, M.D.* (Falmouth: J. Trathan, 1840), 9.

18. Rutty quoted in Arthur Ponsonby, *English Diaries: A Review of English Diaries from the Sixteenth to the Twentieth Century* (London: Methuen, 1923), 218. Alexander Jaffray, *Diary of Alexander Jaffray: to which are added particulars of his subsequent life . . .,* ed. John Baclay (London, 1834), 71–74. Jaffray too was sure to have read Baxter.

19. JRD, November 20, 1733; July 16, 1734; July 22, 1735.

20. *The Rev. Oliver Heywood, B.A. 1603–1702: His Autobiography, Diaries, Anecdote and Event Books: Illustrating the General and Family History of Yorkshire and Lancashire*, ed. J. Horsfall Turner (Brighouse: A. B. Bayes, 1881–1885).

21. JRD, April 8, 1761; *A Call to the Unconverted*, 120.

22. JRD, March 17, 1741/42 (suicidal thought). *The Life of the Reverend Mr. George Trosse, Written by Himself, and Published Posthumously According to his Order in 1714*, ed. A. W. Brink (Montreal: McGill–Queen's University Press, 1974), 80. Seaver, *Wallington's World*, 21–22. There were some twenty thousand reported cases of suicide in England between 1500 and 1800, and by no means was the phenomenon limited to the godly. Michael MacDonald and Terrence R. Murphy, *Sleepless Souls: Suicide in Early Modern England* (Oxford: Oxford University Press, 1990), 357. But the godly may nevertheless have been particularly prone to it and were certainly tuned in to it. Ralph Josselin noted when the deaths he recorded were self-inflicted (Macfarlane, *The Family Life of Ralph Josselin*, 169–70), as did Ryder, although in the main body of his diary more than in his diary lists. See Chapter 6.

23. JRD, May 26, 1735. *Diary of James Clegg*, passim. Ponsonby made the relevant excepts from Rutty's journal in *English Diaries*, 215–20. For another diarist who, like Rutty, struggled with drink, see *The Diary of Edmund Harrold, Wigmaker of Manchester 1712–15*, ed. Craig Horner (Aldershot: Ashgate, 2008).

24. Wallington quoted in Seaver, *Wallington's World*, 128. JRD, June 21, 1733. *A Critical Edition of John Beadle*, 39, 50. Beadle wrote in 1650, but his only book was not published until 1656.

25. JRD, January 17, 1733/34. Ryder often read scripture aloud in meetings and in the 1750s took on the role of distributing his church's charities. JRD, July 8, 1749; February 10, 1748/49. JRD, January 12, 1736/37; January 31, 1740.

26. JRD, March 8, 1749 ("wavering frame"); March 10, 11, 12, 1748 (on his irenicism); April 14, 1750 (on reading, probably, Sherlock).

27. JRD, December 13, 1733; January 29, 1735/36; April 8, 1748.

28. JRD, September 18, 1749 ("Decay in the life"); February 11, 12, 1741/42; October 18, 1749; April 10, 15, 1766. For Ryder's biblical allusions, see 2 Pet. 2:22 and Rom. 6:23.

29. JRD, October 14, 1744.

30. In defining poetry in these formalist terms I borrow heavily from Michael Riffaterre, *Semiotics of Poetry* (Bloomington: University of Indiana Press, 1978), esp. ch. 1.

31. JRD, February 8, 1748/49 (gardening metaphor); December 6, 1735 (hewing wood); January 29, 1735 (pharaohs).

32. JRD, November 5, 1767 and 1748.

33. JRD, March 25, 1734, 1737, 1738, 1741, 1742.

34. JRD, April 5, 1757, 1758, 1759 (after the calendar change in 1752, Ryder began to celebrate his and Elisabeth's birthdays on April 5).

35. JRD, April 21, 1740. Note too that extreme weather did not keep Ryder from his business travels; JRD, May 14, 1741. *Diary of James Clegg*, 5.

36. JRD, April 29, 1742; August 10, 1737; July 14, 1738; August 24, 1733.

37. JRD, August 9, 11, 1745.

38. The quoted passages from the diary here come, in sequence, from JRD, August 6, 14, 1745; September 20, 21, 28, 29, 1745; October 10, 22, 23, 1745; and April 23, 1746. On Jacobitism more broadly, see Paul Kléber Monod, *Jacobitism and the English People, 1688–1788* (Cambridge: Cambridge University Press, 1989), and Daniel Szechi, *The Jacobites: Britain and Europe, 1688–1788* (Manchester: Manchester University Press, 1994).

39. On Elisabeth's death, see Chapter 5. On writing at 11 p.m., see JRD, January 26, 1756. In my research on diaries I have come across no diarist as obsessed with the details of time as Henry Crooke, WYAS, Clarke MSS, "The Diary of the Revd. Henry Crooke."

40. On the emergence of diaries from commonplace books, see Mascuch, *Origins of the Individualist Self*, 81–89. In a note inserted at the end of volume 26, Ryder writes, "June the 2 1757. I hereby testify to my Executors Administrator or Assings That I have Given to Hannah Arey and Grace Arey Her Sister to be Delivered at my Death Two Deel Boxes with all the Manuscripts therein or may be found about the house Witness my hand Joseph Ryder note this was writt before the signing of My Last Will——
——." JRD, July 27, 1754. Note that this might also be a case of pronoun confusion, which could afflict even the most pious spiritual diarists with no avowed interest in audience. See Todd, "Puritan Self-Fashioning," 246–47. JRD, April 26, 1761 (literary rivalry). If Ryder often alluded to other authors, he nevertheless did not make a practice of explicitly quoting them.

41. JRD, March 29–31, 1767.

42. JRD, January 16, 1736 ("coldness"); November 11, 1735 ("weariness"). Cf. JRD, August 4, 1745, when Ryder thoroughly marks out and then rewrites the third line of the poem "Christ a King."

43. Clapham quoted in Walsham, *Providence in Early Modern England*, 159. *The Autobiography of Benjamin Franklin*, 2nd ed., ed. Leonard W. Labaree, Ralph L. Ketcham, Helen C. Boatfield, and Helene H. Fineman (New Haven, CT: Yale University Press, 2003), 48–49.

44. JRD, October 12, 1760. Ryder's recollection of biblical verse is generally very good even if imperfect enough to suggest that he typically used his memory rather than the open book. Evidence that his memory was faltering in old age appears in an entry from June 4, 1761, where he writes, "I read also a little in a book called Allen's call to the unconverted." Here Ryder was confusing Joseph Alleine's *An Alarm to Unconverted Sinners* (1672), to which Richard Baxter wrote the introduction, with Baxter's *A Call to the Unconverted* (1658). It is a useful slip-up, nonetheless, in revealing that Ryder had likely read both works, not surprisingly, given their popularity and the degree to which his own writing reflects their basic message. On the popularity of these works, see Isabel Rivers, "Dissenting and Methodist Books of Practical Divinity," in *Books and Their Readers in Eighteenth-Century England*, ed. Rivers (Leicester: Leicester University Press, 1982), 139–40. JRD, February 21, 1741/42 ("Self Tryal Necessary"); January 22, 1748/49 ("A Good Mans Character"); August 20, 1738 ("Vanity of Vanities"). We will turn to Ryder's verses on death in Chapter 5. For a vivid poem on old age, see JRD, June 22, 1739. JRD, December 4, 1737 (on Caroline). The obituary of George II is in the back of volume 30.

45. Leading up to Whitaker's sermon, Ryder was in a frenzy about the Jacobites: November 20, 1745: "This Day A Great terror prevailed in our Town Upon the news of an Approaching Enemy But before night was Somewhat allay'd by a Contrary account." November 21, 1745: "This day upon the apprehension of Our Enemys approach Great Consternation fill the hearts of Numbers, Not knowing what means or methods to Use for their Safety." November 22, 1745: "This Day our Dangers from our Enemies as we hear Seem to Draw nearer and peoples fears & Perplexities much Increase." November 23, 1745: "This Day in the former part of it Our Towns people were all in Great Consternation being apprehensive of the Approach of this Formidable Enemy that is risen up against us, but in the Evening hearing of his being at a Stand, it afforded Some little Comfort being much like the news of a reprieve of a Condemned Malefactor."

46. JRD, October 13, 1745.

47. See JRD, September 12, 1755, for one example of stray verse. Or consider JRD, October 10, 1752, when he follows a day of busyness (but no sermon)

with this couplet: "From Worldly things O Lord withdraw my Love / And place my Chief delight on things above."

48. Notice too Ryder using the phrase "weariness in well doing" in reference to the meaning of the diary. JRD, March 29, 1736; April 11, 1747. On Wallington and Rastick, see Cambers, "Reading, the Godly, and Self-Writing," 805.

49. JRD, January 14, 1749.

50. For an interesting discussion of the structural similarities, see Webster, "Writing to Redundancy."

51. "Quand le livre reste et que le monde tout autour change, le livre change," Pierre Bourdieu and Roger Chartier, "La Lecture: une pratique culturelle," in *Pratiques de la lecture,* ed. Roger Chartier (Marseille: Rivages, 1985), 236. Charles Edwin Whiting, ed., *Two Yorkshire Diaries: The Diary of Arthur Jessop and Ralph Ward's Journal,* Yorkshire Archaeological Society Record Series, Vol. 117 (Gateshead on Tyne: Northumberland, 1952). Jessop also interestingly reflects the shift from measuring the weather by its extremes to measuring it by its regular patterns that Jan Golinski has written about in *British Weather and the Climate of Enlightenment* (Chicago: University of Chicago Press, 2007). Mather is quoted in Keith Thomas, *Man and the Natural World: A History of the Modern Sensibility* (New York: Oxford University Press, 1983), 38. *Diary of James Clegg,* 925. *The Diary of Thomas Turner, 1754–1765,* ed. David Vaisey (Oxford: Oxford University Press, 1984), xxv.

52. William H. Sewell, Jr., "The Concept(s) of Culture," in *Beyond the Cultural Turn,* ed. Victoria E. Bonnell and Lynn Hunt (Berkeley: University of California Press, 1999), 57–58. Christopher Durston and Jacqueline Eales, "Introduction: The Puritan Ethos, 1560–1700," in *The Culture of English Puritanism, 1560–1700,* ed. Durston and Eales (London: Macmillan, 1996), 1–31.

53. To take only the most immediate examples: Walsham's path-breaking study of providence ends in 1640; the overview of Puritan culture I have just paraphrased ends in 1700; Andrew Camber's short survey of the "Puritan diary" ends in 1720.

54. The fate of the spiritual diary in the nineteenth century is beyond the scope of this book. It is suggestive that Leonore Davidoff and others have argued that over the course of the late eighteenth and nineteenth centuries, "intensely religious men came to depend on women, particularly female members of their family, to act as keepers of their conscience and

protectors or their spiritual self." Spiritual watchfulness may survive in the industrial era, in some sense, in gendered terms. Leonore Davidoff, Megan Doolittle, Janet Fink, and Katherine Holden, eds., *The Family Story: Blood, Contract, and Intimacy, 1830–1960* (London: Longman, 1999), 59.

55. On Methodist diary keeping, see Hindmarsh, *The Evangelical Conversion Narrative*. The fullest account of the relationship between *Robinson Crusoe* and spiritual self-writing is still G. A. Starr, *Defoe and Spiritual Autobiography* (Princeton, NJ: Princeton University Press, 1965). My reading of the book's relationship to Puritan culture is shaped more, however, by the narrative offered in Leopold Damrosch, *God's Plot and Man's Stories: Studies in the Fictional Imagination from Milton to Fielding* (Chicago: University of Chicago Press, 1985). We can still easily let this image of a torch being passed mislead us into believing that the spiritual diary is simply killed by its offspring in an act of profound misunderstanding and misrepresentation. The story is more complicated. As Ryder makes abundantly clear, recognizable "Puritan diaries" continued to be written long after Defoe was dead and buried. Moreover, *Robinson Crusoe* can still be read as a religious book, and Defoe was himself a committed Dissenter—see Defoe's *The Family Instructor* (1715) or *Religious Courtship* (1722), both books that easily could have sat on Ryder's shelves. But it is nevertheless a curious fact of the novel—a fact shrewdly recognized by an earlier generation of literary critics—that Crusoe seems not to know *how* to write a proper spiritual diary. And this failure seems to be tied to more than the general failure of novelists to capture the awkward flow of diary writing that, taking a cue from Lejeune, I discuss in Chapter 6.

56. Michel Foucault, *Discipline and Punish: The Birth of the Prison*, trans. Alan Sheridan (New York: Vintage, 1977), 201. Bentham's work was written in 1787 but is here quoted from a fuller 1791 edition: Jeremy Bentham, *Panopticon: or, the inspection-house. Containing the idea of a new principle of construction applicable to any sort of establishment, in which persons of any Description are to be kept under Inspection* . . . (Dublin, 1791), 201, 2, and the title page. The New England Calvinist is quoted in David Hackett Fischer, *Albion's Seed: Four British Folkways in America* (Oxford: Oxford University Press, 1989), 118.

57. Nicholas Phillipson, *Adam Smith* (New Haven, CT: Yale University Press, 2010), 274. I am not suggesting that Smith was in some obvious sense borrowing from Calvinism. Stoicism was his more apparent source: the

self-command that Stoicism encouraged "meant learning to look beyond the *indifferentia* to the evidence that the moral and natural worlds provided of order and design. Above all, it meant cultivating a love of its benevolent Creator"; Phillipson, *Adam Smith*, 20. But the end result for the Stoic in antiquity was detachment and *apathaeia*. The self-control both Smith and Ryder imagined by way of an ocular trope meant, in contrast, active engagement—with the social, in the former's case, and with the divine for the latter.

58. David Zaret, "The Use and Abuse of Textual Data," in *Weber's Protestant Ethic: Origins, Evidence, Contexts*, ed. Hartmut Lehmann and Guenther Roth (Cambridge: Cambridge University Press, 1993), 245.

## 4. "AN ACTIVE FRAME IN COURTS BELOW"

1. The place to begin in the vast historiography surrounding the Weber thesis is the text itself. The most up-to-date and far and away the best edition for both its lucid introduction and subtle translation (and to which all citations here refer) is Max Weber, *The Protestant Ethic and the Spirit of Capitalism with Other Writings on the Rise of the West*, 4th ed., trans. Stephen Kalberg (Oxford: Oxford University Press, 2009). Also indispensable are the many essays in William H. Swatos, Jr., and Lutz Kaelber, eds., *The Protestant Ethic Turns 100: Essays on the Centenary of the Weber Thesis* (Boulder, CO: Paradigm, 2005), and Hartmut Lehmann and Guenther Roth, eds., *Weber's Protestant Ethic: Origins, Evidence, Contexts* (Cambridge: Cambridge University Press, 1993). Margaret C. Jacob and I first explored many of these connections in our "Missing, Now Found in the Eighteenth Century: Weber's Protestant Capitalist," *American Historical Review* 108, 1 (2003): 20–49. Kalberg's bibliography is thorough, current, and covers various attempts to lend Weber's thesis empirical support. A number of recent studies that have made use of the thesis are also addressed elsewhere in the notes to this chapter. Worth mentioning here is probably the most damning overarching critique of Weber's thesis, which has been put forward by the sociologist Guenther Roth. Roth argues, in short, that the Anglophile Weber had immediate political reasons for idealizing the positive link between religion and the economy in early modern England and America. It is certainly true that the *Protestant Ethic* had domestic rhetorical force because of Weber's opposition to dominant political and religious interests in imperial Germany, but there is no necessary reason to believe that its insights into the psychology of merchants and Protestants in the early

modern English-speaking world must then be disregarded: context doesn't automatically invalidate content. For Weber's idealization of early Anglo commerce and religion to work as a foil for his political agenda, it also had to have a convincing degree of truth. See Guenther Roth, "The Young Max Weber: Anglo-American Religious Influences and Protestant Social Reform in Germany," *International Journal of Politics, Culture, and Society* 10 (1997): 659–71. On Weber's life more generally, see Fritz Ringer, *Max Weber: An Intellectual Biography* (Chicago: University of Chicago Press, 2004).

2. Kalberg makes these points with clarity and elaboration in his introduction to Weber, *Protestant Ethic*, 7–58.

3. The theater metaphor comes from Thomas Beard, *The Theatre of Gods Judgements* (London, 1597), and is discussed at length in Paul Seaver, *Wallington's World: A Puritan Artisan in Seventeenth-Century London* (Stanford, CA: Stanford University Press, 1985), ch. 3, as well as Alexandra Walsham, *Providence in Early Modern England* (Oxford: Oxford University Press, 1999), ch. 2.

4. On Baxter, see William Lamont, *Richard Baxter and the Millennium* (London: Croom Helm, 1979). Lamont more directly addresses the link between Baxter and Weber in *Puritanism and Historical Controversy* (Montreal: McGill–Queen's University Press, 1996), ch. 7, where he argues that while early Baxter may line up at times with R. H. Tawney's and Christopher Hill's view of him as a capitalist in spirit, later Baxter had come to associate the free market so much with spiritually dangerous antinomianism that he had effectively become a socialist ("a seventeenth-century Tawney," 128). In fact, Lamont's take on Baxter is not entirely unlike Weber's, who still finds Baxter at some distance from the capitalist spirit.

5. Weber, *Protestant Ethic*, 81–82.

6. Daniel L. Pals, *Eight Theories of Religion*, 2nd ed. (Oxford: Oxford University Press, 2006), 155–56.

7. For a good visualization of the Protestant-capitalist continuum, see Stephen Kalberg, "On the Neglect of Weber's Protestant Ethic as a Theoretical Treatise," *Sociological Theory* (1996): 63, also reprinted in Weber, *Protestant Ethic*, xlviii. Weber, *Protestant Ethic*, 105, 18. I am not suggesting that Weber's characterizations of Baxter and Franklin are entirely accurate. Baxter was not the predestinarian Weber imagined; Franklin was also one of the most charitable Americans in the eighteenth century. For the former, see Lamont, *Richard Baxter*, passim; for the latter,

see Edmund Morgan, *Benjamin Franklin* (New Haven, CT: Yale University Press, 2002). But in any case, Weber was drawn to Baxter and Franklin because they were so influential, and when it comes to their influence, perception could count more than reality. Moreover, while the early reformers may not have conflated time and money, Calvin and the Reformed tradition more broadly were still obsessed with maximizing time for the sake of spiritual life. See Max Engammare, *On Time, Punctuality, and Discipline in Early Modern Calvinism*, trans. Karin Maag (Cambridge: Cambridge University Press, 2010), ch. 3.

8. On the importance of textiles throughout the early modern world, see Lex Heerma van Voss, Els Hiemstra-Kuperus, and Elise van Nederveen Meerkerk, eds., *The Ashgate Companion to the History of Textile Workers, 1650–2000* (Farnham: Ashgate, 2010).

9. Weber, *Protestant Ethic*, 159 (emphasis in the original). "Economic change in all periods depends, more than most economists think, on what people believe," writes Joel Mokyr at the top of page one of his economic history of Ryder's Britain, *The Enlightened Economy: An Economic History of Britain, 1700–1850* (New Haven, CT: Yale University Press, 2010), 1–12. Keith Wrightson is similarly attuned to the dynamic relationship between the cultural and the material in *Earthly Necessities: Economic Lives in Early Modern Britain* (New Haven, CT: Yale University Press, 2000), as is Deidre McCloskey in *Bourgeois Dignity: Why Economics Can't Explain the Modern World* (Chicago: University of Chicago Press, 2010).

10. On the central role Weber played (by virtue of concepts like elective affinity) in jump-starting the discipline of modern anthropology by so heavily influencing Clifford Geertz and Pierre Bourdieu, see Charles F. Keyes, "Weber and Anthropology," *Annual Review of Anthropology* 31 (2002): 233–55. My understanding of the notion of "elective affinity" is indebted to Patrick Collinson, "Religion, Society, and the Historian," *Journal of Religious History* 23, 2 (1999), 166–67; "the virtues cultivated by capitalism," Weber, *Protestant Ethic*, 89.

11. On Baxter's wariness of the doctrine of predestination, see Lamont, *Richard Baxter*, 127; Dewey D. Wallace, Jr., *Puritans and Predestination: Grace in English Protestant Theology, 1525–1695* (Chapel Hill: University of North Carolina Press, 1982), 136. On the politically radical implications of antinomianism, which Baxter and Laud both saw, if from very different angles, see David Como, *Blown by the Spirit: Puritanism and the Emergence of an Antinomian Underground in Pre-Civil-War England* (Stanford, CA:

Stanford University Press, 2004). On Zwingli, see Philip Benedict, *Christ's Churches Purely Reformed: A Social History of Calvinism* (New Haven, CT: Yale University Press, 2002), 25. Walsham, *Providence in Early Modern England*, 9–10.

12. JRD, September 1, 1749. The distinction between "credal" and "experimental" Calvinism that some historians have used to clarify English attitudes about predestinarianism in the early seventeenth century also inadequately accounts for Ryder's outlook. In one sense, Ryder was no longer interested in the matters of separatism and the visible and invisible church, both of which had so often been tied to arguments about predestination a century earlier. In another sense, and especially when we consider Ryder's views on the Trinity (see Chapter 6), Ryder was apparently uninterested in or, less likely, unaware of the fact that predestination could be such a tricky issue at the conceptual level. When it comes to predestination, Ryder sounds very different from the more nerve-racked Nehemiah Wallington, for example, and the likely reason is that the finer points of this doctrine were simply not the pressing issues for a lay spiritual diarist that they had been in the mid-1600s. Alternatively, it might make sense to describe Ryder's outlook as both "experimental" and "credal"—as someone, that is, who lived the search for election with varying degrees of intensity even as he retained his beliefs in some basic version of predestination. But if Ryder then blurs the line between these two polarities by embodying both, this would only make the distinction between credal and experimental inapplicable from another angle. For the classic statement on this distinction, see the introduction to R. T. Kendall, *Calvin and English Calvinism to 1649* (Oxford: Oxford University Press, 1980). For the distinction where it works better to clarify religious attitudes than it does in Ryder's case, see Peter Lake, "Calvinism and the English Church, 1570–1635," *Past and Present* 114 (1987): 32–76.

13. Kaspar Von Greyerz, "Biographical Evidence on Predestination, Covenant, and Special Providence," in *Weber's Protestant Ethic*, ed. Lehmann and Roth, 273–76, 281, 283. Also see Von Greyerz, *Vorsehungsglaube und Kosmologie: Studien zu Englischen Selbstzeugnissen des 17. Jahrhunderts*, Publications of the German Historical Institute, London, 25 (Göttingen, 1990).

14. JRD, November 20, 1733.

15. A consideration of this anguish is also missing from some older path-breaking accounts of the demoralization of acquisitiveness, which were

also admittedly written to understand social morality rather than the inner workings of individual behavior. R. H. Tawney memorably wrote that "the heart of man holds mysteries of contradiction which live together in vigorous incompatibility," but he also never delved into how difficult it might be to deal with radical ambivalence; R. H. Tawney, *Religion and the Rise of Capitalism: A Historical Study* (New York: Harcourt, Brace, 1926), 212. Albert O. Hirschman, *The Passions and the Interests: Political Arguments for Capitalism before Its Triumph* (Princeton, NJ: Princeton University Press, 1977), and Joyce Oldham Appleby, *Economic Thought in Seventeenth-Century England* (Princeton, NJ: Princeton University Press, 1978), both also shed much light on the conceptual difficulty of demoralizing self-interest but confine themselves to the theorists. A sufficient consideration of psychic anguish is also missing from more recent research that suggests that belief in Hell continues to be an appreciable motivator of economic productivity. See Rachel M. McCleary and Robert J. Barro, "Religion and Economy," *Journal of Economic Perspectives* 20, 2 (2006): 49–72.

16. On some of the problems with the Weber thesis as it is crudely understood, see Benedict, *Christ's Churches Purely Reformed*, xix–xxi, 328–29, 540–41. Also see Paul Seaver, "The Puritan Work Ethic Revisited," *Journal of British Studies* 19 (1980), 44. Seaver is skeptical about the Weber thesis in light of Wallington's case, but Wallington is not all that far from Ryder in avoiding excess. Riches for Wallington came not from honest labor, but from " 'lying and oppression' " and from " 'cruelty and unmercifulness to the poor.' " But Wallington nevertheless implied a distinction between excess and moderate success. If the emerging capitalist ethos was for Wallington "a hazard to one's eternal soul for the sake of vainglorious and temporary show," Seaver also admits that Wallington never praised voluntary poverty as a Christian virtue or actually sought to be poor. Part of the reason we may not find spiritual comments in the writings of eighteenth-century men of commerce is that the surviving sources that tell us about their lives are mostly commercial by design. See, for example, John Smail, ed., *Woollen Manufacturing in Yorkshire: The Memorandum Books of John Brearley, Cloth Frizzer at Wakefield, 1758–1762* (Woodbridge: Boydell, 2001); S. D. Smith, ed., *'An Exact and Industrious Tradesman': The Letter Book of Joseph Symson of Kendal, 1711–1720* (Oxford: Oxford University Press, 2002); K. H. Burley, "An Essex Clothier of the Eighteenth Century," *Economic History Review* 11 (1958): 289–301. More

curiously, Julia de Lacy Mann also found little spiritual concern in the journal of George Wansey, a clothier and Quaker from Wiltshire who was born four decades before Ryder and whose diary is mostly "an impersonal record of the weather and of public events"; de Lacy Mann, "A Wiltshire Family of Clothiers: George and Hester Wansey, 1683–1714," *Economic History Review* 9 (1956): 252. On the types of Dissenters, see Michael Watts, *The Dissenters, Vol. 2: The Expansion of Evangelical Nonconformity* (Oxford: Oxford University Press, 1995), 23. On the survival of the Muggletonians, see E. P. Thompson, *Witness against the Beast: William Blake and the Moral Law* (New York: New Press, 1993).

17. See, for example, Herbert Heaton, *The Yorkshire Woollen and Worsted Industries, from the Earliest Times up to the Industrial Revolution,* 2nd ed. (Oxford: Clarendon, 1965); E. P. Thompson, *The Making of the English Working Class* (London: Victor Gollancz, 1963); W. G. Rimmer, "The Industrial Profile of Leeds, 1740–1840," *PTS* 14 (1968): 130–57; R. G. Wilson, *Gentlemen Merchants: The Merchant Community in Leeds, 1700–1830* (Manchester: Manchester University Press, 1971); Pat Hudson, *The Genesis of Industrial Capital: A Study of the West Riding Wool Textile Industry, c. 1750–1850* (Cambridge: Cambridge University Press, 1986); John Smail, *Merchants, Markets and Manufacture: The English Wool Textile Industry in the Eighteenth Century* (New York: Palgrave Macmillan, 1999). On the stagnation, see Heaton, *The Yorkshire Woollen and Worsted Industries,* 251. Hudson, *Genesis of Industrial Capital,* 31. Also see R. G. Wilson, "The Supremacy of the Yorkshire Cloth Industry in the Eighteenth Century," in *Textile History and Economic History: Essays in Honour of Miss Julia de Lacy Mann,* ed. N. B. Harte and K. G. Ponting (Manchester: Manchester University Press, 1973), 223–46. The extension of this network is visible, for example, in the growth of the Ibbetson-Koster firm; Smail, *Merchants, Markets and Manufacture,* 69.

18. "A Poem Descriptive of the Manners of the Clothiers, Written about the Year 1730," *PTS* 41 (1947): 275–81.

19. According to the *Oxford English Dictionary,* "Sammy" had come to mean a "ninny" or "simpleton" by the nineteenth century. This poem suggests those meanings were already in place in the early eighteenth century.

20. Heaton, *The Yorkshire Woollen and Worsted Industries,* 342, 349. Ryder's first mention of wool occurs in a metaphorical sense on January 9, 1736.

21. See the *Leeds Mercury* and *Intelligencer,* which can be found in the Early English Newspapers microfilm collection; excerpts also appear in several

editions of *PTS*. On Ryder's trip to York and back in a day, see JRD, August 1, 1754; he made the same trip, and was wearied by it, a week later (JRD, August 8, 1754).

22. JRD, December 11, 1751. Ryder mentions robbers on January 14, 1741. International travelers also noted that Britain had no shortage of highwaymen; see Mokyr, *Enlightened Economy*, 401. On the arrival of the turnpike in Leeds, see William Albert, *The Turnpike Road System in England, 1663–1840* (Cambridge: Cambridge University Press, 1972), 48. WYAS, Clarke MSS, "The Diary of the Revd. Henry Crooke," entries from July 2, July 23, and December 2, 1768. Defoe talks about the bad quality of the roads in *A Tour Thro' the Whole Island of Great Britain . . .* (London, 1748), 121. Thoresby mentions them in *The Diary of Ralph Thoresby*, Vol. 1 (London, 1830), 295. Young quoted in Heaton, *The Yorkshire Woollen and Worsted Industries*, 397; Heaton makes the comment about good roads being veritable blessings, 257.

23. Defoe, *A Tour*, 120. If it seems as if Defoe is exaggerating here about the silence of the market, Ralph Thoresby also writes that the cloth markets in Leeds are conducted "in a few Hours Time, and this with so profound a Silence as is surprising to Strangers, who from the adjoining Galleries, etc. can hear no more Noise than the lowly Murmur of the Merchant upon the Exchange *at London,*" *Ducatus Leodeinsis: or, The topography of the ancient and populous towns and parish of Leedes . . .*, 2nd ed. (Leeds, 1816), 17. JRD, September 6, 1737.

24. JRD, January 17, 1736/37. An entry from December 5, 1751, provides an eloquent example of Ryder's gratefulness to God for prosperity, although even this was a thoroughly mixed feeling: "The Evening I have had the account of a Christian Friend of mine who is in a great perplexity by the want of trade & business and likely to be reduced. It helps my admiration of Gods peculiar favour to me who has through life so very plentifully supported me. Yet in the midst of plenty would beg for grace that I may consume nothing upon my lust, or vanity, but endeavour to testify my gratefull frame of heart by Improving whatever God bestows to his Glory and the Good of Others, and would pity Such as want the mercys which I enjoy and crave a Sanctify'd use of afflictions for my Friends, and a Sanctify'd use of my mercys while confined to me, and for a readiness to part with them whenever God calls them from me, or me from them. For mercys I enjoy I would give praise / And in Gods fear would spend remaining Days." JRD, July 9, 1737.

25. Craig Muldrew, *The Economy of Obligation: The Culture of Credit and Social Relations in Early Modern England* (London: Macmillan, 1998).

26. Muldrew, *The Economy of Obligation*, 7. On credit in the West Riding, see Hudson, *Genesis of Industrial Capital*, 140–42, and John Smail, "The Culture of Credit in Eighteenth-Century Commerce: The English Textile Industry," *Enterprise and Society* 4 (2003), 299–325. It is not surprising in light of the length of the repayment period that Ryder on one occasion mentions appraising the goods of a recently deceased man who left his wife a well-furnished home alongside measurable debt: if the man were a clothier, he may have died before completing the work necessary to pay back his debts; JRD, April 2, 1735.

27. We might also note that Ryder's concerns about the debts of others quickly turned religious: "This day has been a fine pleasant day, but many unpleasant accounts have I heard of one and another, great extravagancies which have been found too apparent both among professors and prophane, whereby they are become unable to pay their honest debts, which ought to be warnings to us all that think we stand, to take heed lest we fall. But what is further distressing is that I find my self so cold in religion, and so prone to wander, and to turn with the dog to his vomitt, and with the sow that was washed to her wallowing in the mire . . . . the wages of sin are death"; JRD, April 10, 1766. Ryder did seem worried about his debts in the summer of 1755, during a local economic downturn, but he is very clear in framing his worry about debt in religious terms; see JRD, June 5, 1755. Later in the same summer (August 26), however, he makes clear that paying back debts was not a problem that he actually shared with more unfortunate religious brethren.

28. JRD, June 27, 1749.

29. JRD, November 30, 1757.

30. Ryder's life became intertwined with Darnton's by way of William Lupton, the leading cloth dresser and for a period the effective head of the firm of Sir Henry Ibbetson, one of the town's most prominent merchants and for a time its mayor and the high sheriff of Yorkshire. Lupton became Ryder's kinsman by marriage when Lupton's younger brother Arthur married Ryder's young cousin Olive, the importance of whose relationship to Ryder can be read in the fact that she and Arthur would later end up with their older cousin's spiritual diary. Ryder's link to Darnton, another of Ibbetson's master cloth dressers, was established when Darnton's granddaughter, Anne, married William Lupton's son. See Wilson, *Gentlemen Merchants*, 76, 244–45. Ryder records Sigston's and Sigston's

wife's formal entrance into Call Lane on October 4, 1734; Ryder records
Sigston's death on November 18, 1766, and her death on November 17,
1744. On eighteenth-century doubts about the value of paper money, see
Mary Poovey, *Genres of the Credit Economy: Mediating Value in Eighteenth-
and Nineteenth-Century Britain* (Chicago: University of Chicago Press,
2008); on the changing meaning of money more generally during this
period, see Deborah Valenze, *The Social Life of Money in the English Past*
(Cambridge: Cambridge University Press, 2006).

31. JRD, November 30, 1757. None of the details of what is actually occurring
are ever deliberately made clear. He writes of "a new scene of trouble . . .
rising [between] two persons of my acquaintance . . . at variance about
some accounts, & I may likely be called for an evidence if the affairs do not
take some more agreable turn"; JRD, December 3, 1757. Darnton had just
married, which clarifies an entry two days later: "The day after some
business done I went to visitt a newly married couple, & was very freely
carried to, but withall as an allay I had some renewed account of some
trouble they are likely to have in Law from a troublesome Brother." On
Darnton and Sigston belonging to Call Lane, see The National Archives,
Public Record Office, RG4/3674.

32. Muldrew, *The Economy of Obligation*, 2. JRD, June 2, 1741.

33. JRD, October 12, 1760.

34. JRD, July 4, 16, 1734.

35. JRD, January 16, 1766; November 12, 1767.

36. JRD, April 14, 1748.

37. A similar point might be made about religious history written mostly using
quantitative methods and from a bird's-eye perspective. Like every
historian of early modern religion, I owe an enormous debt to Michael R.
Watts for his two-volume work on Dissent. But when he writes, "It is a
major weakness of Weber's thesis that his evidence is drawn from the
writings of theoreticians and not from the lives of men who were actually
engaged in 'capitalist' enterprises," one is tempted to say that this same
weakness is apparent in his own study, which neglects to give much
attention to the actual reception of doctrine by the laity or to the evidence
that they translated their beliefs into economic terms. See Michael R.
Watts, *The Dissenters: From the Reformation to the French Revolution*
(Oxford: Oxford University Press, 1978), 362, n. 1. His second volume,
surely in part because of the greater abundance of sources at his disposal,
corrects this oversight. See Chapter 7, n. 40.

38. Ryder's bound octavo trade notebook (WYAS GA/B27) is hardly less obscure than his diary. He began it in the 1720s, and the vast majority of the pages consist of long lists of two columns. On the left are dates, typically month and day, although occasionally the year; on the right are lists of names of his weavers. Only one name that appears here, Joseph Theakstone, also appears in Ryder's funeral lists, and the parish register identifies Theakstone as having died while living at the workhouse (see Appendix 2). This is yet more suggestive evidence that Ryder would at least occasionally hire people who lived, or at least would one day live, in the workhouse. The trade notebook also contains other curiosities. It includes twenty-nine recipes for dying wool, as well as "An Infallible Cure for the bite of a mad dog," and it lists some people to whom Ryder lent money. The evidence that Ryder could express his religiosity in the book designated for trade (just as he could very occasionally write practical information in his spiritual diary) comes forth in a prayer, "Give Glory to Almighty God," which is written five times between dying recipes. Along the side of the page is also a note written by Hannah Rider, presumably a relation: "Hannah Rider is my name and with my pen I wrote the same but if my pen had been better I am sure should have write much the better but since that is so you must excuse me and so no more." The biographical information on Williams here is gleaned from Isabel Rivers, "Joseph Williams of Kidderminster (1692–1755), and his Journal," *Journal of the United Reformed Church History Society* 7 (2005): 359–80, and a later edition of an abridged compilation of Williams's diary entries originally brought out in 1779 by Benjamin Fawcett and supplemented with some of Williams's letters in an Edinburgh edition published by Thomas Randall in 1797. The diary entry is from September 11, 1742. See *Extracts from the Diary, Meditations, and Letters, of Mr. Joseph Williams, of Kidderminster . . . To which are now added, A Number of Original Letters to the late Rev. Mr. R[anda]ll* (Edinburgh, 1797).

39. Williams's entry is from May 31, 1747, *Extracts from the Diary . . . of Mr. Joseph Williams*, 173. Matthew Henry, *An exposition of all the books of the Old and New Testament . . . In six volumes* (London, 1721–1725), 363

40. *Extracts from the Diary . . . of Mr. Joseph Williams*, 240–42.

41. *Extracts from the Diary . . . of Mr. Joseph Williams*, 240, 258. The entry comes from Saturday evening, December 1, 1753.

42. The chances to compare are rare, but Wallington is closest to Ryder's counterpart in the seventeenth century and was more one-sidedly negative

in equating providence and commerce. See note 16 above. On the economic theorists who sublimated self-interest in social terms, see Hirschman, *The Passions and the Interests,* passim. For more on Ryder in relation to early Puritan commentary on moderation, see Chapter 8, note 2.

43. Douglas A. Reid, "The Decline of Saint Monday 1766–1876," *Past and Present* 71 (1976): 76–101. Heaton, *The Yorkshire Woollen and Worsted Industries,* 343. WYAS, QS10/18.

44. E. P. Thompson, "Time, Work-Discipline and Industrial Capitalism," *Past and Present* 38, 1 (1967): 56–97; Thompson, *The Making of the English Working Class.* Ryder too was concerned to maximize time, although as much for spiritual as economic reasons. In the spring of 1736 after a long day of business he wrote: "This Day I saw the Evil of Negligence by deferring till night what should have been done in the Day, & Thought it Lookt very like Deferring Repentence to Old Age. I found fear prevailing Lest the Things of Time should Eat out my Concern for a better. Yet was Glad that it was so Near the Sabbath hoping to hear something that might make me wiser and better. Lord help me to Improve Sabbath Time and all my Time Well"; JRD, March 13, 1736. He could have easily added "holiday time." "A Day of Publick Liberty from Labour," he wrote a few years later, "was spent but in a trifling way and manner, Diverted from any thing materially serious by one company or Other. Oh that I could be humbled under a sense of much mispent & misimproved Time," Ryder continued, "& henceforward be enabled by Grace to Walk Circumspectly"; JRD, January 6, 1740. On crowds, see E. P. Thompson, "The Moral Economy of the English Crowd in the Eighteenth Century," in *Customs in Common: Studies in Traditional Popular Culture* (New York: New Press, 1993). On the link between economic change and attitudes toward crime, see Peter Linebaugh, *The London Hanged: Crime and Civil Society in the 18th Century* (Cambridge: Cambridge University Press, 1992); on the novel, see Liz Bellamy, *Commerce, Morality, and the Eighteenth-Century Novel* (Cambridge: Cambridge University Press, 1998); on masturbation, see Thomas Laqueur, *Solitary Sex: A Cultural History of Masturbation* (New York: Zone Books, 2003), chs. 4–5. For merely one fashionista— Elizabeth Shackleton—see Amanda Vickery, *The Gentleman's Daughter: Women's Lives in Georgian England* (New Haven, CT: Yale University Press, 1998). On profit maximization, cf. Smail, *Merchants, Markets and Manufacture,* 9.

45. JRD, July 9, 1735.

## 5. "THE SPARKS THAT FLY UPWARD"

1. Peter Laslett found the anonymous manuscript in a 1705 copy of John
Locke's *Thoughts Concerning Education* and surmised it was written
between 1705 and 1750; Peter Laslett, "A Comment on 'Rules for the
Religious Conduct of a Family,'" *Local Population Studies* 60 (1998):
65–68. We shouldn't fail to note the enlightened emphasis on the criteria of
"nature" and "reason" alongside the more traditional reliance on scripture.
On the eighteenth-century meaning of the word "family," which typically
embraced servants, apprentices, parents, children, and spouses, see Naomi
Tadmor, *Family and Friends in Eighteenth-Century England: Household,
Kinship, and Patronage* (Cambridge: Cambridge University Press, 2001),
27. On eighteenth-century domestic life seen from the perspective of the
sorts of householders who remain hidden in Ryder's diary, see Carolyn
Steedman, *Master and Servant: Love and Labour in the English Industrial Age*
(Cambridge: Cambridge University Press, 2007), and Steedman, *Labours
Lost* (Cambridge: Cambridge University Press, 2009). A useful overview
of the structure of domestic service in Ryder's Leeds can also be found in
Keith R. Wark, "Domestic Servants in Leeds and Its Neighbourhood in the
Eighteenth Century," *PTS* 2, 8 (1997): 2–16.

2. On apprenticing the poor, see Steve Hindle, *On the Parish? The Micro-
Politics of Poor Relief in Rural England c. 1550–1750* (Oxford: Oxford
University Press, 2004), 191–212. The percentages come from Peter
Laslett, "Family, Kinship and Collectivity as Systems of Support in
Pre-Industrial Europe: A Consideration of the 'Nuclear Hardship'
Hypothesis," *Continuity and Change* 3 (1988): 163. It is worth noting that
the percentage of orphans in society more generally was surely lower than
the percentage who worked in households, a point Jane Humphries makes
on the basis of sampling some six hundred working-class autobiographies.
She finds, for example, that between 1627 and 1799, only 72 percent of her
sample reported at age fourteen that their fathers were still alive; the
number reporting living mothers at the same age was higher but still only
82 percent; Jane Humphries, *Childhood and Child Labour in the British
Industrial Revolution* (Cambridge: Cambridge University Press, 2010), 65.
From different perspectives the numbers can be even higher. One study has
shown, for example, that in a town in eighteenth-century Shropshire, 40
percent of sixteen-year-olds lacked at least one parent; Sylvia Watts,
"Demographic Facts as Experienced by a Group of Families in Eighteenth-
Century Shifnal, Shropshire," *Local Population Studies* 32 (1984): 34–43.

For passing but insightful comments on early modern orphanhood, also see Ilana Krausman Ben-Amos, *Adolescence and Youth in Early Modern England* (New Haven, CT: Yale University Press, 1994), 60, 166–68, and Paul Griffiths, *Youth and Authority: Formative Experiences in England, 1560–1640* (Oxford: Oxford University Press, 1996), 7, n. 27.

3. Conception rather than pregnancy was likely the culprit, given the diary's silence on miscarriages. Ryder, however, never assigns blame to Elisabeth.

4. JRD, August 11, 1733.

5. Quoted in Herbert Heaton, *The Yorkshire Woollen and Worsted Industries, from the Earliest Times up to the Industrial Revolution*, 2nd ed. (Oxford: Clarendon, 1965), 348.

6. Why Ryder and his mother lived together is obscure. Under the Old Poor Laws children were under no legal obligation to maintain their elderly parents; Susannah R. Ottaway, *The Decline of Life: Old Age in Eighteenth-Century England* (Cambridge: Cambridge University Press, 2004), 150–55. JRD, March 3, 1742/43; March 26, 1734; September 24, 1734. Herbert McLachlan thought that the source of the difference between what Ryder's mother and God desired was Ryder's future wife. That might make sense if "heart" referred only to Ryder's love life, but in fact he uses this word with reference to his affection for everything from God to "the world." George Trosse, *The Life of the Reverend Mr. George Trosse, Written by Himself, and Published Posthumously According to his Order in 1714*, ed. A. W. Brink (Montreal: McGill–Queen's University Press, 1974), 56.

7. See Thomas W. Laqueur, *Solitary Sex: A Cultural History of Masturbation* (New York: Zone Books, 2003). Whitaker's warning certainly suggests the criminality of masturbation. The fact that this passage is unique in the diary might also suggest that Ryder's concern about solitary sex was not acute. JRD, April 28, 1734.

8. JRD, May 24, 1734. In these early years Ryder also longs for children—a topic explored below. This entry is thus not without ambiguity. But Ryder's invocation of "corrupt affections" suggests the object of desire here is sexual rather than paternal.

9. JRD, November 28, 1734.

10. On Thomas Whitaker the elder, see Thomas Dickenson, *The Fall and Death of an Eminent Person consider'd and improv'd; in two Sermons, upon Occasion of the much Lamented Death of that Excellent Minister of Jesus Christ, Thomas Whitaker, A.M., Late Pastor of a Congregation at Leeds, in Yorkshire. Who died November 19, 1710* (London, 1712), and the preface to

*Sermons on Several Occasions, by the Late Reverend and Learned Thomas Whitaker, A.M., Pastor to a Church at* Leeds *in* Yorkshire. *To which are added, His Character, and Four Sermons relating to his death* (London, 1712). The preface was written by Thomas Bradbury, who claimed that his tutor knew Whitaker for forty-five years. For Whitaker's "Spiritual Marriage," see John Rylands Library, Unitarian MSS G.Q/6, 1–2, 164–65. Ryder acquired the sermons of Thomas Whitaker (1651–1710) in 1723, as indicated by a note at the beginning of the book.

11. JRD, May 20, 1735 (advice from the friend); June 9, 1735 (wedding day); June 20, 1735; August 5, 1735.

12. This information is based on the deaths recorded in the Leeds parish register. For a reprint of these records, see "The Register of the Parish Church of Leeds." *PTS* 25 (1917, 1918, 1920, 1922). At least two of Elisabeth's sisters, Alice and Sarah, also appear as beneficiaries in Ryder's various wills. See Lupton MSS item 126.

13. We cannot know for certain that the draft of the letter was written during the years the diary volume covers: 1736/37 and early 1738.

14. For popular attitudes on marriage, see David Cressy, *Birth, Marriage, and Death: Ritual, Religion, and the Life-Cycle in Tudor and Stuart England* (Oxford: Oxford University Press, 1997), 294–97; JRD, August 16, 1744; August 10, 11, 1737. I am assuming that the implicit pronoun in this final sentence is plural instead of singular.

15. JRD, May 30, 1750; May 25, 1748.

16. JRD, March 28, 1748. Amanda Vickery, *Behind Closed Doors: At Home in Georgian England* (New Haven, CT: Yale University Press, 2009), 9.

17. JRD, March 25, 1745, 1746, 1747; February 8, 1747.

18. See volume 27 for all of Elisabeth's entries. The only indicator that the words are hers is the use of the first-person pronoun to describe feeling sick on days on which Ryder in another volume records his distress about her poor health. This is nonetheless fairly obvious evidence.

19. On handwriting, see Heather Wolfe, "Women's Handwriting," in *The Cambridge Companion to Early Modern Women's Writing*, ed. Laura Lunger Knoppers (Cambridge: Cambridge University Press, 2009), 21–39. Also see Elaine Hobby, *Virtue of Necessity: English Women's Writing, 1649–88* (Ann Arbor: University of Michigan Press, 1988).

20. JRD, December 1, 1753. Although nothing like the phrase Joseph and Elisabeth both use here appears anywhere in the *Eighteenth Century Collections Online* database, Ralph Thoresby uses the phrase "Poor trembling soul ready

to take its flight into an unseen world" in his diary in an entry from 1690 in which he quotes from a moving sermon he had heard a Leeds minister preach. Ryder never mentions Thoresby by name, but it is possible that he read the diary of Leeds's most important antiquarian historian in manuscript form. Thoresby's diary was not published until 1830, but we need to look no further than Whitaker the elder's manuscript to remind ourselves that the manuscript tradition coexisted with print even in the eighteenth century. *The Diary of Ralph Thoresby*, Vol. 1 (London, 1830), 194. Alternatively, the Ryders also may have known the same sermon Thoresby quotes.

21. JRD, June 20, 1738. The nature of Elisabeth's fits is unknowable, although the mention of "reasonable faculties" may indicate a psychological or neurological malady. Men and women took medicinal waters for everything from rheumatism to lead poisoning to skin disease. Anne Borsay, "A Middle Class in the Making: The Negotiation of Power and Status at Bath's Early Georgian General Infirmary, c. 1739–65," *Social History* 24, 3 (1999): 269–86. JRD, July 9, 16, 1750.

22. Alan Macfarlane, *The Family Life of Ralph Josselin: A Seventeenth Century Clergyman* (Cambridge: Cambridge University Press, 1977), 170. JRD, April 13, 25, 1754.

23. JRD, May 2 ("dear friend"); July 12 ("companion of Life"); May 5 (Whitaker's sermon and the poem), 1754.

24. JRD, July 15, 1754 ("At my return home"); September 18, 1754 (boxing up clothes); November 9 and again on December 21 (reading her diary); for the more randomly evoked memory, see JRD, December 16, 1758.

25. On the practical advice of the *Book of Common Prayer*, see Cressy, *Birth, Marriage, and Death*, 296; on the new language of affect that Thomas Cranmer importantly introduced to marriage via his masterpiece, however, see Diarmaid MacCulloch, *Thomas Cranmer: A Life* (New Haven, CT: Yale University Press, 1996), 420–21. On the same page that Ryder felt "desirous of offspring," he comforted himself with the rationalization "that there was a probability of [children] proving otherwise. . . . If I had none for comforts I had none for crosses." JRD, June 3, 1733; April 10, 1735; December 1, 1735; February 9, 1735/36; June 9, 1740.

26. JRD, July 9, 1740. Ryder identifies six people recorded in his death lists as having lived in the workhouse. About only three of these does he give us any more biographical information in his daily entries. Sarah Beckwith he refers to as "one of our society"; Mary Parker he calls a "neighbour." Neither does Ryder indicate as having worked for him. The other name,

Joseph Theakstone (d. February 27, 1767), is more intriguing since it also shows up in Ryder's cryptic notebook beside cloth transactions conducted during 1733 and 1741. See Appendix 2 and WYAS, MS GA/B27. For Whitaker's sermon, see JRD, April 1, 1764.

27. Philip Doddridge, *Sermons to Young Persons on the following subjects, viz. I. The importance of the rising generation. II. Christ formed in the soul the foundation of hope. III. A dissuasive from keeping bad company. IV. The young Christian invited to an early attendance on the Lord's table. V. The orphan's hope. VI. The reflections of a pious parent on the death of a wicked child. VII. Youth reminded of approaching judgment,* corrected 2nd ed. (London, 1737), 28, 30. JRD, February 3, 1750/51 ("Family Order Beautiful"); November 28, 1748.

28. Philip Gorski, *The Disciplinary Revolution: Calvinism and the Rise of the State in Early Modern Europe* (Chicago: University of Chicago Press, 2003), xvi, chs. 2–3. The social and emotional context of domestic life is teased out in Hindle, *On the Parish?,* 210–11.

29. JRD, March 9, 1741/42.

30. See, for example, JRD, April 15, 1748. Some family members might also volunteer to leave. See the entry for June 1, 1749. JRD, January 3, 6, 1736/37 (on the miscarriage and nearly "striking"); April 17, 1747.

31. JRD, February 2, 1734/35. The form and content of such prayers, when Ryder offers us relevant descriptions, can also give us a sense of the coalescence of his interests. He seems typically to have directed morning and evening family prayer by reading aloud passages from the Bible or other works of practical piety, like Matthew Henry's *Expositions.* For Henry, see, for example, the entry from January 28, 1743/44. Sometimes "family worship was not so lively and fervent as it ought to have been," JRD, April 24, 1734. But the blame for lifelessness typically fell on himself and his lack of time; see, for example, JRD, January 22, 1736/37.

32. JRD, January 25, 1740/41.

33. JRD, September 1, 1748.

34. JRD, October 13, 1733. For a reminder that more than materialist interests were at play in the relationships between masters and householders in the West Riding on the eve of industrialization, see Steedman, *Master and Servant.* JRD, February 5, 1738/39. It is interesting that Ryder wrote this sentence at first with just "best for me" and later inserted "best for me in business," which might suggest that what was best for him is almost by definition what he is thinking of with respect to worldly things. It may also

suggest that so much of the time he is thinking of his economic life even if he doesn't express this explicitly.

35. On lying and drunkenness see, for example, JRD, June 24, 1735.

36. The likely date of the entrance of the Arey sisters into the family was early April. Ryder records the death of "Mrs Airey"—a common alternate spelling—on March 31, 1739, and then writes the following on April 5: "This Day having matters of weighty Importance Depending relating to my Family & Increase of it my mind was much Concerned for the Blessing of God upon me & towards me." "Mrs Airey" was undoubtedly their mother. Their father, William Arey, a clothier, had died in 1736 and had listed Ryder as a trustee of his will; Borthwick Institute, York, Leeds Wills, 1700–1830, "Will of William Arey of Leeds." JRD, March 12, 1741/42. On the Arey sisters' attendance of funerals, see Appendix 2. In an ad hoc will composed over ten years before he died, Ryder testified to his executors "That I have Given to Hannah Arey and Grace Arey Her Sister to be Delivered at my Death Two Deed Boxes with all the Manuscripts therein or may be found about the house." The will, dated June 2, 1757, was written on a separate sheet of paper and placed, at some point, inside the back cover of volume 26. (More or less the same bestowal appears in Ryder's will.) The National Archives, Public Record Office, RG4/3674 records admission of Grace and Hanney Airey to Call Lane on March 30, 1750. All Ryder says on this day in the diary is "I was much affected." It is also curious that Ryder makes reference to "Miss Areys" (presumably Grace and Hannah) in an entry from the summer of 1766, where he tells us they "are going to remove to a house after so long a time of being Sojourners, I hope they have committed their case to God, and Craved his direction"; JRD, June 10, 1766. The only other reference he makes to them appears in his will, where he also gives each of them 7p. 10s. The one other householder Ryder named was his housekeeper in late life, Mercy Ross.

37. JRD, January 21, 1748/49.

38. Samuel Wright, *A Sermon Preach'd at the Old-Jury, March 2, 1736–7, to the Society for Relief of the Widows and Fatherless Children of Dissenting Ministers* (London, 1737), 4. Doddridge, *Sermons to Young Persons*, 161–62.

39. JRD, May 1, 1748. This is not the only poem Ryder titled "Of Adoption." Another, written August 5, 1744, also elaborated on the same metaphor of spiritual adoption. "The heirs of heaven Adopted Sons appear / To God their father will be Ever near." Also see Ryder's paraphrase of Whitaker's

sermon from June 22, 1766, where Whitaker references "the great priviledges of Adoption both in this world, and in that which is to come."

## 6. MOURNING, MELANCHOLY, AND MONEY

1. On the consistency in the meaning of depression in the West, see Stanley Jackson, *Melancholia and Depression from Hippocratic Times to Modern Times* (New Haven, CT: Yale University Press, 1986).

2. Key works in the origins of skepticism toward "the fixity of normative categories" are Michel Foucault, *La Folie et la Déraison: Histoire de la Folie à l'Age Classique* (Paris: Plon, 1961); R. D. Laing, *The Divided Self: A Study of Sanity and Madness* (Harmondsworth: Penguin, 1960); and Thomas S. Szasz, *The Myth of Mental Illness* (New York: Hoeber-Harper, 1961). Roy Porter began adding useful nuance to this skeptical consensus with *Mind Forg'd Manacles: Madness and Psychiatry in England from Restoration to Regency* (Cambridge, MA: Harvard University Press, 1987) and *A Social History of Madness: Stories of the Insane* (London: Weidenfeld and Nicolson, 1987). On the "treasured identity badge," Roy Porter, *Flesh in the Age of Reason: The Modern Foundations of Body and Soul* (New York: W. W. Norton, 2004), 179, 192–93. For the artistic uses of melancholy before the eighteenth century, see Douglas Trevor, *The Poetics of Melancholy in Early Modern England* (Cambridge: Cambridge University Press, 2004). The positive link between art and madness continues to find support; for a recent articulation, see S. H. Carson, "Creativity and Psychopathology: A Shared-Vulnerability Model," *Canadian Journal of Psychiatry* 56, 3 (2011): 144–53.

3. JRD, May 23, 1749. On the connection between the Puritan ethos and despair, see Jeremy Schmidt, *Melancholy and the Care of the Soul: Religion, Moral Philosophy and Madness in Early Modern England* (Aldershot: Ashgate, 2007), who importantly notes that although the earliest generation of Puritans saw occasional despair as spiritually healthy, in later years Richard Baxter did his best to disabuse his contemporaries of the view that this connection was inevitable; see chs. 3 and 5. One of the more interesting cases of a melacholic early modern, Hannah Allen, made clear the spiritual dangers of her condition in the title of her autobiography, *A Narrative of God's gracious dealings with the choice Christian Mrs. Hannah Allen (afterwards married to Mr. Hatt) reciting the great advantages the devil made of her deep melancholy . . .* (London, 1683). On Allen and other despairing spiritual autobiographers, see Katharine Hodgkin, *Madness in Seventeenth-Century Autobiography* (New York: Palgrave, 2007).

4. Sigmund Freud, "Mourning and Melancholia" (1917 [1915]), in *The Pelican Freud Library, Vol. 11: On Metapsychology: The Theory of Psychoanalysis*, trans. James Strachey (London: Penguin, 1984), 254. Jackson, *Melancholia and Depression*, ch. 12. For more on Napier, see Michael MacDonald, *Mystical Bedlam: Madness, Anxiety, and Healing in Seventeenth-Century England* (Cambridge: Cambridge University Press, 1981), 150–72. The view Napier held can also be found, for example, in Robert Burton's magnum opus *The Anatomy of Melancholy, What it is: With all the Kinds, Causes, Symptomes, Prognostickes, and Several Cures of it. In Three Maine Partitions with their several Sections, Members, and Subsections. Philosophically, Medicinally, Historically, Opened and Cut Up* (London, 1621). Even many of the experimenters with literary melancholy imply a parallel concern about taking the characteristic features of melancholy too far when they worry that however aesthetically seductive melancholy might be, it could nevertheless lead to suicidal thoughts. See Trevor, *The Poetics of Melancholy*, 9.

5. JRD, March 24, 1748; October 9, 1758.

6. Christopher Durston and Jacqueline Eales, "Introduction: The Puritan Ethos," in *The Culture of English Puritanism: 1560–1700*, ed. C. Durston and J. Eales (New York: St. Martin's, 1996), 11.

7. Chrisopher Hill, *A Tinker and a Poor Man: John Bunyan and His Church, 1628–1688* (New York: Norton, 1988), 64. For a literary and psychoanalytical account of despair engendered by predestinarianism, see John Stachniewski, *The Persecutory Imagination: English Puritanism and the Literature of Religious Despair* (Oxford: Oxford University Press, 1991). *Some Account of Ann Dymond, late of Exeter* (York, 1820), 11. Elizabeth Bury, *An account of the life and death of Mrs. Elizabeth Bury, who died, May the 11th, 1720. Aged 76. Chiefly collected out of her own diary* (Bristol, 1720), 105. Alexandra Walsham, *Providence in Early Modern England* (Oxford: Oxford University Press, 1999), 17.

8. JRD, January 11, 1756. The point of this particular verse, however, was also to express gratitude that he had been saved from such sinful ways.

9. JRD, August 9, 1733.

10. The *Oxford English Dictionary* records the earliest economically tinged use of "depression" in 1793, although Ryder regularly uses phrases like "depressed circumstances" to reference personal economic downturn. On the Enlightenment redefinition of acquisitiveness, see Roy Porter, *The Creation of the Modern World: The Untold Story of the British Enlightenment* (New York: W. W. Norton, 2000), ch. 11.

11. JRD, December 29, 1734 ("Thousands to fall"); July 16, 1735 ("God could bless us"). News of the Lisbon earthquake on November 1, 1755, didn't reach Leeds—or Ryder's ears—for four weeks. See Ryder's entry for November 28, 1755.

12. Given its dearth of details about ritual, funeral costs, and so on, Ryder's diary is mostly a frustrating document for the social historian of death. One might wonder, for example, whether Ryder's funeral invitations arrived orally or in the form of printed tickets, or even, as Ralph Houlbrooke has speculated about their more general function, whether they operated in Leeds to keep away unwanted guests. Alternatively, was Ryder such a funeral heavyweight that invitation was unnecessary? We simply don't know; for such details about the cultural practices surrounding death, the reader should consult Ralph Houlbrooke, *Death, Religion, and the Family in England: 1450–1750* (Oxford: Oxford University Press, 1998); David Cressy, *Birth, Marriage, and Death: Ritual, Religion, and the Life-Cycle in Tudor and Stuart England* (Oxford: Oxford University Press, 1997); and Vanessa Harding, *The Dead and the Living in Paris and London, 1500–1670* (Cambridge: Cambridge University Press, 2002). For elites, Jennifer Woodward, *The Theatre of Death: The Ritual Management of Royal Funerals in Renaissance England* (Woodbridge: Boydell, 1997).

13. JRD, July 14, 1759; August 18, 1734.

14. JRD, April 6, 1748; December 15, 1749; August 25, 1767.

15. On the connections between providentialism and sudden death, which terrified Ryder, also see Walsham, *Providence*, 99–107. JRD, September 12, 1755. The line about "loyns," "lamps," and "lights" is a combination of Matt. 25 and Luke 12.

16. JRD, June 25, 1741.

17. On the sermon of the "stranger," see JRD, May 14, 1749; Walker talked about Purgatory on November 24, 1748. On the uneven response to Purgatory, see Peter Marshall, *Beliefs and the Dead in Reformation England* (Oxford: Oxford University Press, 2002), 313. Ralph Houlbrooke discusses the change in the way grief was expressed in *Death, Religion, and the Family in England*, 228.

18. Francis Atterbury, *Sermons and Discourses on Several Subjects and Occasions*, 3rd ed. (London, 1730), 204, 205. Ryder used remarkably similar language but gives no explicit indication that he read Atterbury. "The day of death will be by far more preferable to the day of our birth, as our birth is our

inlett into a world of sin and misery, distress and temptation," JRD,
November 23, 1767. Laurence Sterne, *Sermons* (London, 1787), 15, 17.
Hugh Blair, *Sermons: Vol. 2* (London, 1780), 374, 376, 389.

19. For citations of Ecclesiastes after funerals, see, for example, JRD March 4,
1735/36 and March 24, 1748. JRD, November 17, 1748 ("be of good
cheer"); November 18, 1748; December 18, 1749; May 8, 1741; July 29, 1733.

20. Porter, *The Creation of the Modern World*, 258. JRD, August 22, 1733.

21. JRD, February 4, 1758 (doctor's bill); July 25, 1750 ("both body and
mind"); April 27, 1743 ("out of order"). The febrifuge recipe is from
volume 36: "Miss [name unclear] receipt for the cure of ague. Take half an
ounce of Jesuitt bark, and make it into a Solid Electuary with an ounce of
the conserve of wormwood. If it be too stiff to mix may add a little
Infusion of Snakeroot. Take half of this as soon as the fitt is off, The rest
12 hours after. Take the same quantity 8 days after for fear of a return."
This is then followed by a cure he attributes to Samuell Walker. "80 grains
of the Salt of wormwood / 60 Grains of Snakeroot / An ounce of bark /
In a Quart of Clarett wine / About a glass at a time when the fitt is off."

22. JRD, October 3, 1734.

23. JRD, May 25, 1735; Whitaker repeats the line from Mark three days later on
May 28. JRD, August 5, 1750 ("Christ the only physician"); May 30, 1757
(we can only wonder why Ryder's physician thought his case uncommon;
this may be evidence that his doctor could find no cause. Alternatively,
"uncommon" could suggest that Ryder suffered from an unusual illness,
but it is then no less curious that he didn't name the condition). JRD,
January 15, 1760 ("hospital of diseases").

24. JRD, October 28, 1758. Ryder also records the death at the back of the
diary volume. After Ryder attends Mary Rider's funeral on the October 30,
having sent his maid to attend the funeral of Hannah, he notes "John
Watson wife dy'd this morning . . . Lord help me so to live as not to fear /
When death to me is also drawing near." This is yet another instance of
four deaths in his purview occurring in fewer than four days; JRD,
October 30, 1758.

25. JRD, July 22, 1735; March 6, 1735/36.

26. Michael MacDonald and Terrence R. Murphy, *Sleepless Souls: Suicide in
Early Modern England* (Oxford: Oxford University Press, 1990), 267,
269–70. Ryder once reasoned that too much attachment to the material was
itself a cause of suicide. From March 13, 1753: "This day being call'd into
Company upon some business I heard some of the Company talking about

a Gentleman of great substance who had traded with another who they say is become bankrupt, and was likely to sustain a great loss, became very uneasy, and not withstanding all arguments used by others urging the unreasonableness of so much sorrow because he was so able to bear it, yet by indulging his sorrow ripened to the Executing of himself by cutting his own throat. The hearing whereof took great place as I apprehended to warn against too great a desire after or concerning about the things of time." The immediate culprit was bankruptcy, but what made bankruptcy so depressing was material attachment. At the same time, Ryder gives us plenty of evidence that living in sustained poverty, especially that brought on by the lethal combination of old age and the inability to work amid the absence of any social pension plans, could also produce suicidal tendencies. In conversation with a friend on June 13, 1761, for example, Ryder heard an account of a "man who Shaves his neighbours" going "to Shave a very old man who is very much afflicted & reduced to poverty, and so Impatient under his burden, That when he is Shaving him, he desires him to cut his throat to rid him of his misery."

27. George Orwell, "Benefit of Clergy: Some Notes on Salvador Dali," in *The Collected Essays, Journalism and Letters of George Orwell: As I Please, 1943–45,* ed. Sonia Orwell and Ian Angus (New York: Harcourt Brace Jovanovich, 1968), 156.

28. Philippe Lejeune, "Composer un journal," *Signes de vie. Le pacte autobiographique 2* (Paris: Seuil, 2005): 63–72. JRD, July 17, 1733.

29. Philippe Lejeune, "Le journal comme antifiction," *Poétique* 149 (February 2007): 3–14. Lejeune's point obviously works best only for truly diurnal accounts and not those mendaciously presented as so, such as *Boswell's London Journal, 1762–62,* ed. Frederick Pottle (New Haven, CT: Yale University Press, 1950). "Patterns of personal significance" is from Ramona Wray, "Autobiography," in *The Cambridge Companion to Early Modern Women's Writing,* ed. Laura Lunger Knoppers (Cambridge: Cambridge University Press, 2009), 197. Julia Kristeva, *Black Sun: Depression and Melancholia* (New York: Columbia University Press, 1989), 33.

30. See JRD, March 29, 1736.

31. JRD, November 26, 1733.

32. JRD, June 21, 1739.

33. JRD, August 24, 1745.

34. JRD, September 22, 1760.

35. Freud, "Mourning and Melancholia," 251–68.

36. JRD, January 10, 1760 ("frailty of human nature"); October 11, 1735 ("slothful in business"); June 24, 1733 ("concerned too much").

37. JRD, March 15, 1735.

38. John Bunyan, *The Pilgrim's Progress from this world to that which is to come* (London, 1678), author's preface, n.p. JRD, May 11, 1734; April 26, 1743.

39. JRD, July 22 ("Oh what a call") and 23 ("Inward conflicts"), 1754.

40. JRD, July 21, 1759. Ryder's death registry indicates that Mrs. Moult lived until December of the next year. See Appendix 2.

41. JRD, October 30, 1758; Ryder's optimism on this day was challenged by the funerals of Hannah and Mary Rider.

42. JRD, June 20, 1735 ("Happy state"); February 17, 1735 ("Happy they who enjoy"); February 2, 1767 ("Oh happy they who are prepared"); November 19, 1767 ("Oh that I may be found").

43. JRD, April 13, 1767. What I am arguing here about the middle class might be applied to the value of moderation more generally. Ethan Shagan has shown that encounters with the spreading "rule of moderation" in Tudor-Stuart society led to resistance to that rule since moderation by its very nature imposes limits on the self and its appetites. Much eighteenth-century historiography would suggest that such resistance faded from view after 1700, when participation in the culture of politeness and sociability could be seen at least partly as self-interested rather than as an involuntary consequence of power exercised on the self by external forces. In Ryder's more commercial age, embracing the ethos of moderation (so the historiography of politeness in one way or another tells us) was an appealing prospect because it gave one greater access to human, social, cultural, and economic capital, some measure of which was also needed to begin making inroads into polite society. The society that offered such forms of capital could benefit by its sale, in other words, and the purchaser of that capital could benefit by the opportunities that its possession opened up. Hence moderation and the middle class could be imagined as appealing ways to satisfy one's own material and cultural needs and desires and to serve a society that was seen to benefit as its middle class grew. What Ryder's case shows, however, is that striving for moderation and the middle class wasn't simply about acquiring various forms of capital; it was about trying to meet his psychological and spiritual needs. And where there was resistance in Ryder's life, it arose not from outwardly political forms of domination that, as Shagan has shown, produced violence in the

Tudor-Stuart era, nor was it allayed by the sort of participation in public life promised by eighteenth-century commercial society. The tension arose as Ryder's spiritual outlook reminded him that disequilibrium, which might very easily come about via a more secular embrace of sociability, was a danger to his soul. See Ethan Shagan, *The Rule of Moderation: Violence, Religion and the Politics of Restraint in Early Modern England* (Cambridge: Cambridge University Press, 2011); Paul Langford, *A Polite and Commercial People 1727–83* (Oxford: Oxford University Press, 1989).

44. JRD, November 13, 1733.

### 7. THE CHANGING MEANING OF GOD AND MAN

1. The only two historians I have come across who read and then wrote about the manuscript of Ryder's diary were both Unitarian Mill Hill ministers; both also focused on the religious change discussed here. See Charles Wicksteed, *Lectures on the memory of the just: being a series of discourses on the lives and times of the ministers of Mill-Hill Chapel, Leeds . . . ; with a farewell sermon delivered on the 14th of March, 1847* (London, 1849), 56–64; and Herbert McLachlan, *Essays and Addresses* (Manchester: Manchester University Press, 1950), ch. 1.

2. Immanuel Kant, *Critique of Practical Reason and Other Writings in Moral Philosophy*, trans. Lewis White Beck (Chicago: University of Chicago Press, 1949), 286.

3. The precise meanings of "Arian" and "Unitarian," among many other terms, were never fixed in early modern times. See John Christian Laursen, ed., *Histories of Heresy in Early Modern Europe: For, Against, and Beyond Persecution and Toleration* (New York: Palgrave Macmillan, 2002), passim. For an overview of rational Dissent, see R. K. Webb, "The Emergence of Rational Dissent," in *Enlightenment and Religion: Rational Dissent in Eighteenth-Century Britain*, ed. Knud Haakonssen (Cambridge: Cambridge University Press, 1996), 12–41; useful too is Roy Porter, *The Creation of the Modern World: The Untold Story of the British Enlightenment* (New York: W. W. Norton, 2000), ch. 5.

4. Article XVII of the Toleration Act, quoted in E. N. Williams, ed., *The Eighteenth-Century Constitution 1688–1815* (Cambridge: Cambridge University Press, 1970), 46. Even though the execution of Thomas Aikenhead in 1696 occurred in Scotland, many in England (like John Locke) were appalled, and the Scottish clergy who thought that "God was glorified by such ane awful & exemplary punishment" would be Britons in

a political sense soon enough. For more on Aikenhead, see Michael Hunter, "Aikenhead, Thomas (bap. 1676, d. 1697)," in *ODNB*. The last person to be burned as a heretic in England, for that matter, was an anti-Trinitarian; see David Como and Ian Atherton, "The Burning of Edward Wightman: Puritanism, Prelacy, and the Politics of Heresy in Early Modern England," *English Historical Review* 120 (2005): 1215–50. On Whiston, see James A. Force, *William Whiston: Honest Newtonian* (Cambridge: Cambridge University Press, 1985). "Ridicule of divine majesty" is from John Marshall, *John Locke, Toleration, and Early Enlightenment Culture: Religious Intolerance and Arguments for Religious Toleration in Early Modern and "Early Enlightenment" Europe* (Cambridge: Cambridge University Press, 2006), 128. Justin Champion and Nabil Matar have shown that in the few years surrounding 1688, association with Islam made Socinianism and Arianism seem particularly dangerous; see J. A. I. Champion, *Pillars of Priestcraft Shaken: The Church of England and Its Enemies, 1660–1730* (Cambridge: Cambridge University Press, 1992), and Nabil Matar, *Islam in Britain 1558–1685* (Cambridge: Cambridge University Press, 1998). In fact, this prejudice seems to be one of the eighteenth century's continuities. A broadside circulating in Birmingham as late as 1790 claimed the belief that anti-Trinitarians had "no more foundation in Divine Revelation than *Mohomet's*"; ten years later the *Anti-Jacobin Review* claimed that Priestley was actuated by the same spirit of proselytizing that led "Mahomet . . . to raise a party against the Christian World." Jan Albers, " 'Papist Traitors' and 'Presbyterian Rogues': Religious Identities in Eighteenth-Century Lancashire," in *The Church of England, c. 1689–c. 1833*, ed. John Walsh, Colin Haydon, and Stephen Taylor (Cambridge: Cambridge University Press, 1993), 323; Stuart Andrews, *Unitarian Radicalism: Political Rhetoric, 1770–1814* (New York: Palgrave Macmillan, 2003), 158. On Priestley, see Robert E. Schofield, *The Enlightened Joseph Priestley: A Study of His Life and Work from 1773–1804* (University Park: Pennsylvania State University Press, 2004), ch. 8. Burke quoted in Andrews, *Unitarian Radicalism*, vi.

5. On Biddle, see Nigel Smith, " 'And if God was one of us': Paul Best, John Biddle, and Anti-Trinitarian Heresy in Seventeenth-Century England," in *Heresy, Literature, and Politics in Early Modern English Culture*, ed. David Loewenstein and John Marshall (Cambridge: Cambridge University Press, 2006), 174–75. Biddle's arguments and writings were printed by John Farrington in *The Faith of One God, Who is Only the Father; and of One*

*Mediator Between God and Man, who is only the Man Christ Jesus; and of one Holy Spirit, the Gift (and sent) of God* . . . (London, 1691). Stephen Nye, *A Brief History of the Unitarians called also Socinians, in Four Letters* (London, 1691), 11–12. On Nye using the word "Unitarian," see H. J. McLachlan, "Nye, Stephen (1647/8–1719)," in *ODNB*. Herbert McLachlan, *The Unitarian Movement in the Religious Life of England, Vol. 1: Its Contribution to Thought and Learning, 1700–1900* (London: Allen and Unwin, 1933), 24. On Locke reading Nye, see Marshall, *John Locke,* 404–5. On the rise of rationalism within Dissent, see Webb "The Emergence of Rational Dissent."

6. For conservative paranoia about the Dissenting Academies, see Henry Sacheverell's infamous *The Perils of False Brethren* (London, 1709). For a more evenhanded view from the leading historian of the subject, see David L. Wykes, "The Dissenting Academy and Rational Dissent," in Haakonssen, ed., *Enlightenment and Religion,* 128–29; JRD, April 20, 1761.

7. For the Salters' Hall controversy, see Roger Thomas, "The Non-Subscription Controversy amongst Dissenters in 1719: The Salters' Hall Debate," *Journal of Ecclesiastical History* 4 (1953): 162–86. Also see David L. Wykes, "Religious Dissent, the Church, and the Repeal of the Occasional Conformity and Schism Acts, 1714–1719," in *Politics, Religion and Dissent, 1660–1832: Essays in Honour of James E. Bradley,* ed. Robert D. Cornwall and William Gibson (Aldershot: Ashgate, 2010), 165–84.

8. G. Fothergill to G. Benson, December 28, 1728, John Rylands Library, Benson Collection, General, B116/26. W. D. Jeremy, *The Presbyterian Fund and Dr Daniel Williams's Trust* (London, 1885). Wykes, "Dissenting Academy," 125. I explore the fuller range of Benson's network in my "Anti-Trinitarianism and the Republican Tradition in Enlightenment Britain," *Republics of Letters: A Journal for the Study of Knowledge, Politics, and the Arts* 2, 1 (December 15, 2010): http://rofl.stanford.edu/node/68. For more on the *Old Whig,* see Christine Gerrard, *The Patriot Opposition to Walpole: Politics, Poetry, and National Myth, 1725–1742* (Oxford: Oxford University Press, 1994), and Andrew C. Thompson, "Popery, Politics, and Private Judgement in Early Hanoverian Britain," *Historical Journal* 34, 2 (2002): 333–56.

9. Priestley is quoted in Alexander Gordon, "Bourn, Samuel (1689–1754)," in *ODNB.* Much biographical information on Bourn can be found in Samuel Blyth, *The good soldier of Jesus Christ characterized. In a sermon preached at Birmingham, March 31, and at Coseley, April 7. occasioned by the sudden and much-lamented death of the Reverend Mr. S. Bourn, who died March 22,*

*1754, in the 66th year of his age* (London, 1754), 12–13. Samuel Bourn, *An Address to Protestant Dissenters. Or an Inquiry into the Grounds of the Attachment to the Assemblies Catechism; Whether they Act upon Bigotry or Reason . . .* (London, 1736), 7. On the general types of philosophical arguments anti-Trinitarians might use—here Bourn points to the problem of individuation—see Udo Thiel, "The Trinity and Human Personal Identity," in *English Philosophy in the Age of Locke,* ed. M. A. Stewart (Oxford: Oxford University Press, 2000), 217–43. Bourn modified the catechism written by James Strong of Ilminster. The antagonistic history is T. S. James, *The History of the Litigation and Legislation Respecting Presbyterian Chapels and Charities in England and Ireland Between 1816 and 1849* (London, 1867), 35. The work of a Birmingham lawyer and conservative Congregationalist, this tendentious history focused on the Wolverhampton Chapel (1817) and Hewley Fund (1830) cases, which ruled against anti-Trinitarians' property rights to certain chapels, and the Dissenters' Chapels Act (1844), by which the Wolverhampton and Hewley rulings were overturned. In many ways the crux of Trinitarians' argument in the first two cases was that anti-Trinitarians had staged a hostile doctrinal takeover of Dissent, and with a sense of paranoia James's one-thousand-page history pursued this theme. For James, early-eighteenth-century Presbyterianism before 1719 was, for example, filled with crypto-anti-Trinitarians who saw Salters' Hall as an occasion to go public, after which they aggressively spread their views. Arianism, for James, had been "the convenient disguise by which to conceal a denial of all that is super-natural in Christianity and carry on war with it to the best advantage. For there is a freemasonry in unbelief, those regularly entered can soon make themselves known to each other, initiate any willing to join their camp or take part in their orgies, and pass each other through the degrees of illumination" (39). "Principles of common Christianity" is from C. G. Bolam, Jeremy Goring, H. L. Short, and Roger Thomas, *The English Presbyterians: From Elizabethan Puritanism to Modern Unitarianism* (London: Allen and Unwin, 1968), 216, 148. Note too that Bourn should not be confused with his equally radical son, also Samuel Bourn (1714–1796), who influence also extended to Europe—or at least we know Voltaire read him. See Letter D15180, "To Jacob Vernes, 19 August 1768," in Voltaire [François Marie Arouet], *Correspondence and Related Documents: Vol. 34: August 1768–May 1769, Letters D15164–D15672,* 2nd ed., ed. Theodore Besterman, 51 vols. (Oxford: Voltaire Foundation, 1968–1977), 24–25.

10. On ministers' salaries, see Michael R. Watts, *The Dissenters, Vol. 1: From the Reformation to the French Revolution* (Oxford: Oxford University Press, 1978), 342. S. Bourn to G. Benson, July 7, 1751, and June 22, 1751, Benson Collection, John Rylands Library, vi, B114/14 and B114/4.

11. The classic work on the political radicalism of Dissent is James E. Bradley, *Religion, Revolution, and English Radicalism: Non-Conformity in Eighteenth-Century Politics and Society* (Cambridge: Cambridge University Press, 1990). "Little democracies" is from Webb, "The Emergence of Rational Dissent," 14. The gender neutrality here is deliberate. To detect the involvement of women, we need to look no further than Priestley's open-minded aunt, Sarah Keighley, or one of the major funders of the Presbyterian Fund, an obscure "Mrs. Loughor." See J. Taylor to G. Benson, March 29, 1748, John Rylands Library, Benson Collection, 3, B111.

12. For the possible allusion to Walker, see JRD, May 21, 1748: "This Day we have the good tydings among us of Persons flocking to hear a minister who according to what I hear from Good Judges is a sound preacher." *Memoirs of the Rev. Dr. Joseph Priestley, to the year 1795, written by himself; with a continuation, to the time of his decease by his son, Joseph Priestley* (London, 1809), 11. On the better-known nephew, see Alexander Gordon, "Walker, George (1734?–1807)," in *ODNB*, and Bradley, *Religion, Revolution, and English Radicalism*, 132–33. The mention of Walker's son appears in an important visual source on the clothing of ordinary people in the early nineteenth century written by Thomas Walker's grandson, also George Walker, *Costume of Yorkshire* (1818), iii. For another brief mention of Walker, see Rev. W. Turner, "History of the Congregation of Protestant Dissenters, Hannover Square, Newcastle," *Monthly Repository of Theology and General Literature* 69, 6 (1832), 587. Turner's article was about Newcastle but mentions Walker briefly because Walker's wife was connected to one of the Newcastle parishioners. Turner's brief comments are based on information provided by a relative who knew and admired Walker.

13. JRD, May 31, 1748. For Owen and for Ryder's delayed response, see JRD, July 28, 29, 1748.

14. The congregation that composed Call Lane had, however, been meeting as early as the 1660s. See James G. Miall, *Congregationalism in Yorkshire: A Chapter of Modern Church History* (London, 1868). On Stretton's persecution and L'Estrange's characterization, see *Letters of Eminent*

*Men, Addressed to Ralph Thoresby, F.R.S., Now First Published from the Originals in Two Volumes,* Vol. 1 (London, 1832), 22–26, 33–36, 47–49. The critical piece of evidence that Stretton wrote *The Case of the Protestant Dissenters* appears in the funeral sermon Matthew Henry delivered for Stretton in 1712. In a short appended biographical note Henry claims that Stretton revealed his identity as the author of *The Case of the Protestant Dissenters* to a "near Relation of his, not long before he died"; Matthew Henry, *A Sermon Preach'd at Haberdashers Hall, July the 13th, 1712. On Occasion of the death of the Reverend Mr. Richard Stretton* . . . (London, 1712), 45.

15. JRD, December 24, 1754 (for the importance Ryder placed on his Dissenter ancestors); October 20, 1754 (for the poem).

16. JRD, October 6, 14, 1748. Isaac Watts, *An humble attempt toward the revival of practical religion among Christians, and particularly the Protestant dissenters, by a Serious Address to Ministers and People, In some Occasional Discourses* (London, 1731), 106.

17. Wicksteed, *Lectures on the memory of the just,* 61, footnote. JRD, April 13, 1749; May 28, 1749.

18. JRD, July 19, 1749; March 2, 1750.

19. There was "one passage in the Authorized Version which appeared to refer to the doctrine [of the Trinity], I John 5:7, 8," Michael Watts has written, but this "was in 1715 rejected as a spurious interpolation by Richard Bentley"; Watts, *The Dissenters, Vol. 1,* 373. JRD, November 21, 1754.

20. JRD, August 18, 1735; February 22, 1735/36; March 28, 1739.

21. JRD, July 30, 1749; September 1, 1749.

22. Whitaker, who preached at Call Lane from 1728 until 1777, also came from a long line of ministers. An early relative, William Whitaker, debated the Catholic polemicist Robert Bellarmine, who considered the Englishman a learned enemy. His grandfather Robert Whitaker was an eminent Lancashire physician. See Thomas Dickenson (a minister at Northoverham), *The Fall and Death of Eminent Person consider'd and improv'd; in two Sermons, upon Occasion of the much Lamented Death of that Excellent Minister of Jesus Christ, Thomas Whitaker, A.M., Late Pastor of a Congregation at Leeds, in Yorkshire. Who died November 19, 1710* (London, 1712). Thomas Whitaker's well-liked father, also Thomas (1651–1710), came to Leeds in 1675 and preached there for thirty-four years, even via sermons written while imprisoned for his nonconformity in York castle for eighteen months during the reign of Charles II and James II. See

H. McLachlan, *The Story of a Nonconformist Library* (Manchester: University of Manchester Press, 1923), 43. A contemporary writes that Thomas the elder possessed a large library, was very learned, and was a liberal in thought and practice: "And here, I may be allow'd to mention his Thoughts upon some few Heads, which he defended with Clearness, and possess'd with Peace: His Way of Understanding the Great Doctrines of Election, Redemption, Justification, Conversion and Perseverance, were agreeable to the Churches of England, Scotland, Holland and Geneva: But yet, I have heard him often call it both a Slavery upon Ministers, and a Damp to their Success, when they suited their Stile rather to the Jingle of a Party than the Nature of their Subject: And he thought that there was to be equal Freedom of Expression in opening a Doctrine and claiming a Duty"; see the (unpaginated) preface to *Sermons on Several Occasions, by the Late Reverend and Learned Thomas Whitaker, A.M., Pastor to a Church at Leeds in Yorkshire. To which are added, His Character, and Four Sermons relating to his death* (London, 1712). The preface author, Thomas Bradbury, writes that his tutor knew Whitaker for forty-five years. Note too that Ryder only indirectly tells us when Whitaker arrived; in any entry from May 8, 1748, he records Whitaker saying that on that day he had been preaching at Call Lane for exactly twenty years.

23. I have searched to no avail for manuscript or printed versions of the sermons Ryder records. Besides Priestley's many writings, and the one sermon of Walker's discussed above, the only other printed tract of one of his ministers to survive is from Nathaniel White (c. 1730–1783), who preached at Mill Hill from 1763 to 1766: *A sermon occasioned by the death of . . . Anna-Maria Poole . . . Nicholas Poole . . . Martha Poole . . . and . . . Lionel Poole . . . who all died in the space of five days. Preached at the Old Jewry, October 27, 1771* (London, 1771). White moved from Mill Hill to Old Jewry. See D. L. Ouren, "Some Major Unitarian Chapels in Great Britain," unpublished MS in 2 vols., Andover School of Divinity, Harvard University, 1984, 296. On Wakefield's wealth, see John Seed, "'A Set of Men Powerful Enough in Many Things': Rational Dissent and Political Opposition, 1770–1790," in Haakonssen, ed., *Enlightenment and Religion,* 149. It is hard not to wonder whether Walker also read the Third Earl of Shaftesbury, who Walker calls to mind when he implies that ridicule is a test of truth. See Shaftesbury's *Characteristics of Men, Manners, Opinions, Times* (London, 1711).

24. JRD, November 1, 1752.

25. Thomas Walker, *The true Christian Worship Explained and Recommended: a Sermon Preached at the Opening of the New Chapel in Wakefield, Yorkshire. Wednesday, Nov. 1. 1752* (London, 1753), 1.

26. Walker, *The true Christian Worship Explained*, 7, 14, 30–31, 32, 38, 38.

27. McLachlan says that Ryder did think of leaving Mill Hill in December, but there is no basis for this in the diary. Ryder talks of others leaving, but he doesn't include himself in this group. JRD, November 15, 1756; December 8, 1756. This was not, however, where matters ended. Two weeks passed before Ryder tells us that "in Severall places where I have been there has been remarks made of what Mr Walker delivered when preaching against Original Sin and many are thereby offended. Oh what need have we . . . to bring what we hear to the Holy Scriptures to try whether these things be so." Ryder's own position is clear enough: he disagreed with Walker on this issue with more explicitness than we ever encounter in Ryder's references to the Trinity. As he wrote the next night in his description of the evening religious meeting—a meeting he was averse to attending given the inevitable heated discussion: "after a little conversation we had a Long debate about two Opposite discourses, One denying Original Sin, Another asserting it, And if Ministers begin to deny the Scriptures, I know not what will become of our Religion." JRD, December 20, 21, 1756.

28. In an oral history recounted by Charles Wicksteed in the mid-nineteenth century, Walker supposedly preached a sermon on original sin that was so offensive it led to "the secession of a number of families from his congregation"; Wicksteed, *Lectures on the Memory of the Just*, 60, note §. The oral tradition may have been referencing the sermon Walker preached in response to Pye. JRD, December 25, 1756 (Walker's caviling); January 3, 1757 (sermon against sloth); January 27, 1757 ("Trinity in Unity"); November 18, 1758 ("not furnished"); February 18, 1762.

29. In an entry from 1755, Ryder makes the observation—as he sees the Methodists erecting a second house of worship, namely White Chapel—that they had been in town for "15 or 16 years"; JRD, July 28, 1755. On Williams and Methodism, see Isabel Rivers, "Joseph Williams of Kidderminster (1692–1755), and his Journal," *Journal of the United Reformed Church History Society* 7 (2005): 359–80.

30. JRD, March 5, 1745; February 7, 1747 (note that in this entry Ryder is not saying that he felt no sense of election as much as that he could not pinpoint the precise time when it happened). McLachlan, *Essays and Addresses*, 33–34.

31. On Whitefield, see Frank Lambert, " *'Peddler in Divinity': George Whitefield and the Transatlantic Revivals, 1737–1770* (Princeton, NJ: Princeton University Press, 1994). On the Methodists in Leeds, see D. Colin Dews, "Leeds and the Methodist New Connexion," *Proceedings of the Wesley Historical Society* 51, 3 (1997): 96–103, and W. G. Rimmer, "William Hey of Leeds, Surgeon (1736–1819): A Reappraisal," *Proceedings of the Leeds Philosophical and Literary Society* 9, 7 (1961): 187–218. For an interesting if brief article on the Unitarian-Methodist connection, see Ralph Waller, "Converging and Diverging Lines: Aspects of the Relationship between Methodism and Rational Dissent," *Proceedings of the Wesley Historical Society* 53, 3 (2001): 81–92. On Methodism more generally, see Phyllis Mack, *Heart Religion in the British Enlightenment: Gender and Emotion in Early Methodism* (Cambridge: Cambridge University Press, 2006), for the personal experience and David Hempton, *Methodism: Empire of the Spirit* (New Haven, CT: Yale University Press, 2006), for the wider angle. JRD, October 9, 1749.

32. Six years later Ryder again turned down hearing Whitefield for fear of giving way to "unsteadiness in temper." Ryder may have feared that Whitefield would make him lose control of his emotions and engage in the sort of enthusiastic behavior Methodists were known for. But even if Ryder had been aware of this in 1749, the point still holds. Maintaining control of his emotions was also part of his religious practice. See JRD, September 9, 1755. On Methodist behavior, see Mack, *Heart Religion*, 1–9.

33. JRD, October 6, 1748.

34. Relations between Presbyterians and Independents were not always so cordial, especially in London. See Bolam et al., *The English Presbyterians*. On Priestley baptizing his son at Call Lane, see McLachlan, *Essays and Addresses*, 20. The numbers of men and women who attended the Independent Call Lane and the Presbyterian Mill Hill are hard to come by in Ryder's lifetime. In 1717 visitation records indicate that Call Lane had eight hundred hearers and Mill Hill six hundred. Earnest Axonn, "Yorkshire Nonconformity in 1743," *Transactions of the Unitarian Historical Society* 5 (1931–1934): 244–261.

35. JRD, December 25, 1757 (Walker thrashing Pye); December 29, 1757 (Ryder mentions favoring Pye); January 16, 1757 (Whitaker on atheism). JRD, May 20, 1766 (for an example of Ryder going to hear a sermon at White Chapel). The Congregationalist history is Miall, *Congregationalism*

*in Yorkshire,* 304–5. Miall provides no dates for the foundation of White Chapel. At the back of volume 24 of his diary, however, Ryder tells us that the foundation for the new building was dug beyond Leeds Bridge on July 28, 1755, and the first sermon preached by Thomas Edwards was on December 14 of the same year.

36. Clifford Geertz, "Religion as a Cultural System," in *The Interpretation of Cultures: Selected Essays* (New York: Basic Books, 1973), 90.

37. JRD, August 8, 1762.

38. On the "Mayor's nest," see Derek Fraser, "Politics and Society in the Nineteenth Century," in *A History of Modern Leeds,* ed. Fraser (Manchester: Manchester University Press, 1980), 287. Much about the Luptons can be gleaned from R. G. Wilson, *Gentlemen Merchants: The Merchant Community in Leeds, 1700–1830* (Manchester: Manchester University Press, 1971). On Ryder's cousin, see JRD, May 18, 1753. "The Register of the Parish Church of Leeds," *PTS* 25 (1917, 1918, 1920, 1922): 262. An added layer of significance here is that Olive and her husband would also inherit their older cousin's massive, orthodox spiritual diary. Ryder had actually bequeathed his diary to Hannah and Grace Arey in his will, but at some point it ended up in the hands of the Luptons, as evidenced by the fact that Edgar Lupton, a descendent of the Arthur and Olive, gave the diary to the Rylands Library in 1925. See McLachlan, *Essays and Addresses,* 20.

39. Margaret C. Jacob, "Commerce, Industry, and the Laws of Newtonian Science: Weber Revisited and Revised," *Canadian Journal of History* 35 (August 2000), 288–90. Seed, " 'A Set of Men' " and "Gentlemen Dissenters: The Social and Political Meanings of Rational Dissent in the 1770s and 1780s," *Historical Journal* 28, 2 (1985): 299–325. E. P. Thompson, *The Making of the English Working Class* (London: Gollancz, 1963), 30; Wilson, *Gentlemen Merchants,* 189–90. Michael R. Watts, *The Dissenters, Vol. 2: The Expansion of Evangelical Nonconformity* (Oxford: Oxford University Press, 1995), 332.

40. While Watts was doubtful of the Weber thesis in the first volume of his study of Dissent (see *The Dissenters, Vol. 1,* 361–62), he wrote in the second volume that "there is no doubt that one of the points made by Weber is valid: that conversion and subsequent membership of a Nonconformist church both produced a conscientious attitude towards work and curtailed opportunities to waste one's time and substance on frivolous pursuits, and so created a situation in which hard work and savings could result in modest

prosperity"; *The Dissenters, Vol. 2*, 333. This seems to be an admission that, in the case of *tempered* worldly striving, religious ideas about ethics shaped economic behavior, even if alongside the business contacts a prosperous church could also provide. What I am suggesting is that we can also find a belief system in Unitarianism that justified accumulating wealth well in excess of moderation. Jacob too takes belief seriously in her "Commerce, Industry, and the Laws of Newtonian Science."

41. Watts, *The Dissenters, Vol. 2*, 339; *The Dissenters, Vol. 1*, 379–80.

42. Watts talks about the philanthropy of Unitarians as he convincingly argues that it was by focusing on wealth at death, and hence by overlooking how charitable Unitarians were while they were alive, that W. D. Rubinstein failed to realize that rational Dissenters dominated the category of the wealthy. See Watts, *Dissenters, Vol. 2*, 330, and W. D. Rubinstein, *Men of Property: The Very Wealthy in Britain since the Industrial Revolution* (New Brunswick: Rutgers University Press, 1981). The sermon of Walker's that Ryder recorded is from JRD, February 21, 1760.

## 8. THE MAKING OF A MIDDLE-CLASS MIND

1. On how to define the middling sort in this period, see Margaret Hunt, *The Middling Sort: Commerce, Gender, and the Family in England, 1680–1780* (Berkeley: University of California Press, 1996), 15–18. For a discussion of the language of class in early modern Britain, see Keith Wrightson, "Estates, Degrees and Sorts: Changing Perceptions of Society in Tudor and Stuart England," in *Language, History and Class*, ed. Penelope J. Cornfield (London: Basil Blackwell, 1991), 30–52. On the financial revolution, see John Brewer, *The Sinews of Power: War, Money and the English State, 1688–1783* (Cambridge, MA: Harvard University Press, 1990). On the Lockean impulse among educationalists, see Roy Porter, *The Creation of the Modern World: The Untold Story of the British Enlightenment* (New York: W. W. Norton, 2000), 339–63. On the various forms of capital in early modern Britain, see Keith Wrightson, *Earthly Necessities: Economic Lives in Early Modern Britain* (New Haven, CT: Yale University Press, 2000), 289–306. On credit, see Craig Muldrew, *The Economy of Obligation: The Culture of Credit and Social Relations in Early Modern England* (New York: St. Martin's, 1998); Hunt, *The Middling Sort*, ch. 1; and John Smail, "The Culture of Credit in Eighteenth-Century Commerce: The English Textile Industry," *Enterprise and Society* 4 (2003): 299–325. On the traditional family order, see Leonore Davidoff and Catherine Hall, *Family*

*Fortunes: Men and Women of the English Middle Class, 1750–1850* (Chicago: University of Chicago Press, 1987). The starting points for the vast historiography on consumerism are still Neil McKendrick, John Brewer, and J. H. Plumb, *The Birth of Consumer Society: The Commercialization of Eighteenth-Century England* (Bloomington: Indiana University Press, 1983), and John Brewer and Roy Porter, eds., *Consumption and the World of Goods* (London: Routledge, 1993). On the drawn-out contest with the French, see Linda Colley, *Britons: Forging the Nation 1707–1837* (New Haven, CT: Yale University Press, 1992), esp. ch. 2; Porter ("stout midriff") is quoted in Wrightson, *Earthly Necessities*, 289. Many insights into the relationship between the middle class and religion can also be found in John Money, "The Masonic Moment; Or, Ritual, Replica, and Credit: John Wilkes, the Macaroni Parson, and the Making of the Middle-Class Mind," *Journal of British Studies* 32 (1993): 358–95, from which I borrowed the title for this chapter.

2. JRD, August 9, 1739. Ryder has a basically Puritan sensibility, but notice the difference between Ryder's concerns here and those of someone like William Perkins, the great sixteenth-century theologian. As Ethan Shagan has recently written, Perkins too recommended moderation in all things. But it was easy enough for Perkins to promise a moderated life by his recommendation to work diligently. In basic form, in fact, Perkins articulated the sort of labor in worldly calling that Weber identified as a defining feature of the Protestant capitalist mindset. Yet Ryder is obviously saying here (as elsewhere) that even *labor* can be overdone. Ryder lived in an age whose commercialism Perkins would have had a hard time imagining, and in that world of far greater materialist possibilities and pitfalls, labor was no longer the simple solution it had once been. It was now a potential part of the problem. On Perkins, labor, and moderation, see Ethan Shagan, *The Rule of Moderation: Violence, Religion and the Politics of Restraint in Early Modern England* (Cambridge: Cambridge University Press, 2011), 232.

3. David Hume, "Of the Middle Station in Life," in *Essays Moral, Political, and Literary,* ed. T. H. Green and T. H. Grose (London, 1898).

4. On the variations, see Albert O. Hirschman, *The Passions and the Interests: Political Arguments for Capitalism before Its Triumph* (Princeton, NJ: Princeton University Press, 1977). In Tudor-Stuart society, recommendations to find the middle way were, as Ethan Shagan has shown, so often driven by a belief that the expansion of the role of the

public depended on steady self-government. But even if the English apotheosis of moderation in this earlier era was therefore mostly political, it no doubt laid the groundwork for the cultural project to demoralize self-interest in a later, more commercial age. See Shagan, *The Rule of Moderation*, 329–35.

5. Michael Mascuch, "Social Mobility and Middling Self-Identity: The Ethos of British Autobiographers, 1600–1750," *Social History* 20, 1 (1995): 59, 61.

6. The habits of the early modern British middling sort and the image they conveyed to others are captured concisely in Wrightson's synthetic *Earthly Necessities*. On the eighteenth century more particularly, see Hunt, *The Middling Sort*, and Paul Langford, *A Polite and Commercial People 1727–83* (Oxford: Oxford University Press, 1989).

7. Thomas Gouge, *The Surest & Safest Way of Thriving, or, A Conviction of that Grand Mistake in Many, that What is Given to the Poor, as a Loss to Their Estate* . . . (London, 1673), 9, 32, 27.

8. Alan Macfarlane, *The Family Life of Ralph Josselin: A Seventeenth Century Clergyman* (Cambridge: Cambridge University Press, 1977), 52. For a more detailed discussion of Josselin's anxiety about money, see Deborah Valenze, *The Social Life of Money in the English Past* (Cambridge: Cambridge University Press, 2006), 109–18. JRD, June 23, 1733. David Edward Owens, *English Philanthropy: 1660–1960* (Cambridge, MA: Harvard University Press, 1964), 401–8. JRD, December 4, 1734.

9. Gouge quoted in Richard B. Schlatter, *The Social Ideas of Religious Leaders, 1660–1688* (Oxford: Oxford University Press, 1940), 134, 133. JRD, December 13, 14, 1734.

10. JRD, Jan. 30, 1735; August 28 1748.

11. JRD, August 24, 1733; December 16, 1740; March 21, 1748/49. On the popularity of giving away clothes, see John Styles, *The Dress of the People: Everyday Fashion in Eighteenth-Century England* (New Haven, CT: Yale University Press, 2007), 247–55. On the Leeds workhouse apprenticing boys and girls, see Philip Anderson, "The Leeds Workhouse under the Old Poor Law: 1726–1834," *PTS* 56, 2 (1979): 79–100. Ryder never details the institutional structures through which he exercised his charitableness. His revelation that he was "publickly employ'd" in offering assistance likely means he was working through Call Lane or Mill Hill when not offering relief privately. He also may have been connected to Anglican philanthropic institutions. Workhouses, for example, were administered by a committee of the Vestry of the Anglican parish church. Studies of Leeds

have not investigated the extent to which Dissenters were included in this parish system of poor relief (see Anderson, "The Leeds Workhouse," and R. Strong, "The Leeds Workhouse in the Eighteenth Century," *Yorkshire Archaeological Society, Local History Bulletin* 12 [1976]), but we know that the relationship between Dissenters and Anglicans could be fluid in the mid-eighteenth century, and it is suggestive that seven names recorded in Ryder's funeral lists—three of whose funerals he attended—are of people who were living in the workhouse at the time of their deaths (Appendix 2).

12. JRD, January 4, 1737/38; September 22, 1747; February 7, 1748/49.

13. We get an indication that Ryder has some role of authority at Call Lane when he records meeting with "Mr Elam," a Quaker who Ryder reveals was willing to give money to Call Lane through Ryder. Interestingly, Ryder then commends Quakers because they "do not confine their charity to their own sect." See JRD, January 28, 1756. On going door to door with a neighbor, see JRD, December 19, 1757. The sardonic "some" Ryder places before "law" and "officer" intriguingly makes him seem less critical of the lawbreaker than the new law, but any willingness Ryder had to overlook whatever authority the man defied is a broken lead in the diary. JRD, December 21, 1757.

14. JRD, January 5, 1756.

15. JRD, February 2, 1739/40; April 11, 1760.

16. The story of Leeds elites moving across town is told in the fastidiously researched book by Maurice Beresford, *East End, West End: The Face of Leeds during Urbanisation, 1684–1842* (Leeds: Thoresby Society, 1988). Susan Wrathmell, *Leeds: Pevsner Architectural Guides* (New Haven, CT: Yale University Press, 2005), 218–19.

17. I owe this observation about the Luptons to conversation with Brett Harrison.

18. Hirschman, *The Passions and the Interests*, 129.

19. Robert L. Heilbroner, *Marxism: For and Against* (New York: W. W. Norton, 1980), 61–62.

# Manuscript Sources

BRITISH LIBRARY, LONDON
Add. MS 32, 557, Letter 142, "G. Benson to Macro, 1 Sept., 1748"

BROTHERTON LIBRARY, UNIVERSITY OF LEEDS
Lupton Box 1, "Ibbetson-Koster Ledger, 1748–60"
Lupton Box 3, "Ibbetson-Koster Journal, 1757–69"
Lupton Box 126, "Joseph Rider will, 1757," "Joseph Rider will, 1764"
Lupton Box 131, "Lists of Call Lane Trustees"

HISTORICAL INSTITUTE, YORK
Leeds Wills, 1700–1830

JOHN RYLANDS UNIVERSITY LIBRARY, SPECIAL COLLECTIONS, UNIVERSITY OF MANCHESTER
Benson MSS, 6, B114/4, "Samuel Bourn to Benson, June 22, 1751"; "S. Bourn to G. Benson 7 July 1751"
Benson MSS, General, B116/26, "G. Fothergill to G. Benson, 28 Dec 1728, JRL"
Benson MSS, General, B116/21, "J. Dolland to G. Benson, 20 May 1748"
Benson MSS, 7, B115, "T. Milway to G. Benson, 6 March 1747/8"; T. Milway to G. Benson, 20 June 1748"; "J. Milway to G. Benson 18 Sept 1748"
Benson MSS, 3, B111, "J. Taylor to G. Benson, 29 March 1748"
Burgess MSS xvii, D18, "Portion of the Diary of Pentecost Barker (fl. 1690–1731)"
Unitarian MSS, Q/6 "Diary of Joseph Ryder, in 41 volumes"
Unitarian MSS, G, Q/6 "The Spirituall Marriage or The Union of Christ to Believers Set Forth and Explained in 22 sermons from Jeremiah 3:14," written by Thomas Whitaker

LEEDS CITY LIBRARY, LEEDS
Reel 36, 3724, "Birth Register from Mill Hill"

NATIONAL ARCHIVES: PUBLIC RECORD OFFICE, KEW
RG 4/3674, Call Lane Chapel Baptisms, 167?–1778
RG 4/3723, Call Lane Chapel, Births and Baptisms, 1778–1835
RG 4/3724, Mill Hill Chapel Births, Baptisms, and Deaths, 1650–1716

WEST YORKSHIRE ARCHIVES SERVICE
MS GA/B27, "Trade Note Book of a Leeds Clothier 'Putting Out' under the Domestic System"
FW/211, Leeds White Cloth Hall Papers
DB/24, Leeds Coloured Cloth Hall Papers
LC/M1–3, Leeds Corporation Court Books, 1662–1835
LC/QS, Leeds Borough Quarter Sessions, Order and Indictment Books, 1662–1835
Clarke MSS, The Diary of the Revd. Henry Crooke
LO/M1–6, The Minutes and Order Books of the Workhouse Committee for Leeds, 1726–1824

# Index

Page numbers in italics refer to illustrations.

death, 102, 122, 137–50, 155; sudden death, 138, 140, 267*n*15; suicides, 146, 243*n*22, 268–69*n*26; wages of sin as death, 60. *See also* Funerals

Debts, 57, 60, 98, 190. *See also* Credit; Poverty

Declaration of Indulgence (1672), 165

Defoe, Daniel: as Dissenter, 247*n*55; on Leeds market, 96; on Leeds's local industry, 5, 11; *Robinson Crusoe* by, and spiritual diary keeping, 81, 148, 247*n*55; tour of Great Britain by, 96, 224*n*9, 254*nn*22–23; works by, 5, 224*n*9, 247*n*55, 254*nn*22–23

Deism, 88, 169, 171, 172, 177

De Lacy Mann, Julia, 253*n*16

Denison, Thomas, 231*n*13

Denison, William, 231*n*13

Denison family, 22–23

Depression/melancholy: Bunyan on, 152; Burton on, 266*n*4; diagnosis and symptoms of, 133, 146; economic meaning of term "depression," 137, 266*n*10; and excessive focus on business, 145–46; and fear of extremes, 137; Freud on, 134, 150; and health problems, 10, 143–45, 151, 152–53; of Josselin, 7, 135; and providentialism, 136; and Puritan ethos, 135; and religiously sanctioned mourning, 115, 134–35, 141–42, 155; and Ryder's emotions summarized, 133; Ryder's experience of, 9, 10, 133–55; and Ryder's fears of and preoccupation with death, 102, 122, 137–50, 155; and Ryder's self-blame and focus on his sinfulness, 9–11, 22, 32, 56–57, 59, 133, 136–37, 142, 145–50, 188, 229*n*8, 230*n*9, 236*n*29, 255*n*27, 263*n*31; spiritual dangers of, 134; and spiritual diary keeping, 135–36; and vanity, 9, 145; and watchfulness, 49, 135–36, 151, 155; of women, 152–53; writings on, 133–34, 150, 265–66*nn*1–4. *See also* Suicides and suicidal thoughts and attempts

Devil: Ambrose on, 48; Calvinists on, 47; temptations of, 49, 146, 149–50, 152; as watchful enemy, 45, 48, 134, 238*n*2. *See also* Sins

Diaries: as antifiction, 148; fictional diaries in novels, 148; as literary genre, 16, 147–49;

marginalia in, 52. *See also* Diary by Ryder; Spiritual diary keeping

Diary by Ryder: audience of, 67–78, 149, 166; and awareness by Ryder of others' diary keeping, 242*n*15; biblical allusions in generally, 245*n*44; birthday entries in, 63–64, 116–17, 123; blank pages in, 32, 51, 241*n*11; bookplates in, 39, *40*, *41*, 237*n*37; daily entries in, 52–53; dates covered by, 53, 202–3; death and funeral lists in, 32, 52, 61, 138, *139*, 204–20; deletions and crossed-out words in, *68*, 69, *70–71*; emotional honesty of, 147–50; final entry of, 32, *34–37*; first entry of, 17–18, 21, 43–45, *44*; formal coherence of, 52–53; handwriting in, *34*, *36–37*, 39, *44*, 51, 201, 237*n*36; inheritors of, and later placement of, in Rylands Library, 130, 222–23*n*2, 255*n*30, 280*n*38; justification for daily writing in, 56–67; length and word count of, 1, 16, 51–52, 183, 201–3; marginalia in, 52–53, 61; McLachlan on, 2, 222–23*n*2; motivations for beginning, 53–56; names of people and places in, 61, 129; neglect of, by scholars, 1–2, 222*n*2; number of volumes of, 1, 51, 52, 104; physical appearance of, 8, 51–52; practical information in, 234*n*20; and providentialism, 61–66; purchase of blank books for, 38, 39; purpose of, 16–17; quotations from authors in generally, 67; reading of, by Ryder, 241*n*13; and relationship between Ryder's religion and his material life generally, 5–8; sample pages from, *34–37*, *68*, *70–73*; as self writing, 17, 61, 77–78; significance of study of, 1–8; specific numbers used in, 66–67; time mentioned in, 66–67; and Unitarians, 2; vagueness and absence of details in, 15–17, 60–61; of Wallington, 56–57, 135; and watchfulness, 6, 43–45, 51, 56, 67; and "weariness in well doing," 246*n*48; weather conditions in, 8, 64, 78–79, 246*n*51; wife's diary entries included in, 52, 117–22, *118*; worries about impact of, on readers, 77–78, 149; worries about lackluster writing in, 69. *See also* Poetry; Ryder, Joseph, religious beliefs of; Spiritual diary keeping